KING OF THE SEVEN DWARFS

GENERAL ELECTRIC'S AMBIGUOUS CHALLENGE TO THE COMPUTER INDUSTRY

IEEE Computer Society Press
Jon T. Butler
Editor-in-Chief, Advances in Computer Science and Engineering

---

SELECTED TITLES

KING OF THE SEVEN DWARFS

GENERAL ELECTRIC'S AMBIGUOUS CHALLENGE TO THE COMPUTER INDUSTRY

Homer R. Oldfield

IEEE Computer Society Press
Los Alamitos, California

Washington • Brussels • Tokyo

Library of Congress Cataloging-in-Publication Data

Oldfield, Homer R.
   King of the Seven Dwarfs / Homer R. Oldfield.
      p. cm.
   ISBN 0-8186-7383-4
   1. Computers—United States—History. 2. Computer Industry—
United States—History.   3. International Business Machines
Corporation.   4. General Electric Company.   I. Title.
QA76.17.O45   1996
338.7 ' 61004 ' 0973—dc20

                    95-51341
                    CIP

IEEE Computer Society Press
10662 Los Vaqueros Circle
P.O. Box 3014
Los Alamitos, CA 90720-1314

IEEE Computer Society Press Order Number BP07383
Library of Congress Number 95-51341
ISBN 0-8186-7383-4

Additional copies may be ordered from:

IEEE Computer Society Press	IEEE Service Center	IEEE Computer Society	IEEE Computer Society
Customer Service Center	445 Hoes Lane	13, Avenue de l'Aquilon	Ooshima Building
10662 Los Vaqueros Circle	P.O. Box 1331	B-1200 Brussels	2-19-1 Minami-Aoyama
P.O. Box 3014	Piscataway, NJ 08855-1331	BELGIUM	Minato-ku, Tokyo 107
Los Alamitos, CA 90720-1314	Tel: +1-908-981-1393	Tel: +32-2-770-2198	JAPAN
Tel: +1-714-821-8380	Fax: +1-908-981-9667	Fax: +32-2-770-8505	Tel: +81-3-3408-3118
Fax: +1-714-821-4641	mis.custserv@computer.org	euro.ofc@computer.org	Fax: +81-3-3408-3553
Email: cs.books@computer.org			tokyo.ofc@computer.org

Assistant Publisher: Matt Loeb
Technical Editor: Jon Butler
Acquisitions Assistant: Cheryl Smith
Advertising/Promotions: Tom Fink
Production Editor: Lisa O'Conner
Cover Design: Alex Torres
Printed in the United States of America by BookCrafters

The Institute of Electrical and Electronics Engineers, Inc

PREFACE

In a speech before a congressional committee in Washington, D.C. on October 26, 1955, Mr. Ralph Cordiner, president of the General Electric Company, stated, in part, "The computer-derived technologies will create new industries and new products that will be a major source of new employment in the coming years."[1]

Mr. Cordiner said a mouthful, but he didn't put his money where his mouth was. While GE had become a major user of computers in its own businesses, Cordiner had forbidden the company's Electronics Division to compete in the commercial computer market. He was content to be a supplier to IBM of vacuum tubes, relays, small motors, and other profitable components, ignoring predictions that computer technology would soon create a completely new and unique category of computer-related components.

GE was well positioned at the end of World War II to compete with IBM in the commercial computer market, with technical and financial resources far exceeding those of the business machine manufacturer. Cordiner's decision not to compete did not sit well with GE's Walter (Doc) Baker, vice president and general manager of the company's Electronics Division. A veteran of the birth of the radio and TV industries, Baker was anxious to compete in what he considered to be the wave of the future.

In 1956, the Bank of America approached the business machine and electronics industries to obtain bids for the development and production of the so-called ERMA system, a unique combination of computers, automated check-handling and sorting equipment, and a revolutionary technique for automatically reading the numbers off checks to permit direct input to the computer. Conceived and brought to research prototype form by Stanford Research Institute under contract from the bank, ERMA was intended to automate the checking account process of the bank's branches throughout California. Cordiner, assured by his staff that the contract would be awarded to IBM or to one of the other companies in the business machine field, permitted Baker to submit a bid. Three months later, to the delight of the Electronics Division in Syracuse and the consternation of the executive office at 570 Lexington Avenue, New York City (referred to throughout the company as "570"), GE received the largest non-government computer contract ever placed up to that time—a total of $31 million (ultimately $50 million)—too large for Cordiner to turn down.

After a great deal of company infighting, the GE Computer Department was established in Phoenix, Arizona, to implement the ERMA program, though without a firm commitment by 570 to remain in the business. It was four years later that President Cordiner finally gave the go-ahead to enter the computer market as a whole. By that time, IBM had achieved a dominant position, including the installation of several dozen 704, 705, and 650 machines in GE's Operating Departments—most under the control of EDP managers inserted or trained by IBM.

During the following decade, the Computer Department was expanded and fragmented to create the GE Information Systems Group, with 25,000 employees worldwide and $1.5 billion in installed equipment. In the process, the Computer Department pioneered in the development of time-sharing and multi-processing techniques that, at one point, threatened IBM's dominance in the field of large computers. By late 1969, Hilliard Paige, GE vice president and group executive, Information Systems Group, announced to Wall Street's financial analysts, "In terms of overall business performance, we are in the best shape of our history."

A few months after this vote of confidence, GE announced the sale of its computer business to Honeywell! The sale was advertised as a joint venture of the two companies to create a strong number two to IBM, but in fact it amounted to a complete withdrawal of GE from the computer hardware business at a time when the company had proclaimed itself to be "in the best shape of our history."

During the 1960s and early 1970s, the U.S. Department of Justice mounted an attack upon IBM's virtual monopoly of the commercial computer market.[2] The sudden withdrawal of GE in 1970 was the subject of intense speculation within government circles, but repeated questioning of GE executives failed to provide any clues. The true story was pieced together 25 years later when former members of the Computer Department compared notes and revealed an intriguing saga during which one of the country's most prosperous businesses had attempted to apply the principles and tools of professional business management to the control of a technologically sophisticated venture into a new and ever-changing market that was expanding exponentially.

This book represents the author's best reconstruction of events, based in part on personal recollections and in larger part on recollections of hundreds of participants in the 14-year history of the GE Computer Department. It is primarily a story told from the bottom looking up, as contrasted to the many company stories generated through the testimony of top corporate executives. Where they could be reached, division and group management of the time have been included in an effort to eliminate or reduce the natural bias of those who struggled in the arena.

Dialog, where used in the story, has been largely invented by the author based on actions taken, opinions expressed, and recollections of the many personal encounters that took place from 1955 to 1970. Surprisingly few of the participants have objected to the author's interpretations, and changes have been made in the case of individuals who protested, "I never said that!"

The term *The Seven Dwarfs* was coined by the business and technical press of the time to denote the seven companies who attempted to compete with IBM during the formative days of the computer industry. They were General Electric, RCA, UNIVAC, Honeywell, Burroughs, Scientific Data Systems (SDS), and Control Data (CDC). GE had been the last to join this list of would-be challengers and was the most feared by IBM. Hence the dubious title of "king."

ACKNOWLEDGMENTS

I left General Electric Company at the end of 1958 and moved into a different industry in the Boston area—eventually I lost all contact with my former colleagues. Some years later, seeking a reference for a major career move, I wrote to Ralph Cordiner who was president and CEO of GE during my time there. He declined to give me a reference and intimated my career at GE had not been entirely to his liking. Chastened, I assumed the ERMA program, with which I had been identified, had been a fiasco despite its promising start—perhaps even responsible for the sale to Honeywell.

This book would never have been written had not Janet Carter, a Bank of America researcher, responded to my request for information about ERMA with the news that the bank had been searching for me for several months to invite me to a celebratory occasion honoring ERMA. The celebration had taken place without me, but Janet sent me a video of the program, which proclaimed ERMA to have been a resounding success. She also sent me addresses of key people involved in the ERMA program, most notably Dr. Bob Johnson, ERMA project manager. A contact with Bob led me to Nate Norris in Phoenix, and thence to the surprisingly large and robust GE Computer Department Alumni Association.

At almost the same time, I received a letter from Eric Weiss, biographies editor, IEEE *Annals of the History of Computing,* requesting a biography for the *Annals.* Flattered to be considered a computer pioneer, I prepared a wordy biography and sent it in. Eric sent a copy to Herb Grosch for comment, initiating a spirited but rather vitriolic exchange of correspondence during which I was exposed to Grosch's autobiography *Computer: Bit Slices from Life,* articles by McKenney of Harvard covering the early history of ERMA, and other stories appearing in the *Annals* and involving the GE Computer Department. I considered most of the stories to contain errors giving a false picture of the Computer Department as I knew it, and this caused me to launch into a series of interviews and correspondence aimed at developing a true history of the 14-year adventure of GE in the computer business.

For this project, I am indebted to certain contributors in particular:

George Snively, an engineer turned financial maven, who developed creative financing and leasing programs to overcome the competitive disadvantages created by GE's conservative accounting policies, and who has been an entertaining and prolific correspondent;

Engineers Gerry Allard, Bill Bridge, John Couleur, Walker Dix, George Jacobi, Bob Johnson, Bob Kettlety, John Paivinen, Karsten Solheim, Arnold Spielberg, Bob Sullivan, Jerry Wiener, and Dave Zeheb, all of whom made important contributions at different points in the history of the Computer Department and helped me to reduce descriptions of complex electronic concepts to layman's language;

Marketeers Art Aschauer, Dick Barnes, Vic Casebolt, Clint DeGabrielle, Bill Duster, John Hogg, Lacy Goosetree, Curt Hare, Don Klee, Dave Lundberg, Nate Norris, Tom O'Rourke, Warren Prince, Vern Schatz, Paul Shapiro, Bob Sheeley, Wes Swanson, Chuck Thompson, and George Trotter, whose exploits versus IBM's numerically overwhelming marketing organization were remarkable;

Programmers Charles Bachman, Bob Bemer, Harry Cantrell, Herb Grosch, Don Knight, Jim Richter, Ed Vance, Joe Weizenbaum, and Greg Williams, who played increasingly important roles in an organization dominated by engineers;

Manufacturing managers Ray Barclay and Cy Statt, who created computer factories in the Arizona desert, and Mrs. Pat Barclay, who furnished important documents and information when Ray passed away;

General managers John Burlingame, Clair Lasher, Harrison Van Aken, and Lou Wengert, who took over the reins of the Computer Department at intervals after my departure from the scene;

GE vice presidents George Metcalf, Hilliard Paige, Lou Rader, and Harold Strickland, who encouraged the development of GE's computer activities at the executive level;

Dick Shuey of the GE Research Laboratory in Schenectady, who supplied an expert and objective view of the activities of the Computer Department as related to the long-term needs of GE as a whole;

Ed Parker of Lou Rader's staff, who assisted the Computer Department in its contacts with the university community;

Howard Lief of the Bank of America, who negotiated the ERMA contract with GE, and Al Zipf, who was the bank's program manager, both of whom provided useful insight into the relationships with GE during and after negotiation of the ERMA contract;

Tom Morrin of SRI, who was in charge of the original ERMA research program; and Bud Feeley of Martin-Marietta, who played an important role as a customer in a critical series of negotiations.

A number of individuals referred to in the book have not been interviewed in person. Some, of course, have passed away, among them Fred Borch, Ralph Cordiner, Vern Cooper, Ken Geiser, John Haanstra, Bob Sheeley, and Bob Wooley, all of whom played important roles in the story. Many others have passed into the invisibility of retirement and could not be located, and a few others have refrained from testifying. In almost all cases, corroborating information has been obtained from two or more persons closely associated with the activities of those individuals personally contributing to the story.

There were so many individuals involved in the 14-year history of the Computer Department that it has not been possible to furnish all but a few with family and professional histories. As an aid to the reader, each major section of the book is furnished with a dramatis personae in partial correction of this deficiency.

My special thanks to J.A.N. Lee, editor in chief of the IEEE *Annals of the History of Computing,* who shared the data-gathering task, made important editorial contributions, and brought my manuscript to the attention of the IEEE Computer Society Press.

Last and most importantly, thanks to my wife, Norma Marcia Oldfield, who acted as a cheerleader, proofreader, and critic par excellence.

CONTENTS

Part I

**The Courtship
of ERMA
December 1955
to
August 1956**

DRAMATIS PERSONAE

(The individuals who participated in the fourteen-year saga of the General Electric Computer Department are introduced and identified briefly in order of their appearance in Part I.)

BARNEY OLDFIELD. An engineer turned marketing manager then laboratory manager, then given the assignment of obtaining the ERMA contract from the Bank of America. He becomes general manager of GE's new Computer Department to be located in Phoenix.

GEORGE HALLER. GE's manager of laboratories, former dean of engineering of Penn State College, and founder of R&D company Haller, Raymond, and Brown.

W.R.G. (DOC) BAKER. GE vice president and general manager of the Electronics Division in Syracuse. A veteran of the radio and early TV wars, Baker is more an entrepreneur than a follower of GE's professional management philosophy.

RALPH CORDINER. GE president and CEO who opposes GE's entry into the commercial computer market. Cordiner is also a firm believer in the philosophy that a competent professional manager can manage any type of business.

FRED TERMAN. Dean of engineering and (later) provost of Stanford University and a strong believer of university-industry collaboration. A brilliant engineer-scientist and visionary, Terman is properly credited with being the father of Silicon Valley.

CONNIE KREHOFF. Oldfield's faithful secretary at the GE Microwave Laboratory at Stanford, which Oldfield headed prior to the ERMA program.

WALT NELSON AND BILL EDSON. Staff members of the Microwave Laboratory.

GEORGE TROTTER. Manager of administration of the Microwave Laboratory and former sales manager of one of GE's large military electronics businesses. He joins Oldfield in the quest for the ERMA contract and becomes sales manager of the Computer Department.

TOM MORRIN. Director of Stanford Research Institute's Electronics Division, responsible for the ERMA research program.

KEN ELDREDGE. Stanford Research Institute (SRI) scientist who invented the magnetic-ink character recognition (MICR) technique employed in the ERMA system and still used worldwide for automated computer input of checks and other banking documents.

ERMA. Electronic Recording Method of Accounting. An acronym used by the Bank of America to describe their (then) revolutionary system for checking-account book-keeping.

HOWARD LIEF. Vice president and controller of the Bank of America, and the chief negotiator and decision maker for the bank in deciding which of the twenty-nine bidders would be awarded the contract.

AL ZIPF. Lief's data-processing expert and the man responsible for the establishment of MICR as the standard banking language throughout the United States.

A.P. GIANNINI. Founder of the Bank of America.

TOM WATSON. President of IBM.

RED LA MOTTE. Executive vce president of IBM.

BOB JOHNSON. Computer engineer with a Ph.D. from Cal Tech; designed an airborne digital computer for Hughes Aircraft prior to joining the GE Electronics Laboratory in Syracuse; technical consultant and, later, program manager for ERMA.

KEN GEISER. Manager of the Computer Section of the company's General Engineering Laboratory in Schenectady. Later to become manager of engineering for the Computer Department.

GEORGE JACOBI. Manager of the Computer Laboratory in Schenectady. First project engineer of the ERMA program.

JAY LEVINTHAL. Manager of Systems Engineering for the ERMA program.

GEORGE SNIVELY. Supervisor of accounting of the Electronics Laboratory in Syracuse and later a key member of the Computer Department's financial team.

CHUCK KEENOY. National Cash Register's manager of engineering. A subcontractor to and customer of the GE Computer Department.

TEXAS INSTRUMENTS (TI). The final competitor in the competition for the ERMA contract.

ART STERN. Bob Johnson's colleague at the Syracuse Electronics Laboratory.

GEORGE METCALF. General manager of the Government and Commercial Equipment Department and creator of the Metcalf Report strongly recommending GE's entry into the computer market.

CLAIR LASHER. Author of the section on computers for the Metcalf Report.

CLARK BEISE. President of the Bank of America.

IKE KAAR. Doc Baker's division manager of engineering.

CLARENCE LINDER. GE's vice president of engineering.

BOB ESTES. Baker's legal counsel, later to become legal vice president of GE.

BILL MORLOCK. General manager of the Technical Equipment Department, under Metcalf.

HAROLD SMIDDY. Cordiner's disciple of "professional management."

LLOYD DEVORE. Manager of the Syracuse Electronics Laboratory.

SOFIA OLDFIELD. Devoted but ailing wife of Barney Oldfield.

DAVE ZAHEB. Charter members of the ERMA engineering team.

BOB YOWELL. Representative of GE's Real Estate and Construction Services in Schenectady, responsible for selecting sites for new GE plants.

DICK HOLMQUIST. Representative of GE's Community Relations Development Services in Schenectady, responsible for evaluating community factors relating to site selection.

RAY BARCLAY. Selected by Oldfield as the manager of manufacturing for the Computer Department. A graduate of GE's Advanced Manufacturing Training Program, he has thirteen years experience in diverse manufacturing assignments and is enthusiastic about computers.

KEN McCOMBS. Plant accountant at GE's Ontario, California, flatiron plant; selected by GE's Accounting Services Division in Schenectady to be manager of finance for the Computer Department.

ART NEWMAN. The new manager of employee and community relations for the Computer Department.

JOHN PAIVINEN. Recruited by Bob Johnson to be manager of computer engineering at GE's laboratory in Menlo Park, California, devoted entirely to the ERMA program.

GERRY ALLARD. Transistor circuit specialist from the Electronics Laboratory in Syracuse, transferred to the ERMA program.

DICK HAGOPIAN. Recruited from Westinghouse to join the ERMA group.

KEN MANNING. A creative GE mechanical designer, assigned to ERMA.

JOE WEIZENBAUM. A former Bendix programmer, self-recruited to the ERMA program and responsible for developing the software for the ERMA system.

HERM GREEN. The engineering administrator for the ERMA group in Menlo Park.

KARSTEN SOLHEIM. A mechanical designer in the ERMA group, later to leave GE and establish Karsten Manufacturing Corporation, based on a proprietary line of golf clubs.

WALLY KATSUNG. Member of the ERMA design team in Menlo Park.

JOE DESCH. Project engineer for ERMA's high-speed printer and check sorter at National Cash Register in Dayton, Ohio.

BOB OELMAN. National Cash Register's executive vice president.

BOB WOOLEY. A Section manager in GE's advanced electronics center at Cornell University, later project engineer for the NCR 304 computer to be engineered and produced in small quantities in GE's new headquarters and factory in Phoenix, Arizona.

"570." The commonly used designation for GE's Executive Office (and its staff) located at 570 Lexington Avenue, New York City.

CHAPTER 1
CALL TO ACTION

The call came during the Monday morning staff meeting of the GE Microwave Laboratory at Stanford. Barney Oldfield stubbed out his cigarette and picked up the telephone.

"Yes, Connie. What's up?"

"What's up, boss, is that Dr. Haller called from San Francisco. He just arrived in town and is planning to catch the early afternoon train to Palo Alto. He has a reservation at Rickey's but will return to Syracuse first thing tomorrow morning. He wants to meet you for dinner at Rickey's and spend a few hours with you, and he'll expect you at six-thirty unless you leave a message at the desk. I told him you'd be there. Did I do right?"

"Right as always, Connie."

The staff meeting was summarily ended. Oldfield automatically lit another cigarette and leaned back in his office chair, musing about the reason for Haller's unexpected visit. Such surprises from the high brass usually meant trouble within General Electric, but George Haller was atypical. Former dean of engineering at Pennsylvania State University, he had come to GE's Electronics Division as manager of laboratories, overseeing the Electronics Laboratory in Syracuse, the GE Advanced Electronics Center at Cornell University, and the GE Microwave Laboratory at Stanford. Haller was an enthusiastic supporter of the concept of locating R&D labs adjacent to universities with strong electrical engineering and physics departments. Not only were such locations attractive to creative engineers, but they were also a source of expert consultants from the teaching staff. It was Haller's responsibility to monitor the activities within each of these laboratories, both to assess the usefulness of the research and to minimize wasteful duplication of effort as well as possible competition with GE's Central Research Laboratory in Schenectady.

Haller was close to Dr. W.R.G. (Doc) Baker, GE vice president and general manager of the Electronics Division in Syracuse, and it seemed possible he had some new project in mind. Oldfield hoped it wouldn't involve another move; the previous one from Ithaca to Palo Alto had been a difficult one for his ill wife. Their present home in Los Altos had proved to be an ideal spot for her recuperation, and he wasn't anxious to make a change.

The cocktail lounge at Rickey's posh restaurant and motor inn was ablaze with Yuletide finery in recognition of the arrival of the 1955 Christmas season. Oldfield, arriving at six-thirty on the dot, found Haller at a table separated from the rest of the noisy before-dinner cocktail throng, old-fashioned in one hand and a file folder in the other.

"Welcome to Palo Alto, George. This is an unexpected pleasure."

"Barney, you may not think so after you've heard my story. Sit down and have a drink while we're still good friends." Haller's sly grin belied his words.

"Okay, let's have it, boss," said Oldfield as he sat down and signaled the waitress to bring another old-fashioned.

Haller's reply was a question." Barney, what, if anything, do you know about digital computers?"

"Not a hell of a lot George. When I was a salesman back in '48 I negotiated a contract with the Air Force for the Electronics Laboratory to develop a digital computer called OARAC. Then, when I went back to being an engineer at our Cornell lab, I was involved in developing digital circuit packages using transistors instead of vacuum tubes. Oh yeah, Bob Wooley and I had visiting professor appointments in the Electrical Engineering Department of Cornell, and we put together the university's first course in computers. That's about it. I've been buried in microwaves for the last three years."

"Son, you've just two months to become an expert. Why don't we move into the dining room where we can hear ourselves think, and I'll give you the whole story."

"I can't wait," said Oldfield.

Over another old-fashioned and a plate of plump Olympia oysters, Haller became expansive. "You're a long way from Electronics Park and even further away from GE's executive suite at 570 Lexington, but I'm sure you're aware that Doc Baker has approached President Cordiner with proposals to enter the commercial computer market. So far, he hasn't had any luck despite market studies showing computers to be the wave of the future in electronics."

"What's the problem?"

"Ten years ago, IBM was in the business of manufacturing and leasing Hollerith/IBM punched card machinery along with associated peripheral devices and supplies. They were an important customer for small motors, relays, switches, and all sorts of components GE makes. The top brass of both companies mingled together in society, played golf at the same country clubs, and the like, so an incestuous relationship developed that is difficult to change. When IBM first began to dabble in electronic computers, they were much smaller than GE but still a good customer, and apparently Phil Reed, our chairman, and Cordiner decided not to upset the apple cart.

"Instead of competing, we became IBM's biggest customer outside the U.S. government, and the company is now loaded with dozens of IBM computers—plus one UNIVAC in Louisville just to keep the Department of Justice quiet. There are some important people on Cordiner's staff who support Baker's view, but what Cordiner says goes at 570 Lexington Avenue."

Haller paused to scan the menu and decided on grilled Alaska salmon. "What's your pleasure, Barney?"

"Make mine Crab Louis, and heavy on the Louis sauce. I've a feeling I'll need some extra energy."

"Okay, I'd better put you out of your misery. Have you ever heard of the ERMA program?"

"Sure. I think ERMA stands for 'electronic method of accounting.' Fred Terman, Stanford's dean of engineering, is on the board of SRI just down the road at Menlo Park, and he invited me to a private showing some months ago. It's a pretty crude prototype, but the system concept seems sound. I understand the Bank of America is anxious for . . ."

Oldfield stopped in mid-sentence as he saw a wide grin spread over Haller's face. "You don't mean . . . you can't be serious?"

"This document I've been waving in my left hand," said Haller, "is the Bank of America solicitation to the office machine and electronics industries to develop a refined version of ERMA and supply enough systems to automate the bank's checking account bookkeeping system throughout the state of California. The bank's willing to give a fixed-price production contract to a qualified company that agrees to resolve the remaining technical problems, and they'll work closely with the successful manufacturer to ensure optimum system performance. Doc knows it's a long shot, but it could be the key to establishing a GE computer department if we could get that contract."

"But, George, we aren't in the computer business. How can we possibly persuade the bank that we're qualified?"

"That's up to you, Barney. You've established a beachhead here at Stanford and with SRI. You know Fred Terman would love to have a substantial GE business on his beloved peninsula. You established yourself back in Syracuse as an expert at selling large systems to sophisticated customers. It should be a snap."

"Right. And what will happen if by some miracle we should succeed in obtaining the ERMA contract?"

"Just to provide a little incentive, Baker has agreed to establish a Computer Department within the Electronics Division and appoint you general manager *if* you should get the ERMA contract.[3] He's confident Ralph Cordiner would have no choice but to go along."

"All right, George. I'll study it. I'm sure you realize there are two tremendous problems here. One is to get the contract in competition with IBM and the rest; the second is to figure out how to accomplish the task if we're successful in receiving the award. We'd certainly have to do the engineering work here in Palo Alto or Menlo Park, so it will involve some major commitments on the part of Doc Baker in terms of facilities and key people. Could you give me a week to investigate the possibilities before deciding to make a proposal?"

"Fair enough. I'll expect to hear from you by next Monday."

Oldfield was thoughtful as he left Rickey's and drove slowly to his home in Los Altos. At the age of 39 he had achieved a position of respect in the Palo Alto community as the representative of GE and manager of a productive research and development laboratory. His family had settled nicely into the informal lifestyle of the area, his ailing wife, Sofia, was apparently making a good adjustment, and his three teenaged children reveled in the atmosphere of life in the shadow of Stanford University. Life was good, and he should have felt content with his role; yet there was an undercurrent of excitement and adventure in the vision created by Haller's proposal. He knew deep down that he'd respond to it.

CHAPTER 2
PRE-PROPOSAL ACTIVITIES

"Connie, round up the usual suspects. We need an emergency staff meeting." It was the following morning, and Oldfield felt a sense of urgency as he contemplated the magnitude of the task he might be undertaking.

The management staff of the Microwave Laboratory consisted of three men. Walt Nelson, manager of microwave tube engineering, was a former member of the famed MIT Microwave Laboratory of World War II. Dr. Bill Edson, research director, was a Stanford University faculty member. George Trotter, manager of administration, had been sales manager of GE's Heavy Military Department. Three good men who straggled into the office holding coffee cups, looking mildly discomfited to be summoned so early in the working day, and all warily expecting some bombshell as a result of Haller's visit. Oldfield wasted no time bringing them up to date on the reason for Haller's sudden appearance.

"For at least the next week," he said, "I'll be occupied full time trying to find out whether it's worthwhile to make the effort required to have a fighting chance for GE to obtain the ERMA contract from the Bank of America. The mind boggles. If Doc decides we should go ahead, then I'll be out of action for another three months or so. If, by some freak of luck, we should get the contract, I'll be out of here. Otherwise, I'll come back to my cushy job.

"Walt, I'm appointing you acting laboratory manager until I return. If I don't return, Haller has agreed the 'acting' will be dropped. Are you comfortable with this?"

"Okay so far, Barney. I already do all the work around here, anyway, so there won't be much change."

"Fine. Don't forget to attend the local Kiwanis Club luncheon tomorrow as my replacement.

"As of now, Connie Krehoff is the executive secretary of the Industrial Computer Section of the Electronics Division. The only other employee besides myself is George Trotter, manager of sales. I'm also counting on borrowing Bill Edson as a part-time consultant to help evaluate the technical risks of the proposal. Is that all right with you, Bill?"

"No problem. Tom Morrin heads up SRI's Electronics Division, and we're colleagues from way back. I'm sure he'll welcome a chance to show off his creation and give us the lowdown on the remaining technical worries."

"Swell. I'd appreciate it if you'd give him a call and see if he can schedule a visit as soon as possible."

"Will do."

"Okay. Let's conclude the staff meeting and get to work. George, can you spare a few moments to go over our strategy for the next week?"

When the two men were alone, Oldfield said, "My apology for springing this on you without warning, but I assumed wild horses couldn't keep you away from this marketing opportunity. Did I assume correctly?"

"You sure did, Barney. I'm hot to trot."

"Spoken like a true Trotter, George." Oldfield had a weakness for bad puns. "I'm going to depend on you to become familiar with the key people of the bank so we can get a feel for the decision-making process. We're getting a late start, so we need to begin right at the top. Here's a copy of the bank's request for proposals. There's a list of names to contact at the bank, as well as a questionnaire to fill out to establish the bidder's qualifications. We should get it filled out in case we decide to bid."

Just then Connie's voice came over the intercom.

"It's Dr. Edson on the inside line."

"Yes, Bill."

"We have an appointment for two o'clock with Tom Morrin at SRI in Menlo Park."

It was late afternoon when the trio of Oldfield, Edson, and Trotter concluded their tour of the ERMA system. They were suitably awed by the immensity of the computer, which contained over eight thousand vacuum tubes, thirty-four thousand diodes, and one million feet of copper wire. The computer included two huge magnetic drums that provided on-line memory, along with a number of tape transports, and had been designed to handle a flow of fifty thousand bank accounts a day on a two-shift basis.

A unique part of the ERMA system was the high-speed pneumatic check-sorting device that routed checks to the appropriate branch or clearinghouse. Printed on the back of each check was a bar code indicating the branch number, the customer account number, and the amount of the check. A bar-code reader entered the account information into the computer and also told the sorter the destination of the check.

"I'm mildly confused," said Trotter. "Obviously, the customer number and the branch number bar codes can be printed when the checks are originally prepared at the printer, but the amount of the check must be added after the check has been cashed. How can the bank clerks verify that the proper amount has been printed?"

"You just asked the key question," said Morrin. "We've been aware of this problem from the start, and we've had a parallel research program to develop an automatic character-recognition system for use with ERMA. We've tried every technique you can imagine, and we finally settled on a method of printing stylized but human-readable numbers along the bottom of each check using magnetic ink. Ken Eldredge

GE's first electronic digital computer (OMIBAC) developed by the Aeronautics and Ordnance Systems Division in Schenectady, 1950.

is the genius behind this development. The research model wasn't ready to incorporate in the bid specs, but our recent results are so good we're sure the bank will want it. Give us a few days and we'll arrange a demo and a discussion of the technical details."

"We'll appreciate it," said Oldfield. "Incidentally, may I ask the origin of the name ERMA?"

"Well, in 1950, when the project began, there were only a few digital computers in the world, and most of them had names like UNIVAC, ENIAC, and OMIBAC. ERMA was actually coined by the bank, and stood for electronic recording machine accounting. There's a move on to change this to electronic recording method of accounting. We think it's silly, but the Bank of America loves it."

Morrin abruptly changed the subject. "Do you really think you'll submit a bid? We'd be very happy to work with GE, but your company has never shown any interest in the commercial computer business. I wish you good luck while warning you the competition is pretty stiff."

"We haven't made a decision yet," said Oldfield, "but don't count us out."

After the meeting, the trio returned to the office and began to compare notes. Edson explained a couple of technical points as he traced out a block diagram of ERMA on the blackboard.

"It's obvious the computer will have to be transistorized to fit into the confines of a bank environment. That's a pretty big job, but the biggest problem is that the system logic has never been tested in practice. Because the computer is hardwired, you'll have to count on redesigning a lot of circuit boards before you're finished. I can't comment on the check sorter and other items of electromechanical equipment, but I suspect they'd have to be subcontracted to one of the business machine companies. The automatic character-reading equipment seems like an important invention, but it probably needs continuing research. It's the biggest technical risk in the program, and I don't think you should get involved without an agreement with SRI to continue work on the project. I'll have a better reading for you after I meet with Eldredge, the SRI guy who invented it."

"Thanks, Bill." Oldfield turned to Trotter. "What's your impression, George?"

"I think we faced just as tough obstacles back in Electronics Park when we made our proposal to the U.S. Air Force for the CPS-6B air defense radar. Remember, it was the first combined long-range detection and height-finding system, and it had the first inflatable radome. The antenna was so huge we had to beat on the Large Turbine Department to design and manufacture the big roller bearing support, and the Tube Department had to develop a new type of T-R tube to keep the receiver from being blown every time a megawatt pulse was sent out. It was a big gamble, but it opened up a market the Electronics Division still dominates. This smells like another of those situations, and I say full speed ahead."

"Spoken like a true salesman, but let's restrain our enthusiasm until after we visit the bank. Connie has made an appointment for the two of us to visit Howard Lief at ten o'clock tomorrow. He's vice president and controller of the bank, and he seems to be the key man in the decision-making chain. He's a good friend of Alf Brandon, Stanford's business manager, and I understand he's a tough negotiator."

The standard executive attire in Palo Alto, with the exception of Chamber of Commerce and Kiwanis Club luncheons, consisted of slacks, polo shirts, and some variation of tennis shoes. Trotter and Oldfield were hardly recognizable in conservative suits, shirts, and ties, but this was the headquarters of the Bank of America, 300 Montgomery Street, San Francisco, one of the country's most sophisticated caverns of commerce, and they had decided they'd better blend with the environment. Briefcases in hand, they took the elevator to the controller's office.

They were greeted by a dignified gray-haired woman who took their business cards (printed the previous night), poured them each a cup of coffee, and ushered them to a leather couch.

"I'm Diane Woodward. Mr. Lief will be with you shortly. He's on the telephone to the president."

Suitably awed, though they weren't sure which president, Oldfield and Trotter sipped the fragrant coffee and looked around at the small, well-appointed outer office.

Just then the intercom lit up. "You may go right in. He'll see you now."

Howard Lief's office was cluttered with stacks of papers, financial spreadsheets, and other odds and ends. His desk held a large Marchant calculator that proclaimed its owner a hands-on accountant. Lief was a tanned six feet of well-tailored middle-aged man, saved from looking natty by the rumples in his jacket. He looked tired, but he bounced to his feet and greeted his visitors with a firm handshake.

After mutual introductions were completed, he said, "Your secretary's call came as a pleasant surprise. We didn't think General Electric was interested in manufacturing commercial computer systems. Frankly, we included GE on the list more as a courtesy than anything else. It's getting late in the game, and we're already evaluating initial proposals, but we're not overlooking any bets, particularly with companies as strong as yours."

"We definitely want to submit a proposal," responded Oldfield, "if the competition is still wide open and we have enough time to plan the program in detail. There seems to be quite a bit of engineering to be accomplished if the system is to be manufactured at a reasonable cost. We'd need about sixty days to submit a proposal."

"Well, we have about ninety days to make a decision, so you're in good shape as far as time is concerned. So far, we're disappointed in most of the proposals we've received. Only one small company—I won't name them—has come up with a reasonably responsive proposal. I can't promise anything, but I can assure you the field is wide open and you'll get a fair shake."

Lief turned to his intercom. "Diane, will you see if Al Zipf is available to meet with these gentlemen from General Electric?"

"He's right here in the office with an appropriation request."

"Then send him in, request and all."

Al Zipf was a handsome man in his late twenties, a George Raft lookalike with a pleasant smile. He held a bunch of bank checks in his hand as he entered the room. Lief made the introductions all around, then said, "Let's dispose of the appropriation request first."

Zipf handed Lief the batch of checks and reached into his pocket for a printed form he placed on the desk. "This is the latest batch of proofs from the printer. The numerics are very good, but the magnetic ink doesn't give as strong a signal as SRI would like. The printer wants to try a more concentrated solution of magnetic powder. I'll need an additional authorization to cover the project."

Lief signed the appropriation request. "You know, Barney, we've spent a small fortune developing magnetic ink and teaching printers how to use it to print numbers on checks. SRI is getting very close to a workable system that will permit direct entry of checks into computers and into high-speed check sorters. In parallel, Al has been a key member of the committee on mechanization of check handling for the American Banker's Association, the ABA.[4] The committee was established last year to evaluate the competing methods for identifying checks and other documents to permit direct computer entry. It's a very important problem because the techniques must be standardized so banks can read checks of all other banks. Burroughs has proposed the use of fluorescent dots on the back of checks, IBM favors bar codes, others have proposed optical readers, but all of these approaches have failed for one reason or another. Al has fought the battle for magnetic character reading ever since

Ken Eldredge of SRI came up with the invention. We're counting on him to win the battle."

"We've already demonstrated the system using travelers checks," said Zipf, "and we're hoping for an ABA decision in our favor during 1956. But the technique still needs a lot of work before it'll be ready for mass application."

"Is there any chance the ABA decision will be made before the bank contracts for ERMA?" asked Trotter.

"I don't think so," said Lief. "In fact, the ABA may even be waiting for us to make a firm decision to ensure the Bank of America is committed to making magnetic ink character reading a commercial success."

Al Zipf rose to his feet, gathered up the checks, and put the appropriation request in his pocket. "If you gentlemen will excuse me, I'd better get back to the printer and put the new project into operation."

"That young man's always attending to business," said Lief after Zipf had departed. "Sometimes I wish he'd relax a bit more, but we couldn't get along without him."

Lief looked at his watch. "It's about that time; would you gentlemen care to join me at lunch?"

"Delighted."

The Biltmore Grill turned out to be Lief's favorite spot for lunch. The three were shown to a quiet corner table and were soon settled with martinis all around. As they discussed the ERMA program, Lief became increasingly frank and open concerning the background of the program.

"We started the project back in 1950 when Mr. Giannini first got the idea to approach the computer manufacturers and ask them to develop equipment that could actually read and sort regular paper checks as well as making the calculations and printing the results. We scoured the country, but we couldn't find anyone to undertake the project, so we decided to explore the subject with one or more of the research laboratories. SRI was an obvious choice.

"Last year I was asked to assume responsibility for ERMA, and I soon found SRI's estimates as to time and cost had been far exceeded. I tightened the screws as much as possible, but as a 'guaranteed' date for completion was approaching, I could see they weren't going to make it. I talked with my boss, Clark Beise, who by then was president, and told him I felt SRI had established the principles but that a capable business equipment manufacturer could do a better job from that point on. He agreed, so we organized a big demonstration and put out a press release indicating the Bank of America and SRI had revolutionized the banking industry, and this brought in all of the computer industry, including IBM."

"What was IBM's reaction?" asked Oldfield.

"Tom Watson and his executive vice president, Red La Motte, came out to see us and offered $10 million for all rights, but with no commitment of what IBM would do with it.[5]

"Our equipment was critical to them, as their forte was computer input by punched cards, and our paper-handling gear could be a threat to them. They might just put it on the shelf to do away with the threat. I refused the offer on the basis that we had invested $5 million to solve an operating problem and not merely for the sake of making a quick profit. "

Oldfield was surprised that Lief would be so open on such short acquaintance. As if reading his mind, Lief continued, "I've told all the other bidders the same thing. We don't care about technical details, and we don't want to sell 'rights.' What we want is sufficient equipment to perform a certain volume of functions of a specified character at a cost that, compared to our present cost of operation, will result in annual savings to the bank. This is a simple concept but very difficult to explain to those who deal with specific products meeting specific technical specifications."

Oldfield and Trotter exchanged glances of mutual understanding. They had discovered the theme of GE's marketing campaign.

The next day they huddled with Bill Edson, who had spent several hours with Ken Eldredge, the head of SRI's character-recognition program.

"It's really a very elegant technical solution," said Edson. "Optical character readers and fluorescent dots turn out to be impractical because cancellation stamps and dirt cause misreading. Magnetic ink characters are unaffected by such impediments. Eldredge has developed unique printed patterns for each number, so shaped that their wave forms can be recognized by a magnetic character reader. The characters have unusual shapes, but they can easily be recognized by the human eye as well. At this stage of development, the character-recognition circuitry takes several racks of vacuum tube electronics and requires continuous adjustment. Also, the magnetic ink doesn't put out as strong a signal as one would like, and the character shapes can stand some additional refinement. I think these are all problems that can be resolved within the next six months, but it's imperative that the SRI team be kept together for at least this period."

"But you think the technical risk is a reasonable one?" asked Oldfield.

"Yes, I do. The concept is sound, and it's really the key to the whole ERMA system. This is where the big cost savings will come."[6]

"Okay, Bill. How about other big technical challenges?"

"Well, the computer is a monster, but we have people in the Electronics Laboratory in Syracuse and the General Engineering Laboratory in Schenectady who would sell their souls for the chance to design a transistorized computer. It's probably not as big a problem as the high-speed check sorter. It reminds me of some of the automated mail sorting equipment I've seen in the newsreels, and I expect one of the companies in that business, like Pitney Bowes, would be happy to act as a subcontractor. If you decide to submit a bid, you'd best find a subcontractor who'll take over responsibility for this and the other electromechanical items."

"Okay. Let's see if we can lay out a schedule and a cost estimate for preparing a strong proposal."

The three men put their heads together and emerged with a figure of $50,000 to develop a competitive bid.

The next few days were filled with follow-up visits to SRI and continuing refinement of the cost justification. Finally, Oldfield took a deep breath and placed a call to Electronics Park.

"Haller here."

"This is Barney, George. We've investigated ERMA to the extent possible, and we've decided it's worth a shot if you and Doc think it's worth the cost of admission. We figure it should cost about fifty K to develop and negotiate a good proposal. The dollar estimate includes time and expenses for George Trotter and myself, plus others in GE who'll help to work up the proposal."

"You know, Barney, I've been talking to some of the local technical and marketing people, and they all think we're out of our minds to think we can get the Bank of America contract. What makes you so optimistic?"

"The word 'optimistic' is stretching it a bit, George. I know it's a long shot, but it's a big system contract and not just a computer purchase. It's going to need a strong organization with a depth of technical talent, a strong financial position, and an understanding of what the customer wants to accomplish. I think our chances are as good as anyone else's, and better than most."

"Barney, I have a meeting with Doc in half an hour. If you'll dictate the details of the budget and schedule to Doris, she'll prepare a requisition and I'll get him to sign it or reject it on the spot. Just a second, and I'll put Doris on the line."

There was a brief pause. "Good afternoon, Mr. Oldfield. I'm ready to take dictation."

"It's a good morning in Palo Alto, Doris. Here's the scoop."

Oldfield awaited the call-back with mixed emotions. It wouldn't do his career much good if he spent $50,000 of the company's money and came up empty handed. And if he should get the contract, what then?

He didn't have to wait long. It was late morning when Connie buzzed him. "It's Dr. Baker on the line!"

He picked up the telephone and took a deep breath. "This is Oldfield, Doc."

"Young man, I understand you think there's a fighting chance of winning the Bank of America competition. Is that right?"

It didn't do to equivocate with Doc Baker. "Yes, sir. I think George Trotter and I have a pretty good idea of what's required to be among the top bidders. It seems like a reasonable gamble to me."

"Okay, Barney, go to it. You've got fifty thousand bucks and two months to bring home the bacon."

CHAPTER 3
THE PROPOSAL TEAM IS FORMED

T he home of GE's Electronics Division in Syracuse was known, appropriately, as Electronics Park. Located north of the city, the campus-like arrangement of offices, laboratories, engineering facilities, and factories constituted an impressive statement of the company's commitment to electronic technology. The Electronics Laboratory, a substantial two-story structure, dominated the entrance to the park. It was here that most of the division's advanced development programs were carried out. Other large buildings were devoted to the design and manufacture of specific products: home TV and radio sets, TV and radio transmitters, military electronics of all types, and a variety of special consumer products.

A smaller building at one corner of the campus housed the executive office of the Electronics Division. The division general manager, a GE vice president, occupied a suite of offices on the second floor. The occupant, Walter R.G. Baker, always addressed as "Doc" in recognition of his honorary degree, had come to GE from RCA where he had been general manager of the Victor Division. A veteran of the early wars between radio and television entrepreneurs, he was a no-nonsense, give 'em hell product of an environment different from that of the typical GE general manager. He had just signed a document authorizing a $50,000 expenditure to develop a computer-based system for the Bank of America; this despite a firm directive from GE's president, Ralph Cordiner, prohibiting any entrance into the "business machine" business. Baker had received a casual go-ahead from Cordiner for this particular project on the flimsy grounds that the Bank of America procurement was a special-purpose process-control system—which it technically was. He was well aware the approval was due to the unanimous opinion of the corporate staff that Baker didn't have a chance of being awarded the ERMA contract.

Across the campus in the Electronics Laboratory, Bob Johnson was laboriously tracing out the wiring diagram of an analog machine tool control system, a product of GE's Specialty Control Department in Waynesboro, Virginia, and a part of the Apparatus Division. This important product used instructions carried on magnetic tape to control the motions of the cutting tool and the carriage on a milling machine, thus greatly speeding up the theretofore lengthy process for creating complex aircraft structures and other intricate machined parts. However, they had found important limitations to the device because the analog instructions were not sufficiently precise for many important applications. Bob's project was to design a digital control system that would solve the problem and add many years to the life of the product.

Bob was well-suited by background for this difficult project. He joined GE right out of college in 1950 and received a basic GE education as a test engineer before migrating to Hughes Aircraft in California while working for his Ph.D. from Cal Tech. His thesis consisted of a small digital computer designed for Hughes, so in 1955 he emerged as one of a small group of young engineers with both a sound background in computers and hands-on experience in computer design and fabrication. He came back to GE as a computer engineer and was contemplating settling down in Syracuse with his wife, Mary, and their two children.

His perusal of the wiring diagram was interrupted by a call from George Haller. "Bob, have you ever heard of the ERMA program?"

"Sure. It's the biggest computer program ever. The whole computer industry is going after the contract. Why? Are we interested?"

"Doc has just signed an authorization to prepare a proposal in the name of General Electric. I think you know Barney Oldfield, manager of the Microwave Laboratory in Palo Alto. He has the job of getting the contract from the Bank of America. While he's had a lot of experience in the electronics field, he's not a computer engineer, and he'll need plenty of help. I'd like you to act as a consultant if you have no objection."

"Sure, I'll be glad to help. It should be fun, though I'm afraid it's a wasted effort. Is Doc serious?"

"Serious enough to allocate fifty thousand bucks."

"Wow! That's serious all right. I'll give Oldfield all the help I can, but I don't think Lou Rader of Specialty Control will be very happy if his project is neglected."

"Do the best you can, Bob. I'll see about getting you some help on the machine tool project."

The General Engineering Laboratory in Schenectady had been created to serve all of the many GE departments as a center of advanced development. One of their large projects was a huge computer in which electrical transmission systems could be simulated and designed. It was the world's largest analog computer, and the project was under the supervision of the laboratory's Computer Section, which included electrical and mechanical engineers, draftsmen, and skilled machinists. There was plenty of funding for this type of activity, but Ken Geiser, the manager of the Computer Section, was anxious to shift the effort from analog to digital computer applications. He responded eagerly when he received Oldfield's call from Palo Alto.

"I'll assign George Jacobi to the proposal effort full time if you wish. He's probably our most creative engineer, and I'm sure he'll jump at the chance. How do you assess your chances?"

"Well, Ken, it's a long shot but I have a hunch we'll be in the top two or three when the negotiating begins."

"That's good enough for me, Barney. You've got my support. I'll have Jacobi contact you at once to arrange for his participation."

While doing graduate work in mathematics, George Snively was working in Ohio State's Research Foundation when he was recruited for GE's Financial Management Training Course. As an undergraduate he pursued a double major in anthropology and electrical engineering. Because of his technical background he was assigned to the Electronics Laboratory as supervisor of accounting following completion of the Financial Management Training Course. He was eager to "join up" having participated in several of the previous business planning efforts to initiate a computer business in GE.

And so the ERMA proposal team was created: one engineer turned entrepreneur, one digital computer engineer, one analog computer expert, one accountant with technical education, and one radar salesman. No member of the team had ever been involved in the development, manufacture, or sale of a commercial computer or piece of office equipment, nor did they have any knowledge of the banking field— just the talent required to go after the world's largest computer contract, to be placed by the world's largest bank.

CHAPTER 4
THE COMPETITION IS JOINED

The ERMA proposal team soon settled into a routine. Trotter spent most of his time with the Bank of America, learning the basics of the checking account processing and accounting system from the tellers, proof operators, and data clerks who had been assigned by Lief to work with potential bidders. One objective was to give the bank the impression they were interested in solving their problems (true) and were not simply out to obtain a lucrative contract. The other objective was to learn as much as possible about the language of banking and the procedures at the branches, the central office, and the clearinghouses.

Oldfield had undertaken the task of developing the written proposal and estimating the costs to develop and produce the many elements of the ERMA system. This began as a series of meetings with SRI in which a general agreement was reached concerning the continuing projects that SRI would undertake, including the indoctrination of the GE engineers, completion of the logic design of the computer, and continuing refinement of the automatic character reader and sorter. All told, the total of SRI subcontracts would come to $1 million. In addition, SRI agreed to furnish space in the building in which ERMA was installed so that GE engineers could set up their offices and laboratory areas adjacent to ERMA. This arrangement was to last for no longer than a year, at which time the GE group would move to permanent facilities that GE would erect at nearby Stanford Industrial Park.

During this period, technical reports from SRI were funneled back to Jacobi and Johnson who would work up the basic technical proposal based on transistorizing the ERMA computer, converting the design information to manufacturing drawings, and doing the same to the rest of the complex system. It soon became apparent that GE had no background in the technology involved in items such as check sorters, and a search was mounted for possible subcontractors. It didn't take long to determine that National Cash Register was the preferred subcontractor and team member. NCR was not in a position to submit a complete proposal because they had no electronic engineering or manufacturing capability in Dayton, but they were anxious to provide the electromechanical portions of the system. An NCR team came to Palo Alto, headed by Chuck Keenoy, NCR's director of engineering. They accompanied Oldfield on a tour of the ERMA facility, visibly impressed with the large computer but skeptical of the high-speed sorter that used vacuum techniques rather than friction belt feed to transport the checks.

"We've spent a lot of money investigating high-speed check-sorting devices," said Keenoy after the tour, "and we've found vacuum techniques susceptible to ambient dust and dirt. We've contracted with Pitney Bowes for a check sorter based on the techniques they use for mail-sorting equipment. If you contract with us for check sorters, we'll give the SRI sorter a close look, but we'd need the freedom to use our own design if you want a firm price."

"We could care less as long as you meet the performance requirements," said Oldfield. "What do you think of the magnetic ink character-recognition system for input to the sorter and the computer?"

"It's fabulous. To be quite honest, it's the main reason we've been interested in the ERMA program. Without automatic input of checks and deposits, the high-speed sorter would be worthless. I'm sure you know all about the program of the American Bankers Association to standardize a machine language for automated check handling. Well, the business machine manufacturers have a parallel committee of which I'm the NCR representative. We're leaning toward magnetic ink character recognition, which we call MICR, pronounced 'mike er.' Burroughs is fighting hard for their system of fluorescent dots, but I think the ABA likes the SRI solution."

"You're telling me we might spend a fortune refining the MICR character reader and be forced to scrap it if the ABA decides otherwise?"

"I don't think that's as big a gamble as making MICR work in practice once it gets out of the laboratory. Incidentally, NCR has a part to play in that project. The system won't work unless there's a reliable way to imprint the amount on the check after it has been processed by the bank teller. This should happen as part of the proofing process at the branch. We manufacture proof machines as a standard part of our banking product line, and the logical thing is to modify them to print the check amount as a part of this routine process. It isn't a simple task because the character reader needs a clear, sharp imprint, and this may be difficult to do with magnetic ink. A branch bank can't be expected to maintain the same conditions of printing control as a professional printer, so the device must be idiot proof. SRI hasn't even looked into these types of practical problems, but you can bet Al Zipf of the Bank of America will be on the lookout for weaknesses in the system."

As they continued to talk, Oldfield began to appreciate the types of complications and pitfalls that would be evident only to those experienced in the banking business. They could use a partner like NCR.

When Keenoy departed, he left an invitation for Oldfield to visit NCR in Dayton and Pitney Bowes in Stamford, Connecticut. "I'd like you to meet Bob Oelman, our executive VP—he'll need some selling from both of us if our company is to make the kind of commitment I think you'll be looking for."

"That sounds great, Chuck. I have to go into Syracuse in a couple of weeks to go over our cost figures with George Snively. I'll give you a call when I know my schedule."

It was mid-January, and the proposal was taking shape. Many of the basic decisions had been made by means of what seemed like continuous conference calls between Palo Alto, Syracuse, and Schenectady. The engineers had decided that it was feasible to redesign the computer using transistors rather than vacuum tubes, even though neither IBM nor Univac had offered a vacuum tube computer as a commercial product. One important decision was to eliminate the costly and unreliable on-line drum memory units from the system and utilize magnetic tapes in their place. But perhaps the most important decision of all, made by Oldfield despite the remaining technical questions, was to include MICR as a basic part of the system. He reasoned that the value of the contract to GE depended on ERMA being well ahead of any competitive banking systems, so that the technical gamble was worth taking.

One day, Bill Edson returned from a visit to SRI with some disturbing news. It turned out that a group of engineers from Texas Instruments was visiting SRI for detailed discussions of processing speeds and banking control functions. They had brought some circuit boards with them to demonstrate transistorized logic on ERMA's sorting functions, and the demonstrations had been impressive. They had talked freely with Edson, even after being told he was with GE. It seemed TI had been working on the project for four months and had submitted a number of detailed engineering analyses along with financial projections of cost savings. The TI group acted as if the contract was already theirs and that it was purely a matter of negotiating details. Their visit to SRI was preliminary to submitting their final contract proposal sometime in February.[7]

This was sobering information indeed. At first, Oldfield wondered if TI had simply been blowing smoke to scare GE away. He didn't know much about TI, a small company in Texas that made instruments for geophysical exploration and was experimenting with transistors. Edson informed him that TI was one of the first companies to procure a license from Bell Telephone Laboratories to produce transistors and had developed a method of fabricating silicon transistors, which were both faster and more reliable than the point-contact germanium transistors GE was planning to employ. The company was well-financed and should be considered a serious competitor.

"Connie, will you see if Mr. Trotter is back from the bank. We need to confer."

Trotter was almost immediately on the line. "Trotter here."

"George, I've just received some interesting information about our competition. I think we need to discuss it."

"Heat up the coffee. I'm on my way."

Fortified with a steaming cup from Connie's carafe, Trotter settled himself and listened while Oldfield went over his conversation with Bill Edson. "TI may be the most serious competitor judging from their close relationship with SRI. Have any of the bank people mentioned them?"

"Not a word," said Trotter. "Howard Lief has been pretty open regarding IBM and Burroughs, but he hasn't said much about RCA, and he's said absolutely nothing about Texas Instruments. This is ominous."

"Maybe it's a good thing to have a specific competitor to fight against rather than submitting a proposal into a vacuum. The fact that the TI engineers are so indiscreet is a sign that the company may be dominated by technical people without much experience in the non-government world. Also, while they're obviously expert in semiconductor technology, they haven't had experience in developing and manufacturing large systems. What other weaknesses can you think of?"

"Well, it's obvious that a project of this magnitude will require substantial capital investment over an extended period. My guess is that TI would ask for progress payments and may not agree to penalty clauses for failure to deliver on time. Also, from what you told me, their whole emphasis is on the computer, without too much attention to the other parts of the system."

"Okay, George. In our proposal we'll emphasize GE's financial strength, suggest favorable financial terms, and treat the transistorization of the computer as a routine chore while emphasizing GE's research capabilities as an important asset in refining the other system elements. I suspect TI may not be planning to contract heavily for continuing research at SRI, so let's make sure we have a letter of commitment from SRI to include in the proposal. What else can you think of?"

"I'm not sure how it can be worked out in a contract, but I think we should pay attention to Howard Lief's desire to have an arrangement whereby the price of the system is related directly to the processing of fifty-five thousand accounts per day by ERMA, with a staff of so many people, in such and such a space, with a power requirement of so many kilowatts, and so on.[8]

"That's a good point, George. I'm not sure whether we know enough yet to incorporate these kinds of details in our written proposal, but let's keep them in mind for future discussions with the bank. Now, do we have all the photographs and diagrams we need?"

"Let's see. I have a good picture of Mr. Cordiner, our revered president, taken when he made a speech on automation last October. We might want to put him on the front page along with a summary of his text stating that the computer-derived technologies will create new products and new industries that will be a major source of new employment in the future."[9]

"Great! I'm not sure how Mr. Cordiner will take this, but he can hardly disavow his own words."

"Then," continued Trotter, "I dug up photographs of computers like the OARAC computer for the U.S. Air Force, the OMIBAC computer developed by the Aeronautics and Ordnance Systems Department, the Network Analyzer, the Power Control Simulator, as well as the Electronics Laboratory in Syracuse and the production line of the Commercial and Government Equipment Department where you plan to have the digital modules manufactured. These should help illustrate the tremendous resources GE has in the electronics field. I also have some fine shots of the Microwave Laboratory machine shop and engineering areas. Finally, I have pictures and resumes of all the key people in the Industrial Computer Section management team."

"Okay. I have some material I can give you. Here's a draft of the summary, the technical proposal, and the business proposal. I'm still waiting for some details from Johnson and Jacobi, so don't put the technical part in final form. Also, there's a design layout of the addition to the Microwave Laboratory building we're proposing

GE's OARAC computer, developed by its Syracuse Electronics Laboratory for the U.S. Air Force, 1954.

to erect to house the ERMA program and serve as the headquarters of the Computer Department. I think the fact that we're willing to locate the business on Stanford Industrial Park property should be a substantial plus with the Bank of America and with SRI.

"Let's see. What's missing at this point? We need a Gantt chart showing the various steps to meet the bank's desired thirty-month schedule to deliver the first production system. I'm working on that with Lasher's help, and should have it for you by the end of the week together with our pricing data. What else is missing?"

"We need a proposal cover. The Drafting Section is working on a couple of alternate designs, and should have samples to show you by the end of the day. It will take a week to get the covers printed up, so we'll need a decision by tomorrow in order to meet your February 3rd deadline for delivery of the proposal to Howard Lief."

"No problem. I'd planned to make a trip to Syracuse next week and stop by Dayton and Stamford, but I think I'd better postpone it until after we submit the proposal. To be honest with you, I'd like to get the commitment made before exposing the program to any more internal second-guessing than necessary. I'll review the proposal with George Haller over the phone as soon as the magnitude of the dollar commitment is firmed up."

"Let's get to work."

It was February 2nd. The proposal and letter of transmittal lay on Oldfield's desk. It covered a quantity of thirty-six ERMA 1A systems, each capable of handling fifty-five thousand commercial checking accounts per day. The total aggregate price was $31 million. Because of the many unknowns in the program, such as the difficulty of implementing MICR, Oldfield had established a target price per system for the first ten systems, to be adjusted upwards by up to 25 percent when all systems were delivered. The proposal included penalties for late delivery, as well as standard legal clauses relating to termination, patents, notices, and so on. It was heavy with financial data, though light on detailed technical information.[10]

Talking the proposal over with Trotter, Oldfield remarked on the one-sided nature of the document. "I'd normally be ashamed to submit a major proposal with such a small amount of technical detail, but I have a feeling the bank will be more interested in finding an industrial partner with the resources and ability to see a very difficult project through to a successful finish. In any event, that's our only possible strategy. Let's make the most of it."

An unseasonable rain slowed traffic on the freeway as Oldfield and Trotter made their way toward San Francisco. In the back seat of Oldfield's aging Mercury were twelve copies of the inch-thick proposal for the ERMA system.

"Every once in a while," said Oldfield, "I wonder why we've spent so much time and money on what must be a worse gamble than the numbers racket. I'm confident we could do the job if we should win the contract, but I can't figure out why they should give it to us."

"Yeah, I know," replied Trotter. "I wake up at night every so often wondering the same thing. However, nothing ventured, nothing gained. I have a feeling the formal written proposal is only the opening gun, and the issue won't be decided until after a lot of wheeling, dealing, and horse trading. We're pretty good at that sort of thing."

They made their way to the Bank of America building, parked the car in an indoor garage, and carried the proposals up to Howard Lief's office.

"Good morning, gentlemen," said Diane Woodward. "I see you came bearing gifts. Just put the stack on my desk and I'll log them in for distribution to the ERMA Committee and the other interested parties. Mr. Lief had to take last night's sleeper to Los Angeles to attend a meeting with some government auditors, but I know he'll be anxious to talk to you as soon as he's read your proposal. I'll give you a call as soon as I know his schedule."

Texas Instruments, Incorporated (TI) went neck and neck with General Electric in the final stages of bidding for the ERMA contract. This artist's conception scale model was presented to the Bank of America by TI in early 1956. It found its way into the GE archives.

"Thanks, Diane," said Trotter. "We'll be at your beck and call."

Two days elapsed before they heard from Lief's office again. Oldfield kept his mind occupied by helping Walt Nelson with the proposal for the microwave oven power package, and Trotter took care of some much needed dental work he had let lapse in the frenzy of getting the GE bid ready for the bank. The silence during the interim was not very encouraging.

Finally the call came through from Diane. "Mr. Lief wonders if you and Mr. Trotter could meet with him tomorrow at the usual 10 a.m. He has some questions about your proposal."

"We'll be there."

As they entered Lief's office the next morning, they noticed a scale model of a computer, sorter, and other peripheral equipment items installed on a file cabinet. The model was mounted on a wooden base bearing a small brass marker on which were engraved the words, "ERMA 1A, Texas Instruments, Inc."

Lief chuckled at their obvious discomfiture. "Just a little indication that the competition is getting pretty serious. Actually, they also gave me a collection of circuit boards that I passed on to Al Zipf. Do you have any samples of GE advanced transistor design that I can show the board as an indication of your work with semiconductors?"

"Why yes," said Oldfield. "I'll bring you a sample or two when we come in next time."

"Fine. Let's talk about your proposal. I thought it was a good one, but there are a number of points that need further discussion. Your price is pretty high, but I'm not going to quibble with it. I'm more interested in pinning down the savings. One important part is the royalty income on sales of ERMA-based systems you make to other banks after you've finished with our order. You've proposed a percentage royalty on these sales. Your competitors have proposed flat know-how and patent royalties ranging from $1 million to $2 million. To make any sort of valid comparison we need to make an estimate of the number of ERMA sales you'll make outside the Bank of America. Your proposal states GE's intent to continue research and development aimed at applying ERMA to broad segments of the banking market and implies a simplified version for smaller banks. I think it would help your cause if you could amplify your proposal to describe the approach you plan to take."[11]

"We'll be glad to do that," said Oldfield confidently, though he had no idea how he would comply. "I think a minimum of one hundred fifty systems would be a reasonable assumption, giving you royalties of at least $6 million. Our target will probably be about five hundred systems before the product is made obsolete by a new system."

Lief seemed pleased with the reply. "Now here are a number of less-important points requiring clarification."

The discussion went on for another hour, with Trotter taking copious notes and Oldfield fielding most of the questions. Finally, Lief ran out of ammunition. "Let's go to lunch."

Lunch at the Biltmore Grill with Howard Lief was always a two-martini affair, usually followed by Olympia oysters on the half shell and a large Caesar salad. These interludes were enjoyable events for Oldfield and Trotter. They were enthralled at Lief's stories of the early days of the Bank of America, starting with the earthquake of 1906 when the "Bank of Italy," as it was then known, helped an untold number of San Franciscans rebuild their shattered lives. (As time went on, these lunches were to become the arena of intense negotiation.)

The winter rain had stopped by the time the two men drove back to Palo Alto. "What do you make of the situation, George?" said Oldfield.

"I have a feeling TI probably has the best proposal but that Howard Lief would be happy to have GE bearing the responsibility for a project of this magnitude."

"I think you're right. Now it's up to us to give him all the ammunition we can to make them confident we can do the job. I'll get on the horn to Johnson and Jacobi first thing in the morning to see what we can drum up in terms of a simplified version of a system we don't completely understand in the first place."

Back at the Electronics Laboratory in Syracuse, Bob Johnson had shifted his attention momentarily from his machine tool control project to the problem of a simplified ERMA for smaller banks. He discussed the project with Art Stern, one of his colleagues who was an expert on digital transistor circuits.

"Why in the world are you wasting time on this proposal?" said Stern. "Do you really think there's a chance GE will get this job?"

"No, there's no chance. I'm working on it because my boss told me to and because it's an interesting diversion. You know, people like Clair Lasher and George Metcalf have been trying to sell GE top management on the idea of getting into the computer business for the last five years, but the answer has always been, 'No.' Most of the engineers who were computer enthusiasts have either left GE or gravitated to other jobs. I can't see how we have a ghost of a chance of getting the Bank of America contract, competing against RCA, which is very hungry with the Bizmac program finishing up, or IBM, which, is, of course, the giant of all, or NCR, or Univac."

"Suppose by some miracle GE should get the contract," said Stern. "Would you want to leave the Electronics Lab and move to Palo Alto and work on the project?"

"Are you kidding? I'd give my eye teeth to take on a digital computer project of this magnitude. However, that's purely wishful thinking. Mary and I are in the process of buying a lot so we can build a house in Syracuse. We're planning on settling down here with the children.

"Now, as to Oldfield's request for alternate ERMA approaches for smaller banks not requiring the large capacity or rapid response of ERMA, I have a couple of ideas I'd better try out on George Jacobi so we can give Oldfield some additional fuel for his proposal."

Johnson was quickly connected to Jacobi using the leased line between Syracuse and Schenectady. "Hi, George. Have you come up with any bright ideas to feed Barney?"

"Well, one thought I've had is to take advantage of the fact that, if the checks are sorted before the information is entered into the computer, the electronic data-handling job is much simpler. This would involve a sorter capable of ordering checks into account-number sequence and entering them into a monthly tape reel revised from day to day. This would eliminate the need for major buffer storage and fast or medium access storage and would greatly reduce the cost of the computer. The disadvantage is that, for fifty thousand accounts, the customer's current balance can be obtained only after an access time of up to ten minutes. For small systems with fewer accounts, this may not be a problem."

"Good thinking, George. I suggest you work it up with a flow chart and block diagram. I have a different scheme in mind that uses a series of successively larger, constantly rotating tape groups to post. The last tape group would have a file of all of the bank's accounts on it. I'll have to do some calculating to see what the access time would be. Anyway, I'll have this version ready by Tuesday when we have our next conference call with Barney. That will probably be our last contact with ERMA."[12]

On March 5, Oldfield and Trotter showed up at Howard Lief's office with a supplemental proposal covering a simplified ERMA design for reduced capacity operation.[13] It had been contributed by Johnson and Jacobi, though it provided no pricing information. It discussed the two options, ERMA IIA and ERMA IIB. Along with the supplemental proposal, they brought a number of transistor circuit boards furnished by Jacobi and Johnson. Lief seemed satisfied with these offerings, but he quickly set them aside and began talking about contract details and possible concessions.

"We're very close to making a decision, and it's important to get very specific so we can make a valid comparison between proposals. I can tell you now that GE is one of three companies whose proposals are being analyzed by the ERMA committee. I'm the chairman, but there are five other Bank of America executives whose votes count as much as mine. The next meeting of the committee will take place on March 14, and we expect our president, Clark Beise, will attend. If all goes well, the committee will make a firm recommendation to the board of directors at that point. I'm going to be up to my neck until then, working with our accountants to prepare the financial exhibits on which the decision will be based. During the interim, please contact Diane Woodward if you wish to provide any additional information. Good luck."

As they departed the Bank of America building, Oldfield remarked, "George, this is going to be a pretty long week for both of us. I plan to spend much of my time with Walt Nelson, getting caught up on Microwave Laboratory problems in case next week finds us back at the old grind. My suggestion is that you continue to spend time with the Bank of America working-level people. You might pick up some information that would be useful if they start asking any last-minute questions. Is that all right with you?"

"No problem."

It was late afternoon, March 15, when Oldfield received a call from Diane Woodward. "Mr. Lief asked me to notify you that he would like to meet with you alone tomorrow morning at the usual time. Can you make it?"

"Yes, ma'am."

Oldfield didn't get much sleep that night. The next morning he carefully studied all the proposals and letters representing GE's formal commitment to the Bank of America, in anticipation of another possible negotiating session. He arrived at Lief's office precisely at 10 a.m. and was ushered in by Diane.

"Congratulations, Barney," said a smiling Howard Lief. "The ERMA committee has selected the GE bid, and the recommendation will go forth to the board of directors today, to be acted on at the April 9 board meeting. In anticipation of the meeting, you and I have some work to do. First, here's a copy of the exhibits on which the committee made its decision. I want you to go over the figures carefully and give me a statement that you either agree or disagree with the analyses. Second, I will need a draft Letter of Intent to present to the board for approval so we can initiate the program immediately after the board meeting."

Oldfield did his best to look unimpressed by the news. "I'll get right on it, Howard. I'm pretty familiar with the clauses our legal people will want in the Letter of Intent. If you like, I'll make up a proposed version that you can shoot at and we can use as a basis for whatever final negotiations may be necessary."

"That will be fine. By the way, I suggest you not make any announcement within GE until after the board meeting. I don't see any problem, but Clark Beise would be upset if anything got out before the board's decision."

"Okay, but how about George Trotter? I'll need his help on the Letter of Intent."

"Of course, so long as he's discreet."

Oldfield floated out of Lief's office.

The board meeting produced no surprises except that Oldfield and Trotter were invited to lunch in the board's formal dining room. They were impressed with Clark Beise, who congratulated them on their fine proposal and stressed the desire of the bank to expedite the program as an important step in the bank's history.

Back in Lief's office they received the final version of the Letter of Intent, signed by Lief. "I assume you'll have to obtain approval from your management in Syracuse before we can start implementing the program."

"Yes, we'll need Dr. Baker's signature on the dotted line. I anticipated a successful conclusion to the negotiation and arranged to take a late afternoon flight to Syracuse. I'll call headquarters the minute I get back to the office and give them the good news."

The mahogany bar in the lounge of the San Francisco International Airport was alive with business travelers stoking up for their long night on one of the red-eye flights to the East. George Trotter, still on a high from the news received from Howard Lief, sipped the dry martini he really didn't need, and said, "I still can't believe it, Barney. We've pulled off the largest order in the history of the computer business and you still haven't cracked a smile."

"I'm just beginning to appreciate the magnitude of the commitment we've made, and it's pretty sobering. Do you realize, George, that we've dragged the General Electric Company into the commercial computer war against the wishes of the company's president. Life is about to get very scary but very exciting.

"Here's to ERMA!" Barney drained his glass, shook George's hand, and made for the boarding area.

CHAPTER 5
THE CONTRACT IS SIGNED

In mid-March, Baker had received a sharp NO! to his latest business plan for GE to enter the commercial computer market on a broad basis. This was followed by a letter of explanation, of which the key passage was: "Under no circumstances will the General Electric Company go into the business machine business. However, sometime in the future, in support of our historical businesses, it may be necessary for us to go into the process computer business."[14]

Baker, considering the ERMA proposal a long shot, had ignored the letter— there was no point in making an issue of it unless a miracle happened. Besides, he did have a prior commitment, probably forgotten by Cordiner, that he could establish a Computer Department if they did win the ERMA contract.

"Dr. Haller is on the line, sir."

"Yes, George."

"Hold onto your hat, Doc. I just hung up from talking to Barney Oldfield in Palo Alto. He's catching a plane in a few minutes to bring us a signed letter contract from the Bank of America in the amount of $31 million for the ERMA system. It looks like you're in the computer business."

Baker was silent for a few moments, then burst into laughter. "That son of a gun has just proved that Ralph Cordiner's staff are a bunch of chumps. Wait until I tell him about this development.

"We'd better set up a strategy session as soon as Barney shows up tomorrow. We'll want to check out that the letter contract is for real, and then I think we need to figure out how to get around Cordiner's stupid mandate."

Oldfield showed up the next day on a Mohawk Airlines DC-4 from Chicago. His eyes were red from lack of sleep, but he was still on a high from his victory at the Bank of America. He checked out a rental car and drove at once to Electronics Park where he finally found a place in the visitors' parking lot. Stopping first at the spacious cafeteria building, he had a quick breakfast, shaved and changed his shirt and tie in the men's room, and called Haller's extension on the inside line.

"Hi, Mr. Oldfield," was the cheerful greeting from Haller's secretary. "I hear congratulations are in order. They're waiting for you in Doc Baker's office."

"They" turned out to be Baker, Haller, and Ike Karr, Baker's division manager of engineering. They were seated at a large conference table, drinking coffee.

"Well, young man," said Baker as he exhaled a cloud of cigar smoke, "it looks like you've surprised the boys at 570 Lexington Avenue. Just last week, Clarence Linder, GE's vice president of engineering, told me the staff was concerned that I was spending $50,000 on a wild goose chase in California. It appears he was wrong."

" I'd say so, sir. It turns out we only spent about half of the appropriation, and it looks as if we've caught the goose." Oldfield laid the letter contract on the conference table. "They made a number of extra copies for me at the bank so we could expedite the review process. The contract is signed by the bank, so it's a legal commitment on their part."

"Okay, Barney. I'll get a copy to Bob Estes at once for legal review. Why don't you give each of us a copy to read while you go over it?" Baker was obviously keyed up and anxious to get into action.

It took an hour to go over the nine-page document, with one or more of the men interjecting questions or comments at each contract clause. When they were finished, Baker said, "Essentially this commits the GE Computer Section to refining and manufacturing a quantity of up to thirty-six complete ERMA systems at a target price of $640,000 each and a ceiling price of $796,000 each. Why the big difference? We normally can estimate manufacturing cost to about 5 percent."

"Well, Doc, there are some major unknowns that can hardly be estimated to within 100 percent. They involve the engineering development work to transistorize the big ERMA computer, make sure it contains the logic to do the bank's job, and integrate it with the automatic character reader and sorter, both of which also require additional development. Johnson and Jacobi both think it's a feasible project, but it's going to take about thirty months before the first system can be delivered."

"Barney, I've read your proposal, but tell me again about your facility plan."

"Stanford Research Institute has a small building—actually a World War II hospital building adjacent to the ERMA building—which they've agreed to lease to us to make into a temporary engineering laboratory. There's plenty of power available, and SRI has already installed desks, chairs, and lab benches in anticipation of the winner wanting to station engineers and draftsmen there for an initial period. TI has had a couple of men there for some time. Maybe we can hire them.

"The temporary lab will work okay for about nine months during which we propose to build a facility adjacent to the Microwave Laboratory. That will contain engineering offices, lab space, assembly areas, and test areas. We propose to use the machine shop of the Microwave Lab for fabricating machine parts and sheet steel cabinetry. We'll subcontract electromechanical items like the high-speed sorter, printer, and mag-tape units. The computer itself will be made up mainly of digital modules, most of which will be identical, and we propose to have the modules built here in the Technical Equipment Department. I believe the repetitive volume will be welcomed by Bill Morlock and his factory people but, if not, Hewlett-Packard would love to act as a subcontractor. We'll have to study this, but there's time to build a separate facility at Stanford Industrial Park once we have ERMA under control and can make a long-range plan. Fred Terman promises to reserve a choice piece of land for us."[15]

"I guess you're right, Barney, but we may have trouble with 570. The company has never favored California as the headquarters of an Operating Department. You may have a fight on your hands." Oldfield was too intrigued with the term *Operating Department* to be concerned about Baker's warning.

Ike Karr, who had not said a word previously, decided to intervene. "Doc, you recently received a mandate from Ralph Cordiner forbidding us to go into business machines. I don't see how you can accept this contract for what is obviously an enormous business machine."

Baker was not fazed. "Haller has told me that ERMA is a process computer system, which would be permitted by a liberal interpretation of his dictate. Besides, we have a prior agreement that if the Electronics Division should obtain the ERMA contract, I can establish a Computer Department. Ralph hates to lose face, and I think he'll accept the liberal interpretation rather than admit he and his staff were dead wrong."

Oldfield was concerned by Baker's words. "Does this mean, when the Computer Department is formed, we'll have to concentrate on process control? That's a pretty small part of the computer market."

"It means you should develop a business plan that includes selling ERMA systems to banks but otherwise concentrates on the industrial control market rather than competing with IBM on a broad scale. The idea is to get the camel's nose under the tent and then expand step by step. In the long run, GE management will accept any product that makes a decent profit.

"Barney, as soon as you can get the engineering operation underway in Palo Alto, I think you should make your headquarters here in Syracuse. You're going to have to go through a lot of misery before the Industrial Computer Section can become an operating department. First, you're going to have to conduct a site selection study together with the Manufacturing Services people in Schenectady. Then you'll have to deal with Harold Smiddy to get tentative agreement on a Product Charter. And of course you're going to have to recruit your management team to go with the engineering team. It's quite likely that all of this may take six months or so before you have all your ducks lined up. Most of that will have to be done here, so if you want to bring your family back temporarily, I'll authorize the rental of a furnished house here and your transportation expenses. During this period, I'm going to assign you to Bill Morlock's Technical Equipment Department. I'll talk with him when the meeting is over to make sure he has an office for you and is prepared to furnish whatever logistical support you need. For the time being, you'll be on his payroll, but all your expenses will be assigned to a Computer Section account."

This was not good news for Oldfield. He knew his wife, Sofia, would be upset at the move, and the thought that their final destination might be up in the air for months was even more troubling. He opened his mouth to argue but decided the situation was complicated enough without getting into an argument with the boss.

"As soon as the letter contract is signed, I'd like to take off for Palo Alto to get things rolling with the bank and SRI. Is it okay to break the news to people like Bob Johnson and George Jacobi so they can start making their own arrangements?"

"I've already told Bob," said George Haller, "and he's ready to go as soon as you give the word. My guess is that he already alerted Jacobi. You can't keep something like this a secret for more than five minutes. Why don't you and I have lunch with Bob and Lloyd DeVore when this meeting is over. Remember, Lloyd is Bob's direct boss and may not be too agreeable about losing him."

"Let me know, George, if you have a problem with DeVore. This project is too important to let organization details stand in the way."

"Sure, Doc. Don't worry."

"Okay, it seems we've covered everything we can for the time being," said Baker. "I think Barney can count on taking an afternoon flight back to the coast tomorrow. The contract looks fine to me, and I see you've even included some of Bob Estes' favorite clauses. You can check with my secretary late tomorrow morning. I'll have it signed by then, with a letter of transmittal back to Howard Lief. Why don't you see Bill Morlock this afternoon and make arrangements for your stay in Electronics Park? Then you'll be all set for your trip home.

Baker broke into a rare smile. "You know, I can't wait to break the news to 570."

Haller took his lunch guests to the Homestead, a favored watering hole not far from Electronics Park. As they sipped their drinks, Bob Johnson said, "I still can't believe we have the contract. In fact, I was so positive we hadn't a chance that I made a deposit on a lot here so I could build a house."

"Would you like to pass it up?" said Oldfield.

"Not on your life. But I think I ought to start off as the chief technical honcho and not the Project Manager, I've never had any experience organizing and managing a large project. I think George Jacobi's experience with developing and supervising the big Power Control Simulator in Schenectady might better qualify him to manage the job."

"How about it, Lloyd?" said Haller. "Are you willing to let Bob go to the ERMA project, at least temporarily?"

"Knowing how Doc feels about the ERMA project, I don't think I have much choice, but I suggest Bob stay on the Electronics Lab payroll for the time being, as a consultant to ERMA to be located in Palo Alto."

"Bob will need to come to Palo Alto almost immediately," said Oldfield. "The contract calls for an initial three-month program at SRI to familiarize GE engineers with the ERMA system and define the production system more precisely. Is that feasible?"

"That's up to Bob," said DeVore.

"I can leave within the next few days," said Johnson, "if you can assign the machine tool control project to someone else." Turning to Oldfield, he added, "I talked it over with Mary last night, and she's excited about California. Our plan is for her to start packing the minute I leave. I'll find us a place to rent in the Palo Alto area and then return and drive the family out to the West Coast. I assume GE will pick up the tab for the move?"

"No problem," said Oldfield. "Actually, I have the same problem in reverse. I'm going to have to move back to Syracuse for six months or so. I'll probably be driving east while you're driving west."

Having disposed of business matters, the quartet settled down to their steaks and french fries. Thus ended the first conference in the history of the Industrial Computer Section, one day to become the GE Computer Department.

True to his word, Baker had the ERMA letter contract ready before lunchtime the following day. With the signed contract was a letter to Howard Lief, signed by W.R.G. Baker.[16] Oldfield was pleased to read in part as follows:

> "I have discussed the program in detail with Mr. Oldfield and his staff and have studied the proposed Letter of Intent Agreement. I am in complete agreement with the commitments made to date and the manner in which they have been expressed in preliminary contract form. I would like to reiterate Mr. Oldfield's statements regarding the long-range nature of our interest in the ERMA program. We visualize ERMA as the first in a series of revolutionary products for use in wide segments of the banking industry and in a number of other industries. We feel our two organizations have joined in a venture which will blaze a trail for all industry to follow, and we can visualize a long and fruitful period of cooperative association during which both organizations should profit."

CHAPTER 6
DOWN TO EARTH

Oldfield had left Palo Alto on a high produced by the award of the ERMA contract. He returned in a sober mood, not quite discouraged but aware of the series of complications, personal and professional, facing him in the immediate future. His first order of business was to break the news to his family that they would be moving back to Syracuse for a period of six months or more. He knew it would be an unpopular move, particularly in the midst of the school term—he had speculated on the possibility of leaving them behind. He knew, however, that his wife, Sofia, couldn't function on her own for such a long period.

In truth, the prospect of returning to Syracuse for a six-month period during the start of the ERMA contract was unwelcome in a number of ways. Oldfield was worried about the interaction between the GE engineers and their counterparts at SRI, and he would have liked to be close to the scene during the early days of the project. As it was, he would barely have time to introduce the initial group when they arrived in a few days. He'd have to trust Trotter to smooth the way and attempt to resolve any personality conflicts that might arise.

Perhaps the greatest concern had to do with the nature of the ERMA letter contract and the fact that it would be necessary to develop and negotiate a formal contract over the following months. He should be available to discuss details with the Bank of America, and it would be clumsy to do this from a Syracuse location. In the back of his mind, there was also a feeling that he was opening a big can of worms within GE.

A week passed. The first four engineers arrived from Syracuse: George Jacobi, Bob Johnson, Dave Zaheb from the Electronics Laboratory, and Jay Levinthal from the GE Advanced Electronics Center at Cornell. Jacobi and Johnson had drawn up a preliminary chart of the local ERMA organization, calling for an immediate infusion of talent to implement the project. Jacobi had a list of engineers who had indicated an interest in becoming members of the ERMA team. He and Bob Johnson had gone over their resumes, discarded some, and ranked the others in terms of probable usefulness. It was agreed to make offers to several.

"As far as the Bank of America is concerned, the Industrial Computer Section is an ongoing operation," said Oldfield, "and not a newly formed activity. We need to build up fast, both from inside and outside GE. I'll help out while I'm on the East Coast, but the main responsibility will be out here. My suggestion is that you, Bob, concentrate on the computer types, and you, George, because you have a number of years of experience in organizing substantial GE technological projects, put emphasis on developing the other capabilities you're going to need here: administration, draftsmen, mechanical designers, technicians, and so on. I'll back you up as necessary."

With words of this sort, Oldfield had left for Syracuse, leaving the technical people to make out as they could with SRI. He left George Trotter behind to handle local contact with the Bank of America.

The Oldfield family—wife Sofia, daughter Wendy, sons Bob and Dick, dog Ragmop, plus a mother cat of many litters, left Los Altos in the family's Dodge sedan, weary and disgruntled from several evenings of arguments and discussions involving school friends, houses, packing, route selection, and so on. By mid-afternoon of the second day, the three children and their animals, crushed against one another in the back seat, hot and sweaty in a car that lacked air conditioning, were on the verge of becoming out of control. They limped into Phoenix, surprised at the cleanliness of the city and the wide, spacious streets. More importantly, they soon located an air-conditioned motel with a large outdoor swimming pool. The kids were soon in their bathing suits, joining the throng of children, and their basic good natures were restored. Later, based on the recommendation of the motel manager, they went to dinner at The Green Gables, a restaurant on Camelback Road that featured a torch-carrying knight on horseback to lead the car to the parking area. The meal was excellent, and the knight made a lasting impression on the kids.

The family left Phoenix in a good mood, and the rest of the trip to Syracuse passed pleasantly except for one evening when they couldn't find a motel with a swimming pool. Phoenix had made a lasting impression.

Oldfield was almost immediately swept into a frenzy of activity. His small office in the factory planning area of the Technical Equipment Department was noisy and inadequate for the traffic that seemed endless. It seemed that a number of GE engineers, salesmen, and manufacturing people were excited by GE's entry into the world of computers, and most of them stopped by the office for a chat and often to apply for a position. This was a rather ticklish business, as it was forbidden to make an offer to any individual without his supervisor's approval in advance. Oldfield solved the etiquette problem by extolling the virtues of the Industrial Computer Section, but then refusing to accept any resumes without an accompanying note of approval from the individual's supervisor. The notes and resumes kept rolling in.

One morning Oldfield received a telephone call that sent him into a state of shock. "This is Bob Yowell from Real Estate and Construction Services in Schenectady. We have instructions to contact you to organize the site-selection study for the Industrial Computer Section. I plan to be in Syracuse tomorrow and would very much like to get together with you when it's convenient."

"I'll be happy to meet with you tomorrow, Bob, but our proposal to the Bank of America, which Dr. Baker has approved, called for us to manufacture the sub-assemblies in Syracuse, and to perform the assembly and test of the computers in Palo Alto. We didn't plan to establish a manufacturing facility at this point in the program."

"As I understand it, you'll be assembling and delivering up to thirty-six identical systems at almost a million dollars apiece," said Yowell. "Is that correct?"

"Why, yes."

"That constitutes manufacturing," said Yowell "and requires a full-fledged site survey regardless of any arrangements you might have made with Mr. Baker. Really, Barney, the site study is for your own good if you plan to have the Computer Section evolve into an Operating Department."

"Okay, Bob. I'll be here all day tomorrow."

"Good. If you've no objection, I'll bring along Dick Holmquist from Community Relations Development Services. He's a plant location expert and can help expedite the study."

"The more the merrier," said Oldfield, still not taking the site-selection survey very seriously.

The two visitors from Schenectady arrived with bulging briefcases and a roll of drawings, one of which was spread out on the small table Oldfield had borrowed for the occasion. It was a map of the United States showing the location of all the GE Operating Departments and other major facilities. Also marked were locations previously studied by GE; approved locations were colored green, disapproved locations were colored red. Oldfield saw to his horror that the entire state of California was red.

"What gives?" he said. "We already have an atomic energy plant in San Jose, the Microwave Laboratory at Stanford, and a flatiron plant in Ontario, California."

"The atomic energy facility and the Microwave Laboratory are both R&D operations and not classified as plants. The Ontario facility was formed by an acquisition some years ago, and its troubles with unions and punitive labor legislation are responsible for California being on the black list," said Yowell. "I have to tell you, Barney, that you'll never be able to sell Palo Alto as the location for the Computer Department."

"But the computer business is several years away from being like other GE businesses. The engineering content is so high we have to locate where we have the best chance of attracting scarce computer engineers. Besides, the customer is here and we already have a facility we can add onto at low cost compared to building a new plant at some remote location."

"I'll grant you that these are good arguments for the short term, but I assume the Computer Department has a five-year plan for expanding into more and more product lines and will require far more employees than you have projected for this one program with the Bank of America."

"Granted, but we have options on sufficient space for a completely integrated facility on Stanford Industrial Park land. We can plan the facility in detail while the ERMA system is being designed. The program is complicated enough without locating the factory hundreds of miles away from the engineering group."

Dick Holmquist from Community Relations decided to enter the debate. "Look at these exhibits, Barney. They'll show you why California is not considered a good place to establish a new GE business. The fact is that California, along with the industrial Northeast, has the worst business climate in the country. It has high taxes, rampant and aggressive unionism, high labor rates, unfavorable labor legislation, and high living costs. California is a good place for laboratories and for military programs where the government pays for all these excess costs, but it's no place for a commercial manufacturing business. We've got to find you a home that is attractive for engineers and also has a good business climate. Just keep an open mind."

"I still think the cost of isolating the ERMA engineering group from the factory where ERMA must be assembled and tested will be much greater than the costs associated with taxes and labor rates. The engineers have no choice but to be located near Stanford Research Institute and the Bank of America until the ERMA development is completed, and when this happens, some thirty months from now, how are we going to persuade them to move away from the country's most attractive location for professional people? We'll lose most of the technical competence created by the ERMA project." Oldfield, normally a mild-mannered man, was becoming perturbed.

"You have some good points, but there's one thing I have to tell you. The highest priority project in General Electric is the nuclear power business, and their main nuclear facility is a few miles from Palo Alto in San Jose. They need computer engineers and physicists as much as you do, and they've been promised by Mr. Cordiner that there will be no new GE facility of a high-tech nature in their vicinity."

Oldfield felt the noose drawing tighter. "How about Berkeley, California? Like the Palo Alto area, it's a magnet for engineers and physicists. It's within commuting distance from Palo Alto, but it's far from San Jose."

"Well, we could include Berkeley in the site-selection process, but I'm sure you'll agree when it's finished that it won't be in the top spot of your rating."

"Just what is your rating system?"

"Well, the company requires that we evaluate six major factors in selecting a site. They include: community desirability, business climate, area factors, transportation, taxes, and utilities. Each of these factors is given a weighting, depending on the type of business. Generally, we establish a figure of a thousand for a perfect site. Community desirability and business climate are given the greatest weight in most cases. Each of the factors is broken down into its components, and each component is rated in accordance with its importance to the particular business involved."

"Who establishes the weighting factors?"

"That's a matter of give-and-take between your people and our offices. Tell you what. I'll leave you a copy of the site-selection study that was made for the Jet Engine Department when they moved from Lynn, Massachusetts, to Evendale, Ohio. It will give you a good picture of what you'll have to go through to establish a site for your business."

"Thanks. I guess I can't get out of it. I'm in the process right now of interviewing and selecting the key section managers of the organization. I hope to have this done by the end of the week. In the meantime, I'll try to develop my own proposal for the weighting factors to be used for the comparison of sites. I'll get this to you so you can criticize and modify it. Will that be all right?"

"That sounds fine. We'll be anxious to hear from you."

A few days later, Oldfield convened a meeting of the group of five individuals he had selected to be the top management team of the Industrial Computer Section. "Our first big job is to find a home for the Industrial Computer Section and ultimately the Computer Department. It appears that we may not be allowed to follow the original plan to locate the organization in Palo Alto, so let's work like hell to ensure we don't end up in Nashville or Little Rock because they have lower labor rates or a good business climate. We haven't had an opportunity to be together before, so I'd like each of you to express his opinion."

Clair Lasher was the first to comment. He was a tall man, dressed more meticulously than the average engineer, and casual in manner. Lasher was understood to be independently wealthy, though the only hint he gave was a certain air of independence. He had been sales manager of Naval Airborne Equipment in the Government Division before he became involved in product planning for the Technical Equipment Department. In that role he was responsible for the computer section of the Metcalf Report, which had, among other things, recommended that GE enter the commercial computer market. It was this recommendation that had been turned down by Ralph Cordiner. He was skeptical of their chance to change Cordiner's mind, but Oldfield had stuck his neck out, and he, Lasher, was willing to ride along as manager of marketing.

"I haven't given much thought to this particular problem," said Lasher. "I was comfortable with your plan to have the digital modules produced here in Syracuse, with final assembly and testing in Palo Alto. However, it's obvious the manufacturing facility in Syracuse won't be able to handle much future growth, so we might as well plan for the long term. I'd be happy to participate in the site-selection study, and I think we should go into it with open minds."

"How about you, Ray?"

Ray Barclay, the newly appointed manager of manufacturing, had received his BSEE from the University of Syracuse in 1942 and had been with GE for thirteen years. He was a graduate of GE's Advanced Manufacturing Training Program, which involved three years of assignments in different functional areas such as production control, quality control, plant supervision, purchasing, and so on. Since 1958 he had held supervisory positions in Electronics Park and had received high ratings as a manufacturing man. Considered a "comer," he was a welcome addition to the computer team.

"I'll admit I haven't been too crazy about having the ERMA manufacturing function split between two locations. I'm all for selecting a permanent site and developing our plant to meet our specific requirements. I'd love to be in a location where we have reasonable labor rates and aren't hobbled from the beginning by union demands. You can count me in."

"Okay, Ray. I'll admit I hadn't given as much thought to the manufacturing side of the picture as I should have. Your point's well taken."

Oldfield shifted his glance to Ken Geiser, who had come up from Schenectady to attend the meeting. As the manager of engineering, Ken would have a key part in the development of the business. Ken had been responsible for the overall data-processing activity of the General Engineering Laboratory in Schenectady. He was widely acquainted within GE engineering circles. Not prepossessing personally, he had a reputation as a firm but reasonable supervisor.

"I'd prefer Schenectady, of course, from a personal standpoint. Both my wife and I are dug into the community and will hate to leave. However, we've decided to make the best of it, knowing that GE would never permit a new business venture to be set up there. I agree with you, Barney, that the most important criterion is to pick a site that will be attractive to high-caliber professional people. The computer business is in its infancy, GE is already several years late in entering the business, and we have to tip the odds in our favor as much as possible. I think either Palo Alto or the Route 128 ring around MIT and Harvard is the place to be."

"I'm with you, Ken, but I have a feeling we'll strike out on either of the two locations. What do you think, McCombs?"

Ken McCombs, manager of finance, had been the plant accountant at Ontario, California. His position had been phased out in an economy move, and he had been recommended by Accounting Services in Schenectady as being ready for a manager of finance position in a small department. His resume was impressive in terms of experience in various aspects of accounting, and he had served a term as traveling auditor, one of GE's prized assignments. Actually, the dotted line that connected McCombs with the central Accounting Services office in Schenectady involved a reporting relationship that was virtually as strong as the solid line to his general manager. One of his major responsibilities was to ensure that the general manager did not indulge in "creative" accounting techniques to enhance or distort departmental financial performance. McCombs and Oldfield had discussed this dual relationship at the time of his interview, and they now felt comfortable with one another.

"I'd strongly prefer being on the West Coast, and lacking that I'd settle for the Northwest or Southwest. Like most Californians, I'd rather not move to the Deep South with its racial problems and poor schooling for the kids. However, I'll approach the site-location study with an open mind."

"Thanks," said Oldfield. He turned to the last member of the fledgling management team, Art Newman, the manager of employee and community relations. It might seem odd that the new organization would have an individual with such a title, considering there were very few employees and no community to be concerned with. However, GE had become very conscious of organizational structure under Ralph Cordiner, to the point where every Operating Department was required to have basically the same management positions and management levels. Reporting to each of the individual section managers were subsection managers, and so on. The objective was to create a structure in which no single individual had more than seven persons reporting to him, so that his "span of control" would be manageable. One of Art Newman's jobs was to deal with these organizational problems as the business expanded.

"How about you, Art?"

"I went through this sort of thing before when the Government Equipment Department was split between Light and Heavy Military, and it was necessary to find another home for the airborne people. The site selected was Utica, and you probably know it worked out very well. I think our biggest problem with the Services people was their desire to establish new departments in the South. We were finally able to get the weighting factors adjusted until we got the answer Doc Baker wanted. I'm not suggesting this is a parallel situation, but I think we'll have to be very careful that Bob Yowell doesn't put too much emphasis on traditional GE factors, such as proximity to steel supplies and costs of shipping heavy products."

"Good point, Art. There seems to be no rebellion among you five concerning this site study, so I hereby appoint you the Site-Selection Committee. I'm appointing Ray Barclay as chairman, responsible for making arrangements for site visits and liaison with the Services people in Schenectady. I'd suggest each of you spend something like half time on the problem and participate in a reasonable number of site visits. It's pretty urgent, because it won't be easy to recruit professional people if we can't tell them where they'll be located."

Oldfield held up the sample site study he'd been given. "Here's a copy of a successful site-selection report. I've read through it a couple of times and suggest we copy the general format and go into the same amount of detail. I've developed an initial proposed slate of weighting factors that relate specifically to our business situation, and I have a copy for each of you. I'd appreciate it if you could make any suggested corrections and get it back to me by tomorrow morning. I'll try to average out our differences and get back to you with the results that we hopefully can argue out. I want to make sure we have a united front in dealing with the Services people. Also, will each of you please develop a list of sites that you feel would be acceptable for our venture, excluding all within fifty miles of an existing GE business. We may as well take the initiative in the hope of getting a corporate decision in the reasonably near future."

Back in Palo Alto, Jacobi and Johnson were busy building up the ERMA technical staff. Jacobi had made arrangements with Art Stern of the Electronics Laboratory to establish a training course in transistor circuits for interested GE engineers who needed advanced instruction in the design of digital devices. Soon there was a flow of good engineers from GE and elsewhere in the industry—some brought in by Jacobi, some by Johnson, and several who had gotten the word through industry sources. Outstanding in the group were John Paivinen from Burroughs who had just completed the design of a large-scale digital computer, Gerry Allard a self-made expert in transistor circuits from the Electronics Laboratory, Dick Hagopian from Westinghouse, and Ken Manning, a creative GE mechanical designer. Very quickly the new people became assimilated as members of the project team.[17]

In the mid-1950s, the computer profession was still a sort of journeyman trade. One finished an interesting job somewhere, heard of something new being begun somewhere else, went there and demonstrated that one knew a little bit about computing, and got hired. Joe Weizenbaum was one of that breed. He had just finished the design of an operating system—small by the standards of the time—for the Bendix Aviation Company when he heard about the ERMA project. Joe showed up unannounced at the ERMA SRI facility and presented himself to Herm Green, the GE engineering administrator who had shortly before joined the group.

"What's your technical specialty, Mr. Weizenbaum?" asked Green.

"I'm a programmer,"[18] said Weizenbaum. "I just finished the design of an operating system and I'm looking for a larger project."

"Well, we have a large project here called ERMA, but I don't know if there are any programs as yet. You see, it's just being developed and we're looking for computer engineers."

Weizenbaum grinned. He'd been through this before. "You see, the program consists of built-in instructions that tell the digital circuits what to do. Programmers are the ones who work with the circuit designers so that the computer can perform the tasks it's being built for."

"I'd better let you talk with Bob Johnson, our computer man," said Green.

The interview with Bob Johnson turned out to be rather important. While Johnson had previously designed a digital computer at Hughes Aircraft, the procedure was one basically of "solving the equations," generally in binary. In the lengthy interview session that followed Bob was introduced for the first time to the term 'programmer' as well as to the technique of programming in symbolic assembly language.

"What a marvelous invention," exulted Bob. "You're hired."

The Palo Alto Computer Laboratory, as the GE ERMA group was called, eventually grew to a size of sixty-five engineers, programmers, technicians, draftsmen, and support personal—actually a modest size for a project of the magnitude of ERMA. The engineers recruited in the early stages became the managers of the five segments into which the work of developing ERMA was divided—Jay Levinthal, Systems Engineerings; John Paivinen, Computer Engineering; Dick Hagopian, Document Sensing and Handling; Joe Weizenbaum, Programming; and Dave Zeheb, Paper Processing. Backed up by such as Karsten Solheim, Wally Katsung, Charlie Asmus, and the rest, they came together to form a potent team that tackled ERMA's monumental technical problems with a dedication unusual in a large corporation.

Meanwhile, back in Syracuse, the site-selection study was rolling along. Oldfield was happy to leave most of the site visitations to his staff and to Yowell and Holmquist. After discussing the matter with Doc Baker, he was resigned to the fact that GE would not permit a site in the San Francisco Bay Area, and he would be faced with a situation in which the department headquarters and manufacturing facility would be separated from the Palo Alto engineering activity. The worst feature of this was the virtual certainty that the bulk of those recruited for ERMA would refuse to leave Palo Alto when the project was completed and would jump to one of the many high-tech activities building up in the shadow of Stanford University. This meant it would be necessary to build up a substantial computer engineering competence at the remote location while the ERMA project was in progress. What to do?

The only answer to this question was to obtain, organize, or invent (if necessary) programs that would finance the engineering and manufacturing activity at the still-undetermined site. One such project was the digital portion of the numerical machine tool controller to be furnished on a subcontract basis to the Specialty Control Department. Another internal GE product was the PRODUCTRON for production scheduling and machine loading, an analog device almost ready for manufacture, based on a design conceived at the company's General Engineering Laboratory. Still another was the military's TPQ-5 computer, provided it didn't get taken away by one of the military departments.

But all these were window dressing. What was needed was a substantial digital computer project. During a visit to NCR in Dayton, Oldfield had spent time with Chuck Keenoy, manager of engineering, and Joe Desch, project engineer on the check sorter and high-speed printer. For the most part, the conversations had dealt with NCR's proposal to act as a subcontractor for ERMA electromechanical equipment. They were joined at one point by Bob Oelman, NCR executive vice president.

"You know," said Oelman, "there seems to be a basic fit between NCR and GE. Our expertise is in the electromechanical systems and components required for business information processing, whereas yours is in electronics. I'm glad to see you fellows working so well together. Maybe it's an omen for the future."

Possibly encouraged by his boss's sign of approval Keenoy outlined the steps NCR had taken to become a factor in the electronic computer field.

"We acquired a small R&D firm in Hawthorne, California, which ran out of money in the process of designing a transistorized general-purpose business computer. They've been spending our money for a long time and still haven't produced. Frankly, I've lost faith in the organization, and we've been discussing the possibility of taking over the project and moving it to Dayton. That seems impractical because we lack expertise and facilities necessary for the production of electronic equipment. Do you think GE would be interested in taking over the project and developing a production prototype on a subcontract basis?"

"I don't think my boss would be anxious to have us dedicate scarce engineering resources just to develop a product for another company. It would be another matter if there were a continuing production contract involved." Oldfield had just been handed a possible solution to his need to have a substantial digital computer project to finance the build-up of the technical group in the remote site. However, he didn't want to appear too eager.

"Suppose we offered you a contract for a reasonable quantity of computers beyond the production prototype? We are in no rush to build up an electronics assembly line. After seeing your manufacturing facilities during my visit to Electronics Park, we appreciate that it's an entirely different business."

"We'd be happy to take a look at it, but we'd have to send a team to Hawthorne to study the computer and determine what we'd have to do to complete the design and put the device into production. Can that be arranged without upsetting the applecart?"

"No problem. They know they're in trouble, and they'd probably welcome a takeover by GE so long as they were offered jobs."

"Okay, Chuck. I'll get back to you as soon as I can put a team together."

On the sleeper train from Dayton to Syracuse, Oldfield sat comfortably in the club car, smoking a Camel and sipping his scotch and soda. He was oblivious to the chatter of the other occupants as he contemplated the possibilities of developing a close business relationship with NCR. Could this be the answer to the long-term dilemma posed by Ralph Cordiner's desire to keep GE out of the business machine business? He knew he was too junior in the GE organization to think of joint ventures between corporations, but the prospects of some type of union with NCR seemed attractive in the extreme. Maybe he could start the ball rolling and, at the same time, obtain the contract he needed to solve at least one part of the problem created by the GE refusal to build up the computer business at Stanford Industrial Park.

Oldfield spent much of the next day with Ken Geiser, Ray Barclay, and Bob Wooley. Bob was manager of the Digital Devices Section at the GE Advanced Electronics Center at Cornell. It was he, in fact, who had developed and fabricated the digital circuits that Oldfield and Trotter had given to Howard Lief as an indication of their competence in the field. A senior engineer, Bob was anxious to join his boss of a few years back if another computer project of substance should develop.

Oldfield explained the possibility of the NCR project as both a means of obtaining additional backlog that would help finance the build-up at what he still thought of as the "remote site" and perhaps initiating a long-term relationship with one of the country's leading business machine companies.

"I realize there's a danger that if we find the relationship not to be compatible in the future, we will have helped a competitor, but then the competitor will also have helped us. The risks seem balanced on both sides.

"Here's the set of specifications covering the computer," continued Oldfield. "Chuck Keenoy smuggled them to me and reminded me they're confidential NCR property. If you three can agree on a few optional times for a trip to California, I'll give him a call and make the necessary arrangements. And please keep quiet about the project until we can determine if we can make a bid covering the cost to complete the engineering, assemble a production prototype, and manufacture an initial quantity of thirty computers.

"Ken, why don't you and Bob start reading the specs while Ray fills me in on the latest results of the site-selection study."

Geiser and Wooley repaired to an empty production office while Barclay unrolled a map and spread it across the desk.

"We've narrowed down the list to six locations," said Barclay: "Austin, Texas; Berkeley, California; Nashville, Tennessee; Phoenix, Arizona; Richmond, Virginia; and Urbana, Illinois. Bob Yowell still wants Nashville, and my guess is that there's some politics involved. He knows you want Berkeley, but my guess is that he'll compromise on Phoenix, which happens to have the highest point rating of the six. All our guys are satisfied with Phoenix as a place to live, though Ken McCombs would prefer the West Coast."[19]

"I hate to accept the compromise, Ray, and I'm going to make one last plea for Berkeley. By the time ERMA is completed, we're going to have a huge stake in the group of technical people who develop the computer, and we're sure to lose most of them if we locate the Computer Department thousands of miles away."

Doc Baker was apologetic but firm. "I've talked to New York and the answer is a flat NO. General Electric is not going to locate any new Operating Departments in the state of California. I agree with your arguments, but I don't have the authority to overrule the president's office on this kind of issue."

The next day, Oldfield gathered his staff together and announced that the final decision had gone in the direction of Phoenix. "Let's firm up some temporary facilities and get to work. We have a business to create."

PART II

Westward Ho,
September 1956
to
December 1958

DRAMATIS PERSONAE

(Names of individuals introduced in Part I are not repeated.)

GRADY GAMMAGE. President of Arizona State College in Tempe, Arizona; anxious to bring the college into University status; a good friend of General Electric.

JOHN JACOBS. Millionaire lettuce farmer and land developer and chairman of Arizona State College's board of trustees; also a member of the Arizona Educational Board of Regents.

WILLIAM DOUGLAS. A lawyer, part-time faculty member of the University of Arizona in Tucson, former Ambassador to Great Britain under Harry Truman, member of Arizona Educational Board of Regents, a director of General Electric, and a foe of Jacobs and Gammage.

AUDREY WHITE. Oldfield's secretary; former executive secretary to William Douglas.

CHARLEY CONROY. Bank of America representative at SRI; an opponent of Al Zipf in the bank's pecking order; a nonbeliever in MICR.

HANS KUEHNI. A prolific inventor and analog solid-state circuit expert in the Schenectady General Engineering Laboratory (GEL). His group developed the transistorized version, which made MICR practical.

JOHN HOGG. Manager of marketing administration for the Computer Department.

HAROLD STRICKLAND. Vice president and general manager of the Industrial Electronics Division, formed when Doc Baker is deposed and the Electronics Division splits into several market-oriented divisions; Oldfield's boss and a former member of Cordiner's staff.

THOMAS WATSON, SR. IBM chairman of the board.

LYMAN (TINY) FINK. General manager of the GE X-ray Department in Milwaukee; Physics Ph.D. who ran one of GE's stable and prosperous businesses.

HARRISON VAN AKEN. General manager of the Communications Products Department; an accountant who made the transition to general manager of a highly successful department.

LOU RADER. General manager of the Specialty Control Department in Waynesboro, Virginia; Ph.D. in electrical engineering. He was an acknowledged leader in the automation field.

FRED MACFEE. Personnel manager for the Jet Engine Department in Evendale, Ohio.

HERB GROSCH. Manager of the Computer Center established by the Computer Department on the campus of Arizona State College. A Ph.D. in astronomy, Grosch learned the programming art at IBM prior to joining GE.

JIM LAPIERRE. Group executive to whom Strickland reported.

BOB and DICK OLDFIELD. Oldfield's two teenaged sons. Their big sister, WENDY, is temporarily in the background.

BARRY GOLDWATER. Congressman, department store owner, and Arizona booster.

FINNLEY CARTER. President of Stanford Research Institute.

ARNOLD SPIELBERG. Recruited from RCA's BIZMAC program, Spielberg is made manager of industrial process computers.

LEMUEL BOULWARE. General Electric's vice president of employee and community relations; an arch foe of labor unions.

CLAUDE TUCKER and BILL FACENDA. Engineers in the ERMA program who made up the "Tiger Team" assigned to solve the AMPEX tape unit and NCR printer problems.

T'SAI LEE. Spielberg's creative programmer.

CHAPTER 7
THE EXODUS TO PHOENIX

By mid-1956 the Oldfield family was on the road, complete with kids, pets, and hopes that Phoenix would be their last stop along the GE highway. Oldfield had stretched the family budget by purchasing a sprawling ranch house with swimming pool, aided by a generous mortgage from the Valley Bank—eager to accommodate the general manager of a business that promised to bring jobs and prestige to this ambitious southwestern city. Even the children were in good spirits, remembering the delights of the motel where they would spend a week or two awaiting their household goods, which had been stored in Palo Alto during their enforced stay in Syracuse. Oldfield was anxious when they arrived in Phoenix and drove by their new home. He had purchased it during a flying trip to Phoenix without an inspection by other family members, and he was braced for a flurry of unfavorable comments. He was pleasantly surprised at the ohs and ahs of approval, highlighted by his wife's dramatic gesture of kissing the ground. Hopefully, they were home at last!

Once the family was settled in the motel and the pets taken to their temporary home at the vet, Oldfield made a beeline for the KTAR television building where Barclay's people had rented fourteen thousand square feet of office space for their headquarters. As he entered, he observed the sign on the door, "General Electric Computer Department." A bit premature, he thought, because they would not reach this status until their appropriation request for a permanent plant facility had been approved. However, there was no point in wasting effort on extraneous details. He let it ride.

Over the next week, families from Syracuse, Schenectady, and elsewhere straggled into Phoenix, and the GE office began to take shape. So many projects were going on simultaneously that Oldfield had to set up a number of task forces to keep track of the details. Art Newman was assigned responsibility for assisting newly arrived families in getting settled, this in addition to recruiting potential employees, dealing with the local newspapers, and working on organizational charts. Ken Geiser was liaising with Herm Green and George Jacobi in Menlo Park to ensure that their support requirements for people and facilities were given top priority. Lasher and Barclay were working on the appropriation request for both rental and permanent facilities, soon due for submission to Doc Baker. Ken McCombs and George Snively were working on the ever-changing budget forecast required for submission along with the appropriation request, a task requiring imagination on a grand scale. Oldfield had assigned himself three major tasks. The first was obviously to stay cur-

rent on ERMA progress both at Menlo Park and at NCR. The second was to negotiate the $30 million contract for NCR 304 computers, a "must" to justify the fore-
cast. It would be the world's second largest commercial computer contract.

Oldfield's third project had to do with nearby Arizona State College (ASC).
Under President Grady Gammage, the college had begun construction of a
Technology Center on the campus. Due to the efforts of Motorola and Sperry, who
had preceded GE in Phoenix, and financed in part by these two companies, the
Technology Center would house the expanded Engineering and Science
Departments. However, it would not be required for two years, and there was talk
of delaying construction. Gammage and Oldfield discussed the possibility of leasing
up to thirty-three thousand square feet of this building for engineering offices and
laboratories to house GE's Phoenix engineering organization pending completion of
a permanent facility, in which case construction might be accelerated. The proposal
was under consideration by the board of trustees, and Oldfield had been invited to
lunch by John Jacobs, the board chairman. Jacobs was a self-made millionaire who
had moved to Arizona before it became a state. He was a lettuce farmer who had
prospered as irrigation had spread through the parched desert and turned it into fer-
tile soil. He had invested in desert land as his business expanded, and many of his
thousands of acres included sections of Scottsdale and Paradise Valley. Jacobs was
one of the most important people in Arizona, and Oldfield was somewhat in awe of
him as he approached the meeting at the Stockyard Restaurant.

John Jacobs, it turned out, was as casual as an old shoe. "Barney," he began, as
they sipped their martinis, "Arizona and Phoenix have been awfully good to me, and
I like to repay the favor when I can. One way is to help build up what used to be a
small teachers' college into a major university. The area needs this sort of thing to
really prosper. Motorola and Sperry have been very helpful in promoting a technical curriculum, and I hope GE has the power to put us over the top. Gammage tells
us you have some background in developing industry-university projects, which
might be helpful."

Oldfield described the programs he had established at Cornell and Stanford, and
emphasized his desire to build a similar relationship with ASC. The proposal to lease
space in the future Technology Building would, he thought, be a good beginning by
bringing the latest in high technology to the campus. If the college could develop a
Master's program in electronics, and eventually a Doctoral program, there would be
benefits to both parties.

"In addition," continued Oldfield, "we have a plan to include a computer center to serve the Computer Department. If the college can furnish us with a building
to install the computer and its staff, we might locate it on the campus so it could
serve the college as well."

Jacobs was openly enthusiastic. "I can tell you right now, the board of trustees
will support you and Gammage. It has already been decided to establish a College
of Engineering, and the staff is already being built up. Within two years we'll be

ready to relocate the department in the new Technology Center. If we could include a large-scale computer in the program, we'd have it all over the University of Arizona. In case you don't know about it, the biggest barrier to Arizona State College becoming a university is the political rivalry between Phoenix and Tucson. We're the state capital and the largest city, but Tucson considers itself Arizona's intellectual center. That's a bunch of baloney, but we've let the myth grow. As a result, the state board of regents has been dominated in the past by the Tucson university crowd. We've recently managed to even the score, but William Douglas of Tucson still holds the whip hand. He's a lawyer, a part-time professor at the university, and a former Ambassador to Great Britain under Harry Truman." (Neither Oldfield nor Jacobs was aware that Douglas was also a director of General Electric. When the *Arizona Republic* broke the story of the selection of Phoenix as the site, he tried frantically to reach Cordiner to divert the operation to Tucson. Cordiner was attending the annual planning function in Florida and not reachable. Had Douglas intervened at an earlier date, it was probable that Tucson would have been selected.)

"You may not know it yet but your new secretary, Audrey White, used to work for Douglas. She can help you make contact."

"I'll talk to her about it, but I don't think I should try to throw my weight around locally for awhile. I still have a lot of internal GE problems to get under control."

"I understand," said Jacobs with an expression of sympathy. "I guess there are feather merchants to deal with even in a great company like GE. Anyway, you'll have no political problems dealing with Arizona State."

"Thanks, John. I appreciate it." Oldfield returned to his office in the KTAR building, happy with the thought that he had a friend of some stature on the local scene.

While Oldfield was dealing with the problems related to establishing the Phoenix headquarters, Jacobi and Johnson were dealing with politics of a different sort.[20] They found surprising differences of opinion both within SRI and within the Bank of America, differences that began to emerge as they continued with their detailed analysis of the ERMA system. Charley Conroy of the bank was their on-site manager. He was a firm believer in the SRI system as built and urged GE simply to transistorize the existing vacuum-tube computer. He also didn't trust MICR and advocated using bar codes on the back of the checks. Al Zipf, whose initial involvement with the project was his crusade for automated character recognition, had, by the summer of 1956, proved to the American Bankers Association through demonstrations at SRI that magnetic character reading was feasible. Thus Conroy's influence began to wane, and Zipf gradually took total control.

Johnson and Jacobi discussed the situation at lunch one day. "I'm nervous about Oldfield's commitment to provide automatic magnetic character reading as the mode of entry into the ERMA system," said Jacobi. "I realize the ABA has now approved it, but you and I know the demonstrations for the bankers were held with

The Arizona Republic *welcomes GE to Phoenix, September 2, 1956.*

specially selected vacuum tubes and a Ph.D. behind the cabinet with a screw driver. Really, you know the vacuum-tube character reader is marginal in performance, and is too bulky and expensive to be practical. We don't have the manpower or skills here in Palo Alto to develop a stable transistorized character reader. I think we need help."[21]

"You're absolutely right, George," said Bob, "but I don't think there's any one back in Syracuse who could do this particular job. How about the Research Laboratory?"

Jacobi laughed. "All they can think of at the moment is how to make diamonds. However, I have a feeling Hans Kuehni's section at the General Engineering Laboratory (GEL) could handle this type of design problem. His group is expert at low-noise analog solid-state circuits, and the character reader is exactly that sort of device."

"By all means," said Johnson, "let's give them a shot at it. We've one hundred K in the budget for the design of the character reader. Let's get a quotation from Kuehni."

Jacobi got on the telephone to Schenectady, and two days later an engineer arrived to examine the SRI prototype. "We can afford fifty K to have this four-by-four-by-six rack on wheels transformed into a shoebox," was Jacobi's challenge. A week later a quotation in that amount was received from the General Engineering Laboratory, and the laboratory was given the contract. This was to prove a wise decision. GEL met the performance specifications at the quoted dollar figure and within the required schedule. From that point on, everyone involved trusted MICR, including Al Zipf. MICR would go on to become the standard of the banking industry worldwide. Al Zipf's reputation was made, and desirably so.

During this period, George Trotter moved to Phoenix to act as manager of sales under Clair Lasher, and John Hogg from marketing was assigned to the ERMA project to hold hands with the customer. He and George Jacobi did not get along very well, and this seemed to exacerbate an already difficult relationship problem with SRI. Both Johnson and Jacobi had decided that the hardwired SRI computer was too inflexible to be used for the checking-account processing operation, the main problem being that flexible procedures were mandatory to solve the bank's problem. This dictated scrapping the SRI design for the computer and developing a stored program approach. The advantage of a stored program computer using high-speed core memory was that, by altering the program, one could change the functioning of the machine after all the hardware had been built. It had become obvious there would be a great many changes in function between what SRI had developed and what GE would ultimately deliver and install.

Again, the GE group was going against the convictions of Charley Conroy and the group at SRI who had designed and constructed the hardwired vacuum-tube computer. It was a more serious dispute than that involving the MICR because it meant that the reliance of GE on SRI expertise would be over as far as the computer went, leading to the reduction of GE dollar sponsorship. In leading this particular fight, Jacobi bumped heads with key SRI people. There were heated exchanges, wounded egos, and an ultimate stalemate that made it virtually impossible for him to continue as the project engineer.[22]

One day, Bob Johnson received a telephone call from Ken Geiser. "Bob, I've just been with Barney Oldfield, and he's decided to reassign George Jacobi to Phoenix, though only if you agree to assume the job of project engineer for ERMA. The relationship between Jacobi, SRI, and the bank has evidently become intolerable, though it really isn't Jacobi's fault."

"I sort of expected something like this to happen, and so did George, I think," replied Johnson. "Hell, yes. I'll take over, but please don't make a big thing about it."

"Okay, Bob. Can you transfer me over to Jacobi? I think the best way to handle it is for me to summon him to Phoenix for a meeting with Barney and me."

Oldfield knew one of his weaknesses as a general manager was his reluctance to fire or displace people. The case of George Jacobi was a particularly distasteful one because Jacobi had been his choice for the job, and Jacobi had made some major contributions to the project. The interview had been a difficult one, but Jacobi took the decision with grace.

"We don't have an Advanced Development Section here in Phoenix, and we don't yet have a budget for the activity. I'm offering you the job of manager of an activity that does not quite exist, but we have the opportunity to obtain contracts with outfits like Niagara Mohawk Power Company for analog computers of the type you had under development when you left Schenectady. Are you game to try it?"

"Well, in some ways it's a relief not to have the pressure of founding a new group, in a new place, for a completely new business. It's tough to give up the project at this stage, but no hard feelings. I'll accept the new job."

As he left the meeting, Jacobi's main concern was for his wife back in Los Altos. On his way to the airport, he stopped by a store in Scottsdale and purchased a western outfit, complete with Stetson and Bolo tie, and wore it on his return. His wife laughed and cried as he opened the door—the tears because she then knew they would move from the beautiful San Francisco Peninsula to the Arizona desert.[23]

CHAPTER 8
THE NEW BOSS

The bad news arrived in mid-September, 1956. Oldfield was holding the regular Monday staff meeting attended by Lasher, Geiser, McCombs, Barclay, and Newman. They were putting the finishing touches on the appropriation request covering the purchase of land and the architectural design of the first permanent facility to be erected in Phoenix. The site, selected after considerable study, consisted of one hundred sixty acres on Black Canyon Highway, just north of Phoenix in a community called Deer Valley. Whereas Geiser would have preferred a location in the Tempe area, close to ASC, the advantages of Deer Valley in terms of local taxes, proximity to inexpensive housing, and cost of land were such that there was no real argument.

The meeting was interrupted by a telephone call that Oldfield was told was urgent and must be answered at once.

"This is Bob Estes." Bob was the attorney assigned to Doc Baker's staff in Syracuse. "Barney, I have some important news for you. Effective today, the Electronics Division ceases to exist. The top level of the company has been reorganized into divisions with common market orientation instead of common technical orientation. You're now a part of the Industrial Electronics Division, reporting directly to the new division general manager, Harold Strickland, formerly a member of Cordiner's staff. His headquarters will remain in New York."

Oldfield was in shock. "What about Doc?"

"He's out of the management loop—promoted to senior consultant to the Executive Office. Just between us, I was with him when he got the news. He seemed to age right in front of my eyes. He knew Ralph Cordiner was unhappy with his independent ways, but he never thought he'd reorganize the Electronics Division out of existence."

"Bob, do you think the ERMA contract had anything to do with this?"

"I don't think so, Barney. Cordiner and his staff have been gradually setting the stage for this organizational structure as a means of implementing Harold Smiddy's concept of a professional manager. The concept is that an adequately educated and experienced manager can manage any type of business regardless of the technology involved or the nature of the market. It's the new religion."

Oldfield's face was grim as he pondered the implications of Estes' bombshell announcement. Baker had been an inspiring leader with the instincts of a true entre-

John Jacobs, land owner and Arizona pioneer, signs the contract conveying property on Black Canyon Highway for GE's Phoenix plant. Ray Barclay, manufacturing manager, and Barney Oldfield, general manager, look on.

preneur and an in-depth understanding of what might be accomplished through the exploitation of electronic technology. His removal from the scene was definitely bad news as far as GE's future in the computer business was concerned.

"What am I supposed to do at this point?" he asked Estes.

"I think you can expect a call from Harold Strickland before the day is over. The next steps are up to him."

Oldfield was still in a state of shock as he summoned his staff to the conference room. He had looked upon Baker as his ally and protector in dealing with the higher echelons of GE, and he suddenly felt himself cast adrift in a sea of uncertainty. He kept the panicky feeling to himself as he broke the news.

"As far as I know," he said, "none of this changes our program. By the way, do any of you know anything about our new boss, Harold Strickland? All I've been told is that he's a member of Ralph Cordiner's staff."

All but Lasher shook their heads. "I had some contact with him when I was working on the Metcalf Report. I recall him as being rather short, about Cordiner's height, and soft spoken, very nattily dressed. He's an electrical engineer, but I don't think he has any background in computers. I assume he has Cordiner's trust, which is an advantage, but he may share Cordiner's fear of IBM, which could be a disadvantage. He didn't seem to have much of a sense of humor when I met with him, but he was always pleasant to me. Also, he asked intelligent questions, so he's no dummy. He's not in Doc Baker's league as an entrepreneur, but we could have done worse."

"Okay, Clair. I guess we'll just have to wait and see. Meantime, let's polish off this appropriation request and hope for the best."

The call from Strickland came in the early afternoon.

"This is Harold Strickland, Barney. I assume you've heard the news of the reorganization."

"Yes, Bob Estes called me earlier. I understand congratulations are in order."

"Thanks. I'm looking forward to working with you and your team. You've undertaken a pretty tough job for the Bank of America, and I plan to help in any way I can."

"We'll appreciate that." As they talked, Oldfield was searching for hidden meanings behind Strickland's words.

"I'm calling a staff meeting in my office for two weeks from today," said Strickland, "so all my general managers can become acquainted and start working as a team. In the meantime, I'd like copies of whatever progress reports or correspondence you think may educate me about your plans and needs. I already have a copy of your letter contract with the Bank of America, and I'll want to discuss the details with you while you're here. Incidentally, I've approved the appropriation request for temporary space, which came from Snively."

"Thanks," said Oldfield, who had already signed the lease. He had a feeling Strickland, unlike Baker, would be a stickler for detail. Well, he'd give him his fill. "Harold, we're just completing the appropriation request for the first phase of our plant facility, and for interim rental space for manufacturing and engineering. It has a good bit of detail on our financial projections. I'll also send you a copy of our proposed contract with NCR. I'm expecting to receive a signed copy before our next staff meeting."

"Did you receive management approval for the NCR program?"

"Why, yes." Whoops, thought Oldfield, sensing a subtle turn of the screw. He'd have to be careful when dealing with Strickland.

"Do you have any specific instructions for us?" he asked.

"Not at this point. A detailed set of organization announcements is on the way to you, and this should pretty well spell out the nature and scope of the new set-up. You'll note in particular the need to firm up the Product Charter of your operation. We can discuss this further when I see you in two weeks."

Oldfield was depressed by the turn of events. His conversation with Strickland had been pleasant and nonthreatening, and there was no reason the two could not work well together, but the abrupt dismissal of Doc Baker from his position as head of the Electronics Division was a chilling example of the autocratic power wielded by the corporate Executive Office of General Electric. The action boded no good for a new business brought into existence by a maverick general manager, now trying to make up for a five-year head start given to IBM.

The relationship between GE and IBM was the subject of much speculation within GE. IBM was a good GE customer for vacuum tubes, relays, and other electronic components, and GE was an even better customer for card punch and sorting equipment, and, then, for IBM computers. GE was, in fact, the largest single user of IBM computers outside the U.S. government, and did much of the initial application work exploited by IBM in dealing with other customers.

As far back as 1948, when there were only a few digital computers in the world, Oldfield, then manager of sales of Doc Baker's Government Division, had responded to a bid request from the U.S. Air Force to develop a vacuum-tube digital computer for the Office of Air Research. The GE proposal was accepted, and the Electronics Laboratory in Syracuse took over the development and construction of the computer, called OARAC. George Metcalf, then general manager of the Commercial and Government Equipment Department, became interested in OARAC during its final testing phase, and he decided to explore the market for the machine, starting with the insurance industry.[24]

Metcalf first visited the Metropolitan Life Insurance Company and then New York Life, and they were sufficiently impressed to ask for a demonstration. In the summer of 1950, Metcalf received a telephone call from Ralph Cordiner telling him that Mr. Thomas Watson, Sr., chairman of the board of IBM, wanted to see him at his New York office at 10 a.m. the next day. He went to New York City and was escorted into Mr. Watson's office—Watson had the slogan "THINK" over his desk. Not asking Metcalf to be seated, Watson said, "Young man, you have been calling on my customers, and I will not tolerate this. You will stop immediately or we will withdraw our substantial annual purchases from General Electric Company. Thank you for responding so soon. Good day!"

Shaken, Metcalf immediately left the IBM building. He reported the one-way conversation to Ralph Cordiner, confident Cordiner would make a fighting response. Cordiner emphatically replied, "You must comply with Mr. Watson's request."[25]

This confrontation was never reported within GE, but there was no question that a fear of IBM permeated the company's Executive Office at a time when some of the company's best young engineers and marketing people were aching to inject GE into the computer business. This fear had not dissipated six years later despite the award of the ERMA contract.

The top management attitude made little impact on the group at Palo Alto. Few of the engineers had known Doc Baker, and the shuffle of vice presidents two layers above them and three thousand miles away was unimportant compared to the technical challenge of the ERMA program. The problems with SRI gradually died down as GE increased the funding for the magnetic-ink development programs in parallel with reducing sponsorship of the computer side. Bob Johnson had sold Al Zipf on the importance of abandoning the hardwired concept in favor of a stored program approach, and Zipf, in turn, had sold bank management. By the end of 1956 the system had been pretty well defined, with circuit and logical design well underway and most of the critical technical problems under attack. The development of the mainframe itself was the largest single portion of the project, and Johnson was very fortunate to have John Paivinen as the manager of this part of the system.

Paivinen had graduated from the University of Michigan with a BS in mathematics and an MS in electrical engineering. He had gone to work for Burroughs in Paoli, Pennsylvania, in 1951, originally as a circuit design engineer and later as project engineer for all logic circuits for the E-101, Burrough's first electronic computer, as well as the logic and circuit design for a mainframe computer. This solid background of experience was just what Johnson needed to complement his own talents. It fell to him to train an inexperienced circuit-design crew and, later, to teach the manufacturing people from Phoenix what a digital computer was and how it had to be assembled and tested.

One of the key people in Paivinen's group was Gerry Allard, a Canadian from Laval University in Quebec and Union College in Schenectady. A physics major, he had started with GE in 1946 at the Knolls Atomic Laboratory, where he was involved in interminable calculations using a Monroe mechanical calculator. Looking for a better way to handle this drudgery, he discovered the world of computers. He later became a member of the Electronics Laboratory in Syracuse, developed expertise in transistor circuits, and joined the ERMA program, assigned to Paivinen's design team.

ERMA used about fifteen thousand diodes, five thousand transistors, and about four thousand pull-up and pull-down resistors. The resistor values had to be individually calculated for the gates, taking into account the number and types of loads imposed on each gate, the voltage tolerances on the DC supply lines, the tolerances in the resistor values, and the capacitance on the connecting wires. It was an awesome project.

"How would you like to take on this project?" said Paivinen.

"Well, it looks like about thirty-six man months of work," said Allard. "Do I have three years to do it?"

"How about seven months, and five guys to help you out?"

"It's a deal, John."

It was a happy moment several months later when Gerry Allard burst into the Paivinen home in the midst of a party to announce that the last loading calculation had been completed. Pandemonium ensued![26] You would have thought he'd just been awarded the Nobel Prize!

Physically isolated from the rest of the organization, funded as necessary to get the job done, unaffected by the company's political changes, and given only a minimum of supervision from above, the ERMA group became a cohesive and harmonious team dedicated to a single objective. It was reminiscent of the MIT Radiation Laboratory atmosphere of World War II, though none of the group was old enough to have such a recollection.

CHAPTER 9
COMPLICATIONS OF EARLY GROWTH

The first of Harold Strickland's monthly staff meetings was held in his suite of offices one skyscraper away from the GE's main headquarters at 570. Present were his four general managers and his own accountant. It was early September, 1956.

"Tiny" Fink, general manager of GE X-ray in Milwaukee, was a six-foot-four-inch beanpole who looked at the world through thick bifocals. He was an erudite individual, a physics Ph.D. who ran what was considered in 1956 to be a stable but unexciting business. The CAT scan and MRI were several dreams away.

Bill Morlock, a scrappy five-foot-ten-inch Irishman, was general manager of the Technical Equipment Department. According to the organizational chart, the Industrial Computer Section was a part of that department, but, in actuality, there was no reporting relationship. Morlock was a veteran of the early television days, and his business interests were in TV transmitters, studio equipment, and FM radio. With television and FM stations proliferating around the United States and Europe, Morlock's production lines were working overtime.

Harrison Van Aken, accountant turned professional manager, had undertaken the job of turning around one of Doc Baker's less-than-promising ventures. This was the Communications Equipment Department, specializing in two-way radio for taxis and police and emergency vehicles. Competition with Motorola in particular was very stiff, with most contracts being awarded strictly on the basis of price, and the situation called for a very tight, cost-conscious style of management. Van Aken, as general manager, was well-suited to the position.

Lou Rader, a large man, though shy of Tiny Fink's height, had earned a Ph.D. in electrical engineering from Cal Tech. He'd come to GE as a development engineer in 1937, left the company in 1945 to be chairman of the Department of Electrical Engineering of Illinois Institute of Technology, and had returned to GE in 1947. General manager of the Specialty Control Department in Waynesboro, Virginia, he was an acknowledged leader in the field of automation.

Listening to the flow of ideas and reports as the staff meeting proceeded, Oldfield wondered what he was doing as a part of this particular group or what he could contribute to the discussion. Strickland concentrated almost entirely on the financial performance of the previous month and the three-month rolling forecast of future performance in terms of return on investment and return on sales. It would be at least five years before the Industrial Computer Section could dream of adding dollar profits to General Electric's coffers, and about all he could report on would be expenditures as compared to the budget and the various technical accomplishments as compared to previous estimates. For the first time, Oldfield wondered whether GE's emphasis on short-term profitability could encompass a radically new business venture with a very long-term payout.

Had he been aware of it, Oldfield would have been comforted by knowing of Lou Rader's distaste of GE's emphasis. Much senior to Strickland, both in terms of education and line experience within GE, Rader had been the logical candidate for the position of division manager. His theory was that Strickland had been picked in part because he could be counted on to do Cordiner's bidding without question and partly because his height matched Cordiner's.

The meeting droned to a close. As planned, Oldfield stayed on after the others had departed.

"Well, young man, how does the NCR contract look?"

"It's in the bag, Harold. I'm going by Dayton on the way back to Phoenix, and they tell me it's ready for signature. As far as I know, it's identical to the copy I sent to you."

"I've hesitated to approve your appropriation request for the first increment of plant space and the leasing of interim space pending receipt of the NCR contract. I'll sign it today with the understanding you won't implement it if you don't get the contract."[27]

Oldfield breathed a sigh of relief. Maybe Strickland wouldn't be so hard to deal with after all.

"Now, update me on ERMA," said Strickland.

"I guess you know we had to bring Jacobi to Phoenix and make Bob Johnson project engineer. It was a tough blow for George, and he really didn't deserve it, but it did clear the air with SRI and the bank. Bank management has finally agreed to accept a stored program computer approach rather than the SRI hardwire solution, so our group is off and running with the design program. One big advantage is that it means the ERMA computer—we've labeled it the GE 100—will be a general-purpose machine we can adapt to other applications as well as to other banks."

"That's one thing I want to talk to you about, Barney. Ralph Cordiner has not changed his mind about GE keeping out of the office machine market. You're going to have to play the game very carefully if you want to stay in business after ERMA. That's why the NCR contract might be very helpful. If you can develop as a supplier to a company like National Cash Register, I don't think Ralph will object, and I believe he'll be willing to have you sell ERMAs to as many banks as you can, but he's not about to invest the company's money in developing a line of products for the business machine market."

"Suppose we developed a version of the ERMA computer for internal GE use? One of Doc Baker's concepts was that GE had such a variety of businesses that a computer that satisfied the internal GE market would be suitable for the rest of the industry as well."

"I don't think you can sell that, at least for the time being. What Ralph would like you to concentrate on is process control, which would fit in with GE's traditional businesses."

"I've got George Jacobi already working on a special computer for Niagara Mohawk Power, and we're studying the problem of data logging for steel mills.[28] One of the problems with the market is that the customers are used to analog technology, so that every different application requires a new design. With the digital approach, the same basic computer with core memory can be adapted to different applications by varying the stored program. We think the market is due for a big change in technology, so we're being pretty careful about how we approach it."

"I understand, Barney." Strickland reached for his appointment book. "I want to schedule a trip to Phoenix and then have you accompany me for an inspection of the Palo Alto group. If it doesn't interfere with your plans, I'd like to block out a week the middle of next month." Oldfield wasn't very happy to have to lose a week while he shepherded Strickland around. However, it would give the other members of the organization a chance to meet him.

The trip to Dayton was successful, and Oldfield arrived back in Phoenix with a signed appropriation request and a contract in the amount of $30 million from NCR. It included the design of a production prototype using the Hawthorne specifications and subsequent production of thirty computers. He was feeling good about Strickland at that point. His first move was to call a staff meeting.

"Audrey, please round up as many of the managers as you can find, and include Bob Wooley."

"Yes, sir. You have an incoming call from a Mr. MacFee of the Jet Engine Department in Evendale, Ohio. Will you take it?"

Oldfield was intrigued. "I'll take it, Audrey—and delay the staff meeting, please, until I'm off the phone."

"This is Fred MacFee, Mr. Oldfield. It's been suggested I contact you about a personnel matter relating to one of our employees, Mr. Herb Grosch. Perhaps you know of him?"

"Sorry, I don't recognize the name."

"Herb is a senior computer programmer who has done a lot of work with IBM computers. He recently developed and put into operation the large computer center for our jet engine test facility. He has a good reputation as a programmer, but his plans are a bit over-ambitious for our department. He has signed an option for an additional IBM 704 and wants to establish a service bureau to perform calculations for a number of GE departments. This sort of thing is completely outside of our jurisdiction, and we wonder if the Computer Department would be interested in talking to Grosch, with the possibility of your organization taking him over. If so, we can send you a copy of his personnel file and rating sheet, and we can arrange an interview if you decide to act on it."

"It certainly won't hurt to take a look. And thanks."

"You bet. I'll get the stuff to you at once."

No sooner had Oldfield hung up the phone than the five staff members, accompanied by Bob Wooley, sauntered into the room brandishing their ubiquitous cups of coffee.

"I'll put you out of your misery quickly," said Oldfield. "The appropriation request is signed covering the lease of engineering space in the Technology Building, the lease of interim manufacturing space on Peoria Avenue, the purchase of one hundred sixty acres on Black Canyon Highway, and the architectural work on the plant facility. It also includes the test equipment and pilot manufacturing facilities we need to get through the prototype manufacturing stage of ERMA. Ray, I suggest you and Ken McCombs get together at once to implement the facilities plan.

"Also, I have a signed contract from NCR covering their computer program in the amount of $30 million. Bob, you're now officially the project engineer. I suggest you and Art Newman get together and begin the interview process so you can build up the engineering staff as quickly as possible. I brought back a list of names and resumes received at Strickland's office as a result of the ad we ran in the *New York Times*. I notice three of the guys who responded are from RCA and worked on the Bizmac program. You have an okay to offer trip expenses for any who look good to you after a telephone interview.

"Clair, I'd like to get together with you and Ken Geiser right after this meeting to develop a plan for Harold Strickland's visit next month. We'll need to plan presentations from each section manager, and we'll need to sharpen up our planning for process control."

"I assume a trip to the ERMA project is a part of the program?" said Lasher. "If so, I suggest George Trotter join us. He's the logical one to make arrangements for Palo Alto."

Oldfield was mildly surprised by Lasher's willingness to share the spotlight with Trotter, manager of sales—their relationship was a touchy one. Although Lasher was Trotter's boss, Trotter and Oldfield had worked closely together for several years and, of course, shared the sales campaign that brought the Bank of America contract to GE. Oldfield had great respect for Lasher's abilities in market research and product planning, but he lacked Trotter's intuitive understanding of customer personalities. Hopefully, they would make a fine team.

Two days later, the package of information on Herb Grosch arrived on Oldfield's desk. It turned out that Herb, an astronomer, had worked for the Bureau of Standards in Washington, and for IBM, before coming to work for GE. He was highly regarded as a programmer, and he had done a good job setting up the Computer Center in Evendale. However, he had become difficult to deal with from a management standpoint because of his disdain for budget restrictions and his aggressive personality. Also, he had a tendency to be an empire builder. Balancing these negatives, he was highly competent professionally in a field where such expertise was scarce.

Oldfield pondered the situation. He knew his hope of a technically upgraded ASC would be enhanced if GE could establish a substantial computer center on the campus, and he figured the technical competence of the GE engineering staff would be increased by the presence of a large scientific computer and an effective programming staff. There had never been any thought that GE would get into the large scientific-type computers as a product, so there seemed to be no conflict of interest in having a big IBM machine in the picture. Why not explore the possibility! Acting on impulse, he put in a call to Evendale to arrange an interview with Grosch. Within a few minutes, Grosch was on the line.

"I can be there tomorrow if you like, and I'd like to bring my new bride with me so she can go house hunting in case I like the setup."

Taken aback by Grosch's assumption that a job with the organization was his for the asking, Oldfield cautioned Grosch that there was no provision in the budget for a large computer center, and that such would involve approval from corporate management.

"Not to worry," said Grosch. "My buddy, Jim LaPierre, will take care of that." LaPierre was the group executive to whom Strickland reported.

Dubious but interested, Oldfield arranged for an immediate visit by Grosch and his bride.

The interview went surprisingly well. Grosch turned out to be a flamboyant character with an obviously larger-than-life self-image, who was witty and articulate in describing his professional background and experiences. It happened that Evendale had ordered a new IBM 704 under a military priority and would be willing to divert it to Phoenix if Grosch went with it.

Grosch exuded confidence concerning the ability of the computer center to pay for itself, in part through contracts for computing from government agencies such as the Army Ballistic Agency at Huntsville, which had a tremendous computing overload, and in part by providing computer services to other parts of General Electric, including the Computer Department itself.

"Herb, what sort of a facility would you need to house an IBM 704 and the programming staff?"

Grosch reached into his briefcase and pulled out a sheaf of drawings and photographs. "Here's what we erected at Evendale. The building itself can be cylindrical or square, with the computer, magnetic tape units, printer, and card reader in the center, and with offices around the perimeter. The only special thing about it is the false floor under which the cabling and air-conditioning ducts are located. You could give these drawings to a contractor and have a computer facility built within three months."

"This would have to be located on the campus of ASC, adjacent to the Technology Center where our engineering staff will be located for the first couple of years. If we can persuade Grady Gammage and his board that it would be a major asset to his quest for university status, I think the board would finance the building so long as we furnished the computer. I'll see if I can arrange a meeting for tomorrow with Grady Gammage and John Jacobs, the board chairman. Meanwhile, why don't you join your bride and go see a bit of Phoenix?"

When Grosch departed, Oldfield immediately got on the telephone to New York to test the water at headquarters. He was surprised to find the way had already been paved. "La Pierre already knows about it," said Strickland, "and he thinks it's a fine idea. Grosch is already on the GE payroll and the IBM 704 is already under a lease contract, so it's a matter of diverting expenses from one division to another rather than an additional major expense. Both divisions report to Jim, so he's perfectly comfortable. He only wants to make sure you don't have to build and own the computer building. If things go wrong, you can always cancel the IBM lease after the first year."

Again, Oldfield was not entirely comfortable with the fact that Herb had been wheeling and dealing under the assumption that his transfer to Phoenix was a sure thing. However, there seemed to be more pluses than minuses to the situation. He'd play along.

The next day, gathered in Grady Gammage's office, Oldfield let Grosch do his own selling to Gammage and Jacobs. He thought Herb laid the charm on a bit too thick, but Gammage seemed receptive and even eager. It turned out the building needed for the computer had already been planned as a part of the Technology Center, although it would have to be expanded to take care of Grosch's needs. The meeting ended with the agreement that, if GE furnished the computer and the initial operating personnel, the college would furnish the building at no cost to GE. Implied in the agreement was that GE would furnish computer time to the college at no cost, sufficient for student training and automating certain college functions such as the burdensome registration process.

This agreement paved the way to make an offer to Herb Grosch, which he accepted. The key provision was that the computer center would have to pay its way through contract services within a reasonable period after installation of the IBM 704. This was to be the start of GE's Service Bureau business.

The subsequent relationship with Grosch turned out to be a thorny one.[29] His contract to accomplish computing services for the Army Ballistic Missile Agency was an up-and-down affair, and Grosch's time and attention became diverted away from the commitment to make the operation self-financing. The situation was exacerbated by his rather lavish lifestyle and Rabelaisian approach to life. This didn't sit well with the other members of the organization, and effectively inhibited the development of in-house sponsorship. It also turned out that when he had left Evendale there was a tacit agreement that he would not compete for GE computer service business, at least in the East where most of the company was located. This was never passed on to Oldfield or Strickland.

Despite these problems, the computer center would prove advantageous in terms of ASC's campaign to attain university status. Oldfield, acting on John Jacobs' advice, decided to visit William Douglas in Tucson to sell him on the project.

"You know, Mr. Douglas," said Oldfield, "the future of GE in Arizona is closely linked with the development of the state university system. We'd like to work closely with the Electrical Engineering Department of the University of Arizona and would hope for their help in upgrading the curriculum of ASC. We'd also like to become familiar with the programs and talents of the faculty and graduate students here with the thought perhaps of sponsoring some research activities of interest to our organization, and we'd hope the university would take advantage of our large computer center on the Tempe campus, both as an aid in solving mathematical problems of complexity and through co-op programs where some of your students would work in the computer center for academic credit."

This sort of thing was appealing to Douglas. The University of Arizona had an excellent reputation, but Tucson was far off the beaten path of commerce, and it wasn't easy to generate major programs or attract top faculty members. Douglas recognized that the price of the preferred collaboration would be to end his opposition to university status for his competitor in Phoenix, but he was sufficiently realistic to recognize such an event was inevitable in the long run as the city of Phoenix continued to prosper.

The meeting ended without the subject of ASC's university status being mentioned, but some weeks later a jubilant John Jacobs announced to Oldfield that Douglas had softened his position. It was some months later that Oldfield learned Arizona State College had become Arizona State University, with a Liberal Arts Department, a Department of Technology, and a Teachers' College. He wasn't sure whether his meeting with Douglas had played a part in the decision, but he was delighted one weekend to be invited to view a football game in Grady Gammage's box on the forty-yard line. Half-time intermission came with ASU comfortably ahead, and the ASU marching band on the field, led by the traditional golden girl with baton raised to the sky and gleaming whistle between her lips. Suddenly she gave a blast on the whistle, and the band formed a perfect GE monogram, holding it as they marched the full length of the stadium. It was probably the first and only time the General Electric Company was honored on a college football field!

Grady Gammage beamed as the band completed its half-time show. "All the faculty and most of the students recognize that GE had a lot of behind-the-scenes influence in breaking the bottleneck that has been holding back the award of university status for Arizona State. I realize we have a long, long way to go before we can even be in the same league with Stanford and Cornell, but there's a lot of potential in our young faculty. I want to thank you and Dr. Grosch in particular for helping the cause."

"It's all been a pleasure so far," said Oldfield, "and of course it's a boon to us to be associated with an up-and-coming university. I enjoyed my time at Cornell, but I never felt our project was enthusiastically endorsed by the upper crust of academicians who abhorred the taint of industrial collaboration. I'm hoping I can get General Electric to donate a Chair of Computer Science at Arizona State as a first step in helping the university attract a computer scientist with outstanding credentials to make Phoenix his home. I'm also hoping you'll be willing to establish a co-op program within the Engineering Department as a formal part of the curriculum so some of our brighter technicians can work part-time for BS degrees. There's an immediate opportunity to develop basic and advanced courses in programming, and I think . . ."

"Hey, Dad, we'd like to get some hot dogs and cokes before the half-time intermission is over, okay?" Bob Oldfield tugged urgently at his father's sweater, bringing him back to the reality of the football game. Arizona State University was leading its arch rival by a score of 20 to 7. Half-time was almost over, and sustenance was in order.

"Sure, Bob. Here's a few bucks. Why don't you and Dick bring back refreshments for all of us?"

Bob grabbed the money, and the two boys ran whooping to the refreshment stand.

"I'm sorry your wife couldn't make it to the game," said Gammage, "so she could see how much the university appreciates your efforts. I hope Sofia's not ill again."

"She's a bit under the weather—nothing serious, I hope. She'll be sorry she missed it."

The boys returned with their loot, the second half began, and Oldfield tried his best to return his thoughts to football.

CHAPTER 10
THE VISIT OF THE NEW BOSS

It was an especially hot day in early October, 1956, as Oldfield watched the huge TWA Constellation settle down on the ten-thousand-foot runway of the Phoenix Municipal Airport bearing Harold Strickland, newly made vice president and general manager of the Industrial Electronics Division. Relations between the two had been cordial so far, though they didn't feel entirely comfortable with one another. This was Strickland's first visit to Phoenix and Palo Alto, and much would depend on his initial impressions.

Oldfield didn't realize it, but Strickland was also nervous about his first encounter with the people who had been assembled to carry GE's banner in the computer industry. He had no prior experience with computers or the computer industry nor had he been a general manager of an Operating Department. He did, however, consider himself knowledgeable in the principles of professional management, and he understood the workings of GE top management. He had welcomed the opportunity to apply his knowledge as a manager and as an engineer. His visit to the Computer Department was important in establishing his authority over what his colleagues at 570 considered to be a risky enterprise. His mandate was to see that the Bank of America program was completed without undue damage to GE's reputation, and that the NCR program was also completed and without any long-range commitment to the retail market. Beyond that, the charter of the Industrial Computer Section was hazy at best.

Strickland had another concern, and that was the shadow of Dr. W.R.G. Baker looming over the computer adventure. He knew Oldfield and most of his crew had begun the computer project under the benign influence of an electronics pioneer who had retained the gambling instincts of the early days of radio. Somehow, he'd have to remove Baker's influence and replace it with a sense of solid adherence to GE policies and practices.

Strickland's first thought as he stepped out of the plane and onto the stairs was one of utter shock at the oven-like heat that enveloped him. Even though it was late in the year, the dry heat of the desert was a startling contrast to the air-conditioned interior of the Constellation. He wondered how people could work under such conditions.

Oldfield greeted him at the foot of the stairs, looking cool in a lightweight suit and sport shirt. "Welcome to paradise," said Oldfield.

"If you'd said, 'Welcome to hell,' it would have been more appropriate," replied Strickland.

"You'll find if you stay here a month or two your body will adapt to local climate and you'll think nothing of playing golf or tennis with the temperature 110 degrees or so in the shade, just as skiers adapt to freezing outdoor temperatures in the winter. All our transplants from the East revel in the local lifestyle."

As they drove down Van Buren Avenue, Phoenix's east-to-west main drag, Strickland was impressed by the clean streets and buildings. "There really isn't much in the way of dirt here," explained Oldfield. "Everything is sand for hundreds of miles, and they even have to import dirt for lawns and flower beds. It's the cleanest city I've ever lived in, but I'd welcome a mud puddle now and then. The natives tell me it rained a couple of times last year, but I'll believe it when I see it."

They turned right at the next light. "We're now on South Central Avenue, and that's the Westward Ho on our right. The top floor of the hotel is the highest point in Phoenix, and it's occupied totally by the Thunderbird Club. It's a pretty exclusive spot frequented by such as Goldwater and the other prime movers, one of whom is John Jacobs, a lettuce and real estate millionaire and a power behind a number of thrones. He's also chairman of the board of trustees of Arizona State. Anyway, he invited the two of us to dinner tomorrow night at the Club, and you'll be meeting the president of the Valley Bank, the general manager of the Salt River Power Company, and the editor of the *Arizona Republic*. I assumed you'd want to accept, but I gave only a qualified acceptance in case you had other plans."

"I'm in your hands, Barney. I'd be delighted to meet with them," said Strickland, obviously pleased. So far, so good, thought Oldfield.

"Would you like me to take you to the Camelback Inn first so you can freshen up from your trip? If not, we can go right to the office, which is coming up in a few blocks."

"Why don't we go right to the office. I'm anxious to get acquainted with your team. The only one I've met is Clair Lasher, and he only in passing."

The temporary offices of the Industrial Computer Section were on the second floor of the KTAR Radio and Television building. As they ascended the staircase, they faced the entrance door to the GE space. On it were the words, "General Electric Computer Department."

Strickland stopped in his tracks, pointed to the door, his face purple, and shouted, "You're not a department and won't be one until I say the word. I want that door repainted with the words, 'Industrial Computer Section,' before I'll go inside."[30]

Strickland's voice had echoed through the temporary office partitions, but none of the group dared interfere with what had become a tirade. Oldfield was dumbfounded, embarrassed more for Strickland than for himself. "I'm sorry, Harold. None of us have paid any attention to the sign since we first moved in. I guess we assumed, from what Doc Baker had told us, that we'd be classed as a department, and it never entered our minds that we should act otherwise in our dealings with people outside GE. I'll have the sign repainted while you and I have a bite of lunch at the KTAR cafeteria."

Mollified, and feeling he had asserted his authority in a positive manner, Strickland let himself be led down to the first floor to the cafeteria. Oldfield excused himself and hurried back, to find Ray Barclay busily chipping the paint from the door.

"What kind of a piss ant do you have for a boss, Barney? He acted like a spoiled child." Oldfield privately agreed, but he couldn't afford to let the incident get out of hand.

"He was within his rights, Ray, and you know the upper echelons of GE are organization and rank conscious. You can't expect him to act like another Doc Baker. Just be sure the right title's on the door when he comes back, and check that there aren't any references to the Computer Department anywhere else."

"Okay, boss."

The rest of the day passed without any other embarrassing incidents. Strickland was introduced to each of the section managers, and each gave a flip-chart presentation covering the present projects and the future plans and product areas. The most important topic of the afternoon was the forthcoming appropriation request for the Deer Valley facility

"We have fourteen thousand square feet here in the KTAR building, which is devoted entirely to headquarters, marketing, accounting, and employee and community relations. Engineering has about twenty-seven thousand square feet of rented office and laboratory space on the campus of Arizona State University in Tempe, and we have fifty thousand square feet of rented manufacturing and office space on Peoria Avenue. The separation is not good, but we can live with it through 1958. After that, we must have additional manufacturing space to cope with ERMA and the NCR 304. Also, we must vacate the rented engineering space at that point. Appropriation Request AC-416 will provide permanent space for our headquarters building, engineering, and interim manufacturing space, which, together with the Peoria Avenue space, will see us through 1959. We'll need additional manufacturing space at that point, but we can add it in increments as warranted by our business plan in late 1958. We have one hundred sixty acres in Deer Valley and can expand as required—enough for about five thousand employees. The present appropriation request is the key, and it sets the stage for an orderly expansion."

"It all sounds logical," said Strickland, "but how many millions are we talking about. My authority for a plant expansion stops at $5 million."

"I have good news for you," said Ken McCombs, manager of finance. "We have firm quotations on the building and associated items of equipment, and it comes to only $2,635,000 of investment and $185,000 of associated expense. Because our land is level and firm, and because wages here are much lower than in the East, building costs are far less than you're accustomed to."

"I guess I walked into that one," said Strickland, with his first show of humor. "Get it into formal shape and I don't think there'll be any trouble getting it through. If there's anything GE management loves, it's good manufacturing facilities."

"It just happens we have the formal document ready for your perusal," said Oldfield, handing him the bound appropriation request.

"I'm impressed," said Strickland. "I'll need a sign-off from Manufacturing Services; otherwise I'd review it and sign the document during this visit."

"Sir, if you'll look at the approval sheet on the first page," interjected Barclay, "you'll see it's already been reviewed and approved by Bob Yowell from Manufacturing Services. He was out here a few weeks ago helping us with the details. As a matter of fact, we made some important changes based on his advice."

"It looks like I've booby-trapped myself," said Strickland. "I'll take it back with me to Camelback Inn and read it tonight."

"I think we can wait that long," said Oldfield.

The remainder of the afternoon was devoted to a presentation from the marketing people covering the long-range product plan, including process control. The first speaker was Clair Lasher.

"As you know, Mr. Strickland, many of GE's core businesses involve the generation and application of electrical power to the manufacturing process. Large and small motors, voltage regulators, relays, measuring instruments, transformers, and all sorts of switch gear are traditional products of our company. The most technically sophisticated application to date has been the machine tool controller developed by the Specialty Control Department in Waynesboro, Virginia. Not a computer, it is an analog device utilizing a magnetic tape on which is recorded information necessary to position the machine tool, change its rate of orientation, turn on and off the cooling oil, and other operations usually done manually. The analog signals go from the tape to a set of servomechanisms that execute the commands. It's really pretty slick, and it allows an unskilled operator to carry out complex operations that would otherwise require a skilled machinist, and at greater speed. Someday the system will probably be digital rather than analog, and our place in the picture would be to supply the general-purpose computer to prepare the magnetic tapes.

"A true process control computer would be directly involved in the production process, either to capture and organize information in a rapidly changing process for quality control purposes or, at a higher level, to accumulate and analyze data during the process, compute changes necessary to optimize the process while it is still going on, and send control signals to control mechanisms."

"Are there any immediate practical applications?" asked Strickland.

"Absolutely," said Lasher. "One example, important to GE, would be the control of a large utility, where the efficiency of the process is optimum when the temperature and boiler pressure are matched to the load. The load can vary rapidly depending on the time of day, the weather, the cycle of industrial processes, and so on. We already have instruments that measure the demand and the variables that affect electrical output, and we have meters to display the information so operators can make adjustments; but they're not fast enough to follow sudden shifts in demand. If we can insert a computer in the loop, it will act like an automatic pilot, making optimum adjustments continuously, but will still be capable of being overridden by a human operator."

"Isn't that a lot of complication to go through just to speed up some small adjustments?" asked Strickland.

"Not at all," said Lasher. "The utilities have determined that fuel costs could be reduced by 15 percent if the output were perfectly matched to the load. That's millions of dollars a year in savings for a medium-size utility. Considering that such a utility costs about $500 million, an investment of $5 million or so in control equipment would be chicken feed."

"You've sold me. What are you fellows doing about it?"

Ken Geiser, who'd been quiet during much of the meeting, said, "We've established a three-man group to research the technical requirements as a first step in developing a program. In addition, we hired a senior engineer from RCA's Bizmac project to head up the Industrial Computer Section. He's still in the East, visiting departments such as Industry Control and Specialty Control, and we're making arrangements for him to meet some of the key GE industrial customers so he can get a feel for their requirements. He'll also spend some time in the Electronics Laboratory in Syracuse to become familiar with the work they're doing to support the machine tool control program, an activity we'll probably have to become involved in at some point. By the time he arrives here at the end of the year we should be in a position to define the technical characteristics of our basic general-purpose industrial computer."

"In the meantime," added Lasher, "we'll be building up a relationship with the Apparatus Sales Division. We're in no position to sell directly to industrial customers because we don't have the application engineering knowledge, so we'll have to work out a commission arrangement with Apparatus Sales."

"Okay, that all sounds reasonable," said Strickland. "Are there any other major product areas to be considered in developing your long-range plans?"

"There's one other category of computers we ought to consider," said Oldfield. "As you know, GE itself is IBM's largest customer outside of the U.S. government. Most of what we have in the company are mainframes like the IBM 650, 701, and 704; and we probably have developed more capability as users than any other organization in the world. It's a cinch that every GE Operating Department will want its own computer within a few years. It seems important to focus on the needs of all departments because they represent a cross section of American industry as a whole. If we can meet GE's needs, we should be able to meet most of the needs of the market.

"You know also that Herb Grosch, one of the GE users, has joined our organization to run the computer center at Arizona State University. Grosch is on leave of absence at the moment—on his honeymoon, as a matter of fact. However, he's been quite vocal in his claim that GE should go full bore into scientific mainframes, develop a machine similar to the IBM 704, and then 'sell' the first dozen internally to replace the mainframes IBM is now moving into the larger departments and laboratories. His argument is that big mainframes will be at the heart of most major computer applications. We don't disagree that there is a big market for the large machines, and at some point we'll have the resources to enter this particular market, but it doesn't seem sensible or feasible right now for us to challenge IBM's strongest product line. However, Herb has been promoting his philosophy at higher company levels, for instance with your boss, Jim LaPierre. We'd like your opinion."[31]

"I'm quite sure Mr. Cordiner would come down like a ton of bricks on the computer business if we proposed to throw out IBM's computers and replace them with a machine we haven't even developed yet. Herb Grosch has a reputation as a scientist with no business sense. You'll have to try to control him."

Strickland looked at his watch. "You know, fellows, it's after eight o'clock New York time, and I think I'd better repair to the Camelback Inn, have a little supper in my room, and read through your appropriation request before I get too sleepy. Barney tells me I have a full day tomorrow."

As they made their way to the Camelback Inn, Strickland and Oldfield discussed the next day's program.

"The plan tomorrow is for Ray Barclay to pick you up after breakfast and take you for a tour of the leased factory building on Peoria Avenue and then the site of the permanent headquarters building on Black Canyon Highway. Unless you feel differently, I think it will be beneficial if you spend some time with the key people without me being in between."

Strickland nodded his approval. "Some of the department general managers get upset if I'm with one of their people without them being present."

"Being only a section general manager, I haven't yet learned to be paranoid," said Oldfield with a grin.

"Ouch," said Strickland. "I didn't mean to embarrass you, but it seemed important to draw some sort of a line at the start. Actually, Mr. Cordiner has been holding up the organization announcement pending my inspection trip. Based on evidence to date, I can see no reason to delay it further."

"That'll be good for morale," said Oldfield. "Now, as to the rest of tomorrow's schedule, Ray will bring you back to the KTAR office by about 10 a.m., and turn you over to Ken McCombs and George Snively. They're prepared to go over our budget in any detail you wish, including the financial data included in the appropriation request. Then I'll take you over to the university where we're slated to have lunch with Grady Gammage. After lunch I'll turn you over to Ken Geiser and Bob Wooley for a tour of our engineering set-up on the campus and a presentation covering the NCR 304 computer. At about 3 p.m., Art Newman, our manager of employee relations will pick you up and bring you back to the office for a discussion of personnel problems and possible union approaches to our employees. That will complete your introduction to the key Phoenix people and permit you to ask any embarrassing questions you wish.

"Art will drop you at the Camelback Inn by 6 p.m. so you'll have a chance to freshen up and change before dinner. I'll plan to show up an hour later to take you to the Thunderbird Club. Okay?"

"You seem to have thought of everything, Barney. I'll look forward to tomorrow."

The next day went like clockwork. When Oldfield picked up Strickland that evening it was evident that he had enjoyed the direct contacts with each of the men and was suitably impressed. As evidence, he had signed a copy of the appropriation request. "Just don't proceed with this for a few days so I'll have time to brief Cordiner. I'll give you a call when I've done so."

The dinner at the Thunderbird Club went without incident, although Oldfield winced every time John Jacobs referred to the Computer Department, seemingly

The GE Computer Department staff meets with company top brass in Phoenix, 1957. Left to right around the conference table are Dr. Herbert Grosch, manager, computer applications; Kenneth Geiser, manager of engineering; Kenneth McCombs, manager of finance; Clair Lasher, manager of marketing; Arthur Newman, manager of employee and community relations; Barney Oldfield, general manager; Raymond Barclay, manager of manufacturing; James LaPierre, group vice president, Defense and Electronics group; and Harold Strickland, vice president and general manager, Industrial Electronics Division.

Missing from the picture are Dr. Robert Johnson, manager of the ERMA Systems Laboratory; and George Jacobi, ERMA project engineer. At that time, both men were located in temporary facilities at Stanford Research Institute, Menlo Park, California, pending completion of a permanent laboratory facility in Sunnyvale.

emphasizing the word department. Strickland didn't react, so apparently it would remain a closed issue. He was obviously flattered by the attentions of these important local dignitaries, and, after two cocktails and some excellent local wine, he grew expansive about GE's ambitions in the computer field. As the dinner drew to a close, Oldfield had to remind Strickland they had an early morning flight to catch.

By contrast to Phoenix, the weather at the San Francisco airport was brisk and breezy.

"This is more like it," exulted Strickland.

"I agree. You'll remember I fought hard to locate the computer activity at Stanford Industrial Park, but I had no chance against the corporate hate of California."

"Before my time," said Strickland.

"I think I should warn you, Harold, that the group here in Palo Alto is dedicated to the ERMA program, but not all that dedicated to GE. Bob Johnson has put together a number of talented people who are gung ho to solve the technical problems involved in ERMA, but they have little use for what's happening in Phoenix. They were told originally that the Computer Department would be established here, and they feel betrayed. So did I, for that matter, but I accepted the heavy hand of corporate management. I anticipate you may encounter some hazing on the subject."

"Okay, I'll be prepared. The sole reason for my visit to Palo Alto is to become educated quickly in the ERMA concept and understand the technical problems involved. I won't be upset by any anti-Phoenix propaganda. The deed is already done and over with."

As they drove south along the Bayshore Highway, Oldfield pointed out the many small electronics companies located along the route to Menlo Park where Stanford Research Institute was located.

"Many of these companies are outgrowths of the electronics research and development programs carried out by the Stanford EE Department and Physics Department. Hewlett Packard got its start there. So did Varian Associates, Eimac, Ampex, and a number of others. They're all thriving and quite competitive, though most of them have unions. It's hard for us to understand that GE can't do the same thing."

"You've got to realize, Barney, that the top management of General Electric hates unions like poison, and also hates unemployment compensation, sales taxes, and states that don't have a right-to-work law or have punitive labor legislation. California has all of these sinful things in abundance."

"Granted, but along with the Route 128 area around MIT and Harvard—which are in the sinful Commonwealth of Massachusetts—the Palo Alto area is a world-renowned center of high technology. The high-technological content of most electronics products far overshadows the cost of factory labor and overhead. ERMA is just one example of the many computer-based products that can flow from the industry-university collaboration in this region. It's too late to rectify GE's mistake in not locating the computer headquarters here, but I hope the company will be receptive to locating a computer research laboratory here when ERMA is completed. It would be a big boost to morale of the ERMA group if they had a possible long-term future here."

"I don't think you're right, Barney, but I'll keep your point in mind." Strickland obviously wanted to change the subject.

"We're coming to the Menlo Park exit," said Oldfield, "and we'll soon be at SRI. The plan is to take you first to Finnley Carter's office. He's the president of SRI. Bob Johnson will be there, as will Tom Morrin, SRI's director of research. We'll socialize for a few minutes and then go with Bob over to the rented GE space to meet the project group.

The SRI interview proceeded predictably, with pledges of mutual cooperation. Oldfield noticed Strickland becoming increasingly expansive when he talked to Finley Carter. He apparently spent so much of his time with top corporate officials that he was more comfortable in their presence than with the lower echelons. He wondered if others gained the same impression.

Bob Johnson led the way to the GE laboratory building. As they approached, they saw a section of bamboo fishing pole about five feet high, stuck on a rubber suction cup and with a sign hanging from it saying, "Phoenix Shade Tree." It appeared that some of the group had visited Phoenix and had noticed people lined up in a straight line waiting for the bus. It did not occur to them until they had seen this two or three times that what the people were doing was standing in the shade of a tall telephone pole. This had evidently struck the observers as both ridiculous and indicative of the shabbiness of Phoenix as compared to Palo Alto. It was a not-too-subtle statement of protest.[32]

Oldfield glanced at Strickland to see how he had taken the rather clumsy joke. Strickland's cheeks were red and his jaw was set a bit firmer than before, but he said nothing. The incident passed without comment, but Oldfield wished Johnson had kept his group under control. Their petulant complaint had diluted the impact of his own appeal to Strickland.

As the demonstrations and discussions progressed, Oldfield noticed that Strickland often asked questions of Johnson and his people that he had previously asked in Phoenix and presumably had been answered to his satisfaction. As it happened, the answers were substantially the same as before, or were finessed with the statement, "You'll have to ask Barney. He negotiated the contract," or "Ray Barclay's the expert on that." Oldfield recognized Strickland's use of one of GE's professional management techniques of probing an extra level of management or two in case he was getting sugar-coated answers from his direct subordinate. How different it was from Doc Baker's policy of selecting men he trusted and then leaving them alone to do the job. Oldfield realized, however, that Strickland had not selected him in the first place. He was entitled to a period of appraisal, and it would be some time before the two men would be completely comfortable together—if ever.

Later, as the two men sipped after-dinner coffee at the San Francisco airport's restaurant, Strickland warmed up a bit. "Barney, I'll admit I'm scared to death of the Bank of America obligation. You and Bob seem to have done a good job so far, but the technical risks are tremendous. If you have no objections, I think I should send out a few of the more experienced Services people from New York and Schenectady from time to time to appraise technical progress and perhaps look for areas where they can be helpful."

"I have no objections." Oldfield lied in his teeth. The last thing he wanted was a continuing flow of Services people dropping in on the ERMA group and feeding rumors and casual complaints back to 570. "I'd appreciate it if Bob and I were notified in advance, and if they'd stop by Phoenix on their return so I could have the benefit of their observations."

"Of course," lied Strickland in return.

It was the start of a polite but rather sterile relationship.

After Strickland's flight left for New York, Oldfield returned to Rickey's where he was to meet Bob Johnson for a drink.

Bob's first words were, "How did things go with Strickland?"

"Okay, I guess. He seemed to be impressed with you and the group, although he thought the business with the mock shade tree was contrived by me. I'd been giving him a long speech about the importance of maintaining a strong presence in Palo Alto once ERMA is completed, so he obviously thought I'd put you up to it."

"Sorry. The guys just didn't think."

"It's not important," said Oldfield. "What is important is that he plans to send out technical people from the Services to review progress from time to time. He seems frightened about the magnitude of the commitment to ERMA, and I can't say I blame him. Also, he and I have never worked together before, and I don't think he has a great deal of faith in my technical judgment. I don't blame him for this, either, but I'm anxious to make sure this situation doesn't cause a rift between the two of us, or between Palo Alto and Phoenix."

"Say no more," said Johnson. "I'll make sure his experts always return to New York fat, dumb, and happy."

CHAPTER 11
THE PRODUCT CHARTER BATTLE

Most of 1957 passed in a blur of frantic activity, both in Phoenix and Menlo Park. The detailed design of the ERMA computer was occupying most of the efforts of the northern California contingent, while the Phoenix activity was split into three major efforts. One of these was the development of the manufacturing skills to implement the production phase of the ERMA program, another was the push to engineer the NCR 304 for production, and the third was the development of a process control capability to meet the expressed desire of GE's president, Ralph Cordiner.

Oldfield dreaded the mandatory monthly trips to Strickland's staff meetings, but he took advantage of the visits to New York to interview potential candidates for the Computer Department. During one of those trips he met Arnold Spielberg.

Born in Cincinnati, Ohio, Spielberg had graduated from high school during the depression, worked in a Kentucky department store until World War II, and enlisted in the army where his interest in ham radio eventually led him to the Radar Advanced Development Section at the Wright-Patterson Air Force Base. From there he had used the GI Bill to obtain a BS degree at the University of Cincinnati while co-oping at the Crosley Division of AVCO Corp. The next step was graduate school at the Moore School of Electrical Engineering at the University of Pennsylvania where he completed the course work for a Masters in electrical engineering while working in the Advanced Development Department of RCA. Since 1950 he had been assigned to RCA's entry into the digital computer field, the BIZMAC Computer System. Promoted to department manager by 1956, he had a group of forty engineers and some programmers reporting to him. His resume indicated that he and his wife, Leah, had four children—Steven, Anne, Sue, and Nancy. (Steven was to rise to prominence many years later with his films *Jaws, Jurassic Park*, and most recently, *Schindler's List*.)

"That's a pretty impressive resume," said Oldfield as the two sat at a conference table in GE headquarters. "You seem to be doing well at RCA, so I obviously wonder why you're interested in joining GE."

"The big thing at RCA is television," said Spielberg, "and I don't think the company has the resources to make it in TV and computers at the same time. I guess you know we were one of the final three bidders for the ERMA contract. We never even knew GE was bidding on the project, and we thought we had a good chance of beating out Texas Instruments because of their small size. The ERMA program was to be the nucleus around which RCA would build a commercial product line.

When we lost the big order, the steam went out of our computer development program, and I don't think RCA will ever make it in computers. That's why I'm looking around."

"That makes sense," said Oldfield, "but you'll appreciate the ERMA program is pretty well organized, and with good people. The opportunity for someone at your level would be in Phoenix where our permanent headquarters will be. We have two major programs in addition to developing a production facility to manufacture the ERMA system. One of these is a contract from NCR to engineer the prototype NCR 304 for production, and that's already well-established at the sub-section level. The second program is to develop a product line of industrial process computers. I don't need to tell you that one of GE's major markets consists of industrial customers such as steel mills, aluminum refineries, utilities, cement plants, and the like. There we have a big advantage over companies like IBM and RCA because GE has sales engineers in constant touch with these businesses at almost all levels. There's a big trend toward automation in all of those industrial fields, and we're pretty sure digital computers will play an increasingly important role. Ralph Cordiner, our president, is still lukewarm about business machines, but he wants us out in front in process control computers."

"This is beginning to sound exciting," said Spielberg. "I've been doing a lot of advanced development of on-line real-time applications, and I think some of what I've learned would be applicable to process control; but I don't know enough about industrial processes to know where to start. Is there any way I could be educated if I should come to GE?

"Probably the best way would be to plan a series of visits to key company locations, starting with the General Engineering Laboratory in Schenectady. It happens that Ken Geiser is there at this moment, making arrangements for some subcontracting work. Ken's our manager of engineering. His background is in analog computers, but he has a great deal of experience in developing systems for industrial applications. If you and I make a deal, I'd recommend you plan to visit Schenectady at once. I'd leave it up to him to organize an indoctrination program before you report to Phoenix."

"That sounds great. I'm ready to deal."

The two men sparred briefly over matters of salary, benefits, moving expenses, patent agreement, housing assistance, and job title. Satisfied that Spielberg was an outstanding candidate, Oldfield said, "It seems we have a meeting of the minds. I'll put this in the form of a letter that will constitute a formal job offer and get it in the mail to you tonight. The sooner you can get going the better, so I suggest you call Geiser within the next few days. I'll talk to him tonight so he'll be prepared to process you on the payroll in Schenectady. I'll look forward to seeing you in Phoenix as soon as your education program is complete."

It would be four months before Spielberg, his wife, and their four children moved to Phoenix. The interval was well spent in visits to a number of GE Operating

Departments, Field Sales Offices, and selected industrial customers. Also involved had been a number of late-night discussions between Leah and Arnold concerning the wisdom of making the move. It had originally taken quite a bit of persuading to get Leah to move from the Cincinnati area to Camden, New Jersey, and now he wanted to take off for Arizona, which she considered a territory just liberated from the Indians. This scene was to be repeated in a number of households as the GE Computer Department recruited much of its staff from the effete East. Fortunately for the Spielbergs, the whole family came to love Arizona. Leah had cheered up considerably when they arrived on a balmy February day from a frigid Philadelphia climate. They built a nice home in an orange grove and, like most of the rest, quickly succumbed to the beauty of the desert setting.

Spielberg arrived at the office bubbling with enthusiasm. He had not only visited every GE department involved in products for industrial applications, but he had spent time with application engineers and sales engineers dealing with each of the major types of industrial customers. He had been welcomed by the Apparatus Division salesmen who were seeking new and more technologically advanced products they could exploit, and they had taken him to a number of factories so he could obtain a feel for the difficult environmental conditions under which process control equipment would have to operate. Describing his visitations at a hastily called staff meeting, he concluded with the revelation that he had been given a request for proposal from the Jones & Laughlin Steel Company covering a desired automatic inspection system for their high-speed tinplate line.

"It's an ideal opportunity for us to take our first step in process control," said Spielberg. "The system is pretty straightforward but it has to operate reliably in an environment that is hot, dirty, noisy, and subject to intermittent shock and frequent power fluctuations. I learned a lot about that when I visited the Industry Control Department in Lynchburg, Virginia, where they produce all sorts of process control equipment using components furnished by other parts of the company: relays, switch gear, thyratron tubes, rectifiers, voltage regulators, and the like. Many of these components are physically delicate, so they use massive cabinets with built-in air conditioning and vibration isolation to obtain reliable performance under the most difficult conditions. They've done an excellent job, and they're well-established and highly profitable, but they don't know beans about digital data processing."

"Do you think they're likely to resent it if we encroach on what they must think of as their turf?" asked Oldfield.

"I think they might, but they seem overly confident, and we should be able to outflank them."

"Wouldn't we be better off acting as a subcontractor to Industry Control rather than competing with them?" asked Lasher.

"You'd think so, but I made a few exploratory overtures while I was there, and their engineering manager didn't think they needed any help from the outside. Besides, their attitude is that digital computers are too unreliable to be used for industrial applications. They're happy with their tried-and-true product line, and I don't think they'd be very easy to work with."

"Okay," said Oldfield, "Let's go after the Jones & Laughlin job and see what happens. We may end up having a Product Charter fight with Industry Control, but the best way to win it will be to have a detailed technical proposal completed and costed out as soon as possible. I'll start probing the Product Charter procedure so we'll be completely prepared for the battle. There's a two-inch thick manual issued by Harold Smiddy, Cordiner's guru for corporate organizational decentralization, and it includes a long dissertation on the Product Charter procedure. Let's get busy."

A month later Harold Strickland called with the word that the Apparatus Division general manager had told him the Industry Control Department was upset because they had learned we had approached one of their customers, the Jones & Laughlin Steel Company.

"They want you to cease and desist."

"Is that an order?" said Oldfield.

"It is unless you can show it's a legitimate Computer Department product. I'm told it's a routine instrumentation project."

"You've been told wrong, Harold. This is a hardwired transistorized computer, simple by comparison with ERMA but definitely a process control computer system—exactly what Mr. Cordiner says we should be doing. You haven't met our project engineer, Arnold Spielberg. He and two younger engineers are hard at work on the project, and we've scheduled a design review for next week. Ken Geiser's very enthusiastic about it as our first step into process control computers. So am I."

"All right, Barney. I'll protect you if I can, but you'd better be prepared for a Product Charter fight."

"I've been reading up about Smiddy's procedure for adjudicating Product Charter disputes, and I've already started the chain of paperwork that will lead to a decision according to Smiddy's rule book. J&L wants a quotation by the end of October, and I'm hoping I can use that as a lever to speed up the process."

"That all sounds okay, Barney, but be careful not to stick your neck out too far. Industry Control's a favorite of the corporate staff."

"I'll do my best, Harold."

The call was mildly disturbing. First they want us to emphasize process control computers, thought Oldfield, and now we have to fight our way through a jungle of red tape to be able to make a modest quotation for a process control computer. For the first time, he wondered whether the people at 570 had any conception of the single-minded determination it would require to succeed in this fast moving new industry, particularly after giving a five-year head start to IBM.

The basic design of the Jones & Laughlin tinplate inspection system was completed by mid-September, 1957, and the key components and circuits had been selected and tested. It was to be a hardwired computer; Spielberg recognized that he did not have a sufficiently experienced staff to permit a stored-program approach, and, besides, the application was primarily one of data accumulation and data storage rather than computation. The system included an assortment of specialized instruments for measuring thickness, presence or absence of pinholes, coating consistency, footage of tinplate, and so on. As the tinplate was fed down the line at speeds up to thirty-six hundred feet per minute, these instruments would send their measurements to the computer consisting of transistorized logic circuits that would, in turn, feed the data to a magnetic storage drum. At the end of the run, the data would be channeled to an automatic typewriter that would print out a complete record of the automated inspection and classify the coil of tinplate as prime, standard, or substandard.

The concept was straightforward, except that the use of semiconductor circuits and magnetic drums had not previously been attempted in an industrial environment such as a steel mill. Spielberg proposed to build the electronic cabinet from rugged fiberglass-insulated steel with rubber-gasketed doors to protect the already plastic-sealed electronic equipment. Heavy-duty switches and mercury-wetted relays (to eliminate burned relay points) were to be used, and the electronics cabinet would have built-in air conditioning along with heavily filtered air intakes to remove dust and corrosive agents. The entire unit would be shock-mounted to isolate it from shock and vibration.

"This thing is going to be as rugged as a tank," said Spielberg during the design review, and we've used worst-case techniques in all the electronic assemblies. We've also added a couple of features the customer didn't think of, such as a manual input panel so the operator can enter data on visually observed defects such as oil and grease, abrasions, anode streak, sliver, and quench stains."

"What are sliver and streak?" asked Oldfield. "Sounds like the name of a vaudeville act."

"I'm glad you asked that," said Spielberg, launching into a detailed description of the tinplate process. "As you know, tin is a malleable silvery metallic element obtained chiefly from cassiterite. It is used to coat other metals such as steel to prevent corrosion. The process is essentially electrolytic, and one of the problems has to do with . . ."

"Enough, already. You've convinced us you're the expert. Are there any technical problems to be solved in order to meet the specifications?"

"Very few,'" continued Spielberg. "This is a pretty easy data handling problem. While the tinplate line is quite awesome when you see the steel plate whipping along the rollers at thirty-six hundred feet per minute, the speed of data flow is rather slow in electronic terms. The system is hardwired so there aren't any programming problems. We can release the entire job to manufacturing within sixty days. The rest is up to Ray Barclay."

"No problem," said Barclay. "We have the transistors and diodes in stock, and we have quotes on all the other hard-to-get components, including the magnetic drum and the battleship-type cabinetry. The biggest job will be assembling and wiring the hundreds of circuit boards. It'll give us a good chance to use our new wire-wrap system to eliminate solder joints, and then to test each board before final assembly. We estimate the whole system can be put together and checked out within three months from final engineering release."

Clair Lasher, who had been quiet up to that point, stubbed out the cigarette he'd been nursing and said, "We've given this product the nomenclature GE 302 Automatic Inspection Computer, mainly to confuse the Industry Control Department. However, let's not fool ourselves that it's really a computer. It's a small step along the way, but I don't think it's worth the effort unless we have a clear mandate to go ahead and exploit the field of process control computing by developing a complete product line."

"You're right," said Oldfield. "I've gone to some lengths to follow Harold Smiddy's procedure for adjudicating Product Charters, and I hope we're near the end of the trail. The final step is to hold a meeting attended by the interested parties, at which time Smiddy will hand down a verdict. He's agreed to hold it here in Phoenix by mid-October, in time to meet the deadline for the Jones & Laughlin submission. I suggest you organize a flip-chart presentation showing how the GE 302 will evolve into a product line of process control computers applicable to a wide range of industrial applications. I doubt if Industry Control will bother to do anything of this sort, so we should have a leg up."

Oldfield's prediction proved correct. The Product Charter meeting, held in Phoenix in mid-October, 1957, turned out to be a triumph for both Harold Smiddy and the Computer Department. Smiddy had successfully implemented his rather convoluted process for eliminating competition between GE Operating Departments, and the Computer Department had obtained a clear charter for process control computers. It had resulted in one of the very few satisfactory interactions between the new organization and the dreaded 570 corporate management team.

Following the Product Charter meeting of 1957, a barbecue was held for the participants. As the group feasted on ribs, biscuits, french fries, and beer, a radio played western ballads in the background. Suddenly there was an interruption.

"Flash . . . Moscow, 10 p.m. Eastern Standard Time . . . Marshall Nikolay Bulganin, premier of the Union of Soviet Socialist Republics, announced today that the U.S.S.R. has successfully launched a Sputnik, or satellite, to create the world's first artificial moon. The revolutionary device was propelled into space by a giant rocket that reached the incredible speed necessary to free the Sputnik from the earth's gravity. It is now circling the earth, sending radio signals announcing the triumph of Soviet science and engineering, and it will be visible from the United States as a bright star streaking across the heavens. Stay tuned to NBC for further details." The announcement, with its implications for the Cold War, silenced the group momentarily, but was followed by excited chatter. Ken McCombs argued that the whole thing was probably a hoax created by the Russians.

No hoax, the dawn of the satellite age would have an undreamed of impact on the future of worldwide communications and, ultimately, the nature of computers as they would emerge into the twenty-first century. None of this was apparent in October, 1957—only the cold fact that we had lost the first space race to the Russians.

CHAPTER 12
PROCESS CONTROL ACHIEVEMENTS

While the Jones & Laughlin Tinplate Inspection Computer was processing through the manufacturing cycle, Spielberg and his group were busily working on what would be known as the GE 312 Digital Control Computer, to be a general-purpose stored program computer, adaptable to all types of industrial applications requiring on-line input, high-speed computation, and continuous feedback to the process being controlled. T'sai Lee, a programmer, was added to the group, and he developed the first process control computer operating system, analogous, he said, to "little sausage links."

During the development of the GE 312, a contract was received from McClouth Steel Corporation for a computer to provide computer control for a hot strip mill. This was an exceedingly difficult problem because the temperature control of each of the five "hot stands" through which the strip steel was heated and squeezed was highly irregular and subject to hysteresis. This meant that temperature controls would have to be reset at each of the hot stands depending on the measurements made at the previous hot stand—a process requiring continuous recalculation as the steel strip proceeded along the way. This was not only labor intensive, but it slowed down the process and made it more expensive. What was needed was a control computer that could receive the measurements from the sensors, calculate the adjustment to be made to the subsequent hot stand, and feed the required signal to the control mechanism. This type of on-line real-time operation required speed of computing and flexibility not possible with any existing process control equipment.

When the McClouth Steel request for proposal was received, the application engineer from Apparatus Sales warned Lasher that the job had previously been turned down by Westinghouse as being beyond state of the art. Lasher passed on the comment to Spielberg.

"It's a toughie, all right," responded Spielberg, "but I think we can do it if we can add about five hundred words of high-speed core access storage to augment the drum memory. This is about as difficult a process control job as we're ever liable to encounter, so the computer that can do it will be able to handle most any process control problem we'll face in the future. Let's go for it."

The biggest problem in the McClouth Steel five-stand strip mill was the programming of a mill that had hysteresis in the rollers. There were also many problems with the sensors, particularly the gage (thickness) sensor that had great difficulty in measuring accurately because of scab; eventually McClouth went to a beta-ray thickness gage to solve the problem. The original plan that came to Spielberg from the

Apparatus Sales engineers was to use a "rolling formula" that calculated the reduction and speed of the inputted roller-stand settings in order to predetermine the setting of the next roll. That formula didn't work because the roll deflected—the steel was not uniformly hot and, therefore, as malleable, so the predictions for the next roll were wrong. Finally, Spielberg had to resort to a feedback loop in which the output of the farthest roll thickness was compared with calculated thickness, and corrected roll settings were reapplied to earlier rollers to bring the steel on gage. It took almost a year after shipping the GE 312 before the GE 312 could roll steel to spec. It was a major accomplishment that established the GE Computer Department as a leader in process control computers.[33]

The GE 312 Digital Control Computer weighed three thousand pounds!

CHAPTER 13
PROBLEMS AT PALO ALTO AND AT HOME

Most of the newcomers to Phoenix made a rapid and joyful transition to the dry desert climate and casual way of life. An unfortunate exception was Barney Oldfield's wife, Sofia. She suffered from a severe and poorly understood nervous condition at a time when Phenobarbital was prescribed in liberal quantities "to quiet the nerves." Her inevitable addiction had been brought under control by physicians at the Concord Clinic during the period when Barney had been an MIT faculty member, but it returned after the move to Phoenix. Year by year, her condition deteriorated despite apparently competent medical care.

The situation reached a crisis in mid-1958 when Sofia and Barney were guests of honor at a cocktail party hosted by Dr. and Mrs. Grady Gammage of Arizona State University. Sofia had run out of Phenobarbital and had quieted her nerves before the party with a rather liberal dose of vodka. Her nerves still on edge, she continued to imbibe at the party, soon reaching a point just short of delirium. It came on quickly, and Barney was able to get her home and in bed before any real damage was done, or so he thought. From that time on, Sofia became increasingly reclusive, withdrawing from social contact with the Phoenix community and most of their GE friends. Many thought she was being snobbish, but, in fact, she was seriously ill. She was convinced the only solution was to return to the Boston area where she could get proper treatment. The pressure to do so increased month by month, and it became apparent to Barney he would have to take drastic action—either break up the family or move them back to Boston.

It was a particularly difficult time to be faced with a decision of such magnitude. Ground had been broken for the new Deer Valley plant where the various components of the Computer Department—management, marketing, engineering, manufacturing, and finance—were to be consolidated. This was a signal for union organizers from the International Union of Electrical Workers to begin their campaign to organize the factory workers, a fate worse than death in the eyes of Lemuel Boulware, General Electric's vice president of Employee and Community Relations. Oldfield, together with Ray Barclay, manager of manufacturing, was plunged into a round of meetings with corporate staff experts attempting to guide the union negotiations, as well as to oversee the nitty-gritty of plant design. Much of the burden fell on Ray Barclay, an expert himself in electronic fabrication, assembly, and testing. Barclay more than held his own in dealing with those who had cut their industrial teeth on the manufacture of transformers and light bulbs. Nevertheless, the deluge of discussions and decisions was continuous and time consuming and left little time for the resolution of personal problems.

Other worries diverted Oldfield from his domestic agenda. There was word from Johnson that the ERMA project had run into unexpected technical snags that might delay beyond the contract date acceptance of the first system.[34] Achievement of this goal was an important key to keeping the naysayers on the corporate level at bay. Most of the staff at 570 Lexington were unsympathetic with GE's attempt to enter the commercial computer market via the technically risky ERMA program. Oldfield and Johnson likened them to a pack of coyotes, waiting just outside the campfire, fangs bared and tongues hanging out, ready to pounce at the first sign of weakness.

The instant Oldfield put down the telephone after his conversation with Johnson, Audrey was on the intercom. "Ken McCombs needs to see you in the worst way."

Oldfield groaned and reached for a cigarette. "Send him in."

McCombs was inclined to be a nit picker, but this time he had substantive news. "We've just finished a routine audit of Herb Grosch's expense account and capital commitments," he began. "They're way out of line, as George Snively suspected, and Herb recently made a four-day trip to New York when we thought he was in Huntsville. We've just heard through financial channels he approached your group executive, Jim LaPierre, with a proposal that you should be removed and Grosch made department general manager. He struck out with LaPierre so he then went to Harold Smiddy with the same proposal. Smiddy thought it was some sort of a joke.[35] Anyway, his financial people believed you should know what's going on."

"Son-of-a-gun!" Oldfield whistled and shook his head, more in amusement than anger. "I'm not completely surprised. Herb's been on a collision course with the rest of us for some time. I'm glad he's brought it to a head."

An astronomer by education, Herb Grosch had been with IBM as a card-punch machine programmer during the early days of IBM's entry into the digital computer field. He had no engineering background, but he did have a feel for computation. Unsatisfied with the career opportunities available in IBM, but inculcated with the IBM mystique, he joined GE's Jet Engine Division at a time when that part of the company was establishing computer centers using IBM equipment with which he was familiar. He was managing their center in Evendale, Ohio, when he heard about the new Computer Department. No shrinking violet, Grosch offered his services to Dr. W.R.G. Baker, Electronics Division vice president. Informed that the job was filled, he settled for the position of manager of the planned GE Computer Center at Arizona State University. The center was to be planned around a powerful IBM 704 mainframe, and Grosch was permitted to bring along a number of programmers from Evendale to man the center. His arrangement with Oldfield permitted him to finance the venture through either government or commercial contracts, and he was free to sell his programming and computing services to other project groups within the Computer Department as well as to other GE departments. He had not told Oldfield that before leaving Evendale he had agreed not to compete for computing services for any of the eastern departments of GE. This agreement was one he would live to regret.[36]

One of Grosch's extracurricular activities prior to joining the Computer Department had been as a member of the American Rocket Society. As an astronomer, he was naturally drawn to the blossoming missile and space program where he became acquainted with Wernher von Braun and other scientists working frantically to catch up with the Russian satellite program. He was able to put these contacts to good use in developing a computer services contract with the Army Ballistic Missile Center in Huntsville, but this turned out to be his only paying customer. He had proposed to computerize ASU's registration process, but this turned out to be a comedy of errors, due probably to students' resistance to being automated. Grosch found the problem of financing a $44,000-a-month computer much different in the commercial world than in a government-contract environment.

The problem of financing the Computer Center became a continuing source of friction between Herb and much of the rest of the Computer Department. It had been hoped that the Computer Center would become a source of expert programming to serve the needs of the project groups in both Menlo Park and Phoenix, and Grosch journeyed to Johnson's laboratory to make his pitch. He gave Johnson a lecture about the senior IBM experience he and his group could bring to bear in solving the problems of the ERMA project and proposed an arrangement whereby ERMA would pay the Computer Center a regular monthly fee for his services. Grosch returned to Phoenix without a contract, furious at being turned down. He accused Oldfield of poisoning Johnson's mind against him. Puzzled, Oldfield called Johnson and asked what happened.

"I'm sorry, Barney," said Johnson, "but he rubbed us all the wrong way with his trumpeting about IBM and his superior knowledge. We weren't particularly interested in the first place since we were confident we could do the job and felt we didn't need the 'help' of IBM-type veterans. You know, I was an IBM Fellow at Cal Tech, and I saw a lot of IBM, especially IBM San Jose and engineering executives from Poughkeepsie. Those fellows looked down their long noses at what we had accomplished at Hughes with our operational airborne computer and told me I should come to San Jose to see real computer engineering. I went, saw nothing compared with what we had done at Hughes, and came home intending to have nothing more to do with IBM. I feel Joe Weizenbaum knows more about programming than Grosch, and I know John Paivinen can design and build a transistor computer better than anyone Grosch knows. I'm sorry if this creates a problem for you."[37]

Oldfield sighed. "The problem is Herb Grosch and not you. I won't push him at you again."

Grosch's relations with Bob Wooley and the other engineers in Phoenix were no better. Grosch considered them second-rate and made no effort to hide his feelings. It was true that many in the group, though experienced and capable electronics engineers, were still in a learning phase as far as computer design was concerned.

Nevertheless, they were human, and they were not about to place their trust in someone who openly despised them.

In Grosch's defense, it must be said that, in the mid-1950s, computers were considered a field for electronics engineers rather than programmers, so Grosch's sales pitch was a difficult one. Unfortunately, he was not a very good salesman. He became increasingly bitter, resulting in his unsuccessful approaches to LaPierre and Smiddy. It became obvious to Grosch that he was not going to be allowed to run GE's computer business, so he contacted his old boss at IBM and went back to New York.

After Grosch's departure from the scene, it became evident he had attracted some talented people to the Computer Center and had made a contribution by establishing GE's first venture into the computer services business. He was never cut out to be an organization man, but he had some good ideas that others would later bring to reality.

CHAPTER 14
ERMA PASSES THE TEST

B ob Johnson's internal schedule was to have the first ERMA system complete and installed in the San Jose branch of the Bank of America by the end of 1957, a full year before the contract delivery date. This would have given him the luxury of a full year to debug the system and train both operators and service personnel prior to full-scale operation. As 1957 passed into history, it became evident that his schedule would not be met, and Bob worried for the first time about the ability of the Computer Department to meet the contract date. There were severe financial penalties for any delay, not to mention the panic at 570 Lexington Avenue.

It was a rainy and rather depressing day when he and John Paivinen, manager of computer engineering, sat in Bob's office, sipping black coffee and discussing the schedule.

"I'm relaxed about the computer," said Paivinen. "When we started the project, I worried about our ability to use a worst-case design approach with germanium transistors, but Gerry Allard came through like a champion. Then I started to worry about the ability of the fellows in Phoenix to develop the necessary manufacturing capability, but Ray Barclay and his crew have delivered a quality computer to San Jose. It's checking out fine."

"That's not what I'm worried about, John. We seem to have solved what we thought would be our worst technical problems. We can read checks. We can sort checks at high speed. We can compute. What we can't do yet is get the blasted AMPEX magnetic tape units to work properly so we can post the customer accounts to long-term memory, and we can't get the NCR high-speed printer to print out customer statements legible enough to satisfy Al Zipf.[38] The specs we gave AMPEX in the beginning aren't adequate to meet our needs, and it turns out AMPEX can't even meet the original specs, much less our new requirements. We may have to modify our tape controller along with putting the fear of God into AMPEX. I'm not quite so concerned about the printer because NCR has its reputation on the line, but AMPEX is another story. Any ideas?"

"I have some thoughts on what might be done to help the tape unit problem. The weak point in the AMPEX unit is the lousy tape transport. It's an old design that is over-stressed for our application. I hear by the grapevine that they've engineered an entirely new transport for higher speed operation, but they're reluctant to use it for ERMA because they have a large inventory of the old units. We'd probably have to redesign our controller electronics to use the new transport, but that's no big problem."

"I'm glad you're optimistic, John, because I'm going to ask you to put together a Tiger Team to expedite both the tape system and the printer. Are you game?"

"Sure, Bob. As I told you, I think the computer itself is in pretty good shape, so a change of pace might be welcome. It wouldn't seem normal around here without a crisis or two to worry about. I think Claude Tucker would be my first choice for the team. He's a good manager as well as being a damn good engineer, and he has a diplomatic way of dealing with people. Bill Facenda would be an excellent team member. He's a real creative problem solver and likes nothing better than to chase down mysterious troubles. Yes, I think the two of them can do a job for you. I'll just put my feet on the desk and point them in the right direction."

"Okay, John. You've got six months to identify the problems with the tape unit, persuade AMPEX to install an improved transport, re-engineer our electronics to fit within the specs AMPEX can meet, and then make the two work together. Now, how about the printer?"

"I really have no idea what to do about the printer, but I have a lot of confidence in National Cash after the terrific job they and Pitney Bowes did on the high-speed check sorter. One of the first things I'll do is visit Dayton and get together with their design engineers. I may have to prevail on Jay Levinthal to let me have his mechanical genius, Karsten Solheim. I'll get back to you on this after my trip to Dayton."

"Sounds reasonable. Now, if you'll excuse me, I have to meet with Al Zipf and Joe Weizenbaum in San Jose to go over some problems having to do with the detailed operation of the system after all the hardware bugs are worked out. Some of the systems people at the bank think ERMA will never really do the job even if the character reading and the check sorter are near-perfect. They're worried about the time it will take reconciling and tracking those few errors. We're going to have to develop a procedure to make the operation foolproof. An error once every few thousand checks isn't good enough when you're handling other people's money."

As Johnson entered the ERMA area of the Bank of America's San Jose Branch—the first to put the new system in operation—he could not suppress a feeling of satisfaction as he glanced at the computer with its gleaming control console, racks of electronics, MICR, futuristic-looking high-speed sorter, magnetic tape units, and high-speed printer. True, the latter two peripheral devices were still not fully operational, but he had little doubt John Paivinen's Tiger Team would solve these remaining hardware problems. As he watched, an engineer fed a batch of sample bank checks into the hopper of the character reader where the checks were flashed down the sorter belt and deposited in the appropriate bins based on electronic instructions received from the character reader. Simultaneously, the printer chattered away as it registered account identity and check amount. It was a truly impressive example of things to come.

The historic meeting at Rickey's Motel in Palo Alto, July, 1956, during which the Technical Committee on Mechanization of Check Handling of the American Bankers Association adopted magnetic ink character recognition (MICR) as the standard for computerized check handling. On the left, standing second from left is Al Zipf, Bank of America representative to the ABA and major proponent of MICR. Sitting, third from left is Ken Eldredge from Stanford Research Institute, inventor of MICR. GE representatives are John Jogg, marketing representative, third from left, standing; George Jacobi, second from right standing; and Bob Johnson, third from right, sitting.

Johnson found Zipf in the small conference room, working on a complex flow chart. "Good afternoon, Al," said Bob, "I understand you're concerned with a possible operational problem in utilizing the ERMA system."

"Yes, I'm worried about the procedure of reconciling the checks. We know the character reader and sorter are near-perfect, but we also know some errors always creep in due to all kinds of unavoidable human problems, and we have to make sure we have the means of correcting any errors during the period between when the batched checks are received from the branches for processing at the ERMA center and when they must be returned to the branches the next morning along with the revised statements. Let's trace this process."

Zipf then went into a detailed discussion of what errors might creep into the processing of the checks from the time they were put into the hopper of the character reader until the data were captured on magnetic tape together with an accumulated total and a listing of checks against member accounts. If the accumulated total was the same as the entry total received from the branch, all was well. If the total should

The first ERMA system is shipped from Phoenix, February, 1958.

vary from the correct amount it would be necessary for an operator to compare the listings and determine where the errors occurred, and why. If this process took too long, the ERMA system would be a failure.

"Unfortunately," said Zipf, "there is no way of determining whether the system will work until we can process real checks with real customers and real employees, and then measure the results."

"I get the message," said Johnson. "We'll put every resource we can into bringing the total system up to specs before the end of the year so we can start processing enough accounts on a daily basis to permit us to measure the magnitude of the problem."

When Johnson went home that night, his mind full of problems and possible solutions, he told his wife, Mary, "I don't know whether to curse Barney Oldfield for plunging us into a contract with the Bank of America where we'd be responsible, at least in part, for the success of the system they ordered from GE, regardless of its technical performance, or to praise him and Howard Lief of the Bank for establishing an arrangement where both organizations had to work together for a common objective regardless of contract details. I'm a little bit scared at this point, but it's a thrill to know we may be making history in the application of computers to the field of banking and finance, instead of designing devices to make war."

By mid-October, 1958, the tape system problem seemed to have been resolved by Herculean efforts on the part of the Tiger Team, combined with an improvement in performance characteristics of the AMPEX unit.[39] All components necessary for interconnection of the tape unit to the data processor were being debugged in anticipation of a complete system test before the end of 1958. Software available at that point was tailored to handle only one hundred accounts per day initially in order to permit a controlled series of engineering and programming tests with the entire system in operation.

All seemed to be in order as December, 1958, rolled around, but Bob Johnson was still worried about the NCR high-speed printer designed to operate at seven hundred fifty lines of copy per minute, pushing the technical limits of the period.

Johnson and Zipf were huddled over a sheet of computer printout one bright December morning, using a straightedge to measure the amount of skew and waviness in a sample bank statement.

"It still isn't good enough for a statement going to a Bank of America customer," said Zipf. "Your Tiger Team has made a distinct improvement, and the statement is perfectly legible, but the numbers and letters are still enough out of registration to look amateurish to a customer. Don't you agree?" Johnson looked at a number of statements and frowned his reluctant agreement. He knew how hard the team had worked to clean up the printer.

"Okay, Al. I'll get back to Paivinen and Levinthal and read them the riot act for the umpteenth time. We'll solve the problem somehow."

Back at the laboratory, Johnson found Jay Levinthal up to his elbow in gear trains and grease. "I have a sort of half-baked idea I'd like to try out if you'll agree. Have you noticed that if we align the printer at seven hundred fifty lines per minute, it produces virtually perfect type when we run it at half speed? The printer is designed with a huge factor of safety because of the expected heavy usage. We can gear it up to operate at fifteen hundred lines per minute for a brief period and do the character alignment at that speed. Maybe that will cut out the wavy tendency at seven hundred fifty lines per minute . Worth a try? We've got nothing to lose but a printer that won't work."

"That's the dumbest thing I've ever heard of—let's do it!"

By the next day, the shop had constructed a modified gear box that would permit operation of the printer at three speeds: half speed, design speed, and what Levinthal had optimistically labeled, "alignment speed." A crowd of concerned and skeptical engineers hovered around the test area as Levinthal started the printer, phasing past design speed and up to fifteen hundred lines per minute, computer paper spewing out at an amazing rate. Levinthal went through the alignment procedure methodically, and then shifted down to seven hundred fifty lines per minute. There was no trace of waviness or skewed numbers.

Bob Johnson couldn't contain his excitement. "Jay, it looks as if you've done it at last. Let's let her run at design speed for eight hours or so and see how the alignment holds up. If it's still this good tomorrow, we'll install it at San Jose."

A multiple ERMA system installed in a Bank of America branch. (Computer and peripherals shown in top photo and MICR and check sorters shown in bottom photo.)

Their luck held, and the next day, December 28, 1958, the first complete ERMA system was assembled and put into operation. Al Zipf gave a smile of approval as customer statements emerged from the printer in perfect alignment.[40] The GE 100 computer hummed its cybernetic ballad, the MICR fed checks into the hungry belt of the high-speed check sorter, the multiple magnetic tape reels spun back and forth as they recorded data and were accessed by the computer, and the printer chattered in unison. There was a functional beauty to the blend of noises that heralded the introduction of automation to the world of banking.

It was New Year's Eve day, 1958, when Al Zipf accepted the first ERMA system capable of processing the bookkeeping of one hundred accounts per day. However, there was no breaking out of champagne or other forms of celebration. Though the accomplishment was a great one, the task still remained to develop procedures and techniques to reconcile processing errors within the time constraints required to meet the bank's daily operating cycle. The entire system of equipment and operators would have to be tightened up and optimized to handle the design volume of fifty-five thousand accounts per day. The weary could not yet rest.

CHAPTER 15
THE CHANGE IN MANAGEMENT

Barney Oldfield and Clair Lasher were seated at a window table in the Stockyards Restaurant—a South Phoenix institution devoted to thick steaks, strong drinks, and pretty waitresses in attractive cowgirl costumes. Outside, the almost empty stockyards were a stark reminder of the days when Phoenix was a major assembly area for cattle drives wending their way north to the railroad. The onset of widespread irrigation had turned the city into an agricultural center, but many of the remnants of the Old West clung to the region and enhanced its culture.

Oldfield had been talking for some time, picking his words very carefully to emphasize the importance of the conversation.

"Well, that's the story, Clair. I'll be out of Phoenix by the end of the year. It's agonizing to leave the best job I've ever had—probably the best I'll ever have—but there simply isn't any other choice. I haven't told anyone but Harold Strickland, and I'd appreciate it if you'd not tell anyone for a bit. It's important to have a smooth transition, which means the avoidance of gossip and speculation until a decision on my successor can be announced."

"Thanks for the confidence," said Lasher. "I'll keep it under my hat, but I think you know the wives are aware of Sofia's problems and are already uneasy."

"I'm aware of that." Oldfield paused to light a cigarette and take a healthy swig of his martini. "The reason I wanted to have lunch with you today away from our usual haunts was to make sure you knew the background and to sound you out concerning your personal ambitions. You're the logical one to take over as my successor, and I plan to recommend you for the job if I'm sure you really want it. My only real concern is my recollection of what seemed to be a not-so-enthusiastic attitude on your part when we first obtained the ERMA contract and gambled on our ability to pull it off. How do you feel about it today?"

"I'll admit I was skeptical at first, but it was the only game in town as far as computers were concerned. Since then we've erased my original worries, which had to do mainly with our ability to handle a program like ERMA, with all its technical unknowns. I think ERMA's going to be a winner, and I think there's a good chance to build the Computer Department into an important part of GE if the powers that be will back us up.

"You know, Barney," continued Lasher. "I'm a great believer in long-range product planning, and I don't think I'd have had the nerve to go after the ERMA contract without a lot of lengthy study. I see now that the only way to have overcome the inertia within GE was to seize the ball and run with it the way you did. If I should become general manager, I'll be grateful for your contribution, but my inclination will be to base new product decisions on detailed market analysis and product planning. Do you have a problem with this?"

"Not at all, Clair. It's obviously time to shift gears, which is one reason I plan to recommend you as my successor. I'm meeting with Harold Strickland and Jim LaPierre next week to develop a transition plan. I'll let you know the results."

Oldfield never felt comfortable at 570 Lexington Avenue. It was the same feeling he had when being ushered into the principal's office at school. He realized that here was the court of last resort, where spur-of-the-moment decisions could initiate or undo the work and accomplishments of many thousands of others throughout the organization's complex channels of management. He approached the interview with Jim LaPierre with some apprehension, concerned that pressure would be applied to make him change his mind, or, conversely, that he would be ushered out of General Electric with a cry of "good riddance."

LaPierre surprised him with a warm greeting when he was ushered into his office by Harold Strickland.

"I'm sorry you find it necessary to leave the Computer Department and settle in the Boston area, but I admire your decision to put your family at the top of your priority list. I wish we had a job to fit you in the Boston area, but the fact is that most of GE's activities are moving in the other direction. Do you have anything specific in mind?"

"I'm not sure, because I haven't sought out any other opportunities, but I've talked to Hal Geneen, the executive vice president of Raytheon, and I think there's a good opportunity there. It's not competitive with anything I've been doing with the Computer Department, so I'll probably end up there."

"I've read over your personnel record," said LaPierre, "and it's apparent you've been involved in one way or another in just about every branch of electronic technology. I'd like to take advantage of this before you leave the company, and I've a proposition to offer you. I'd like you to head up a three-month study program to explore the applications of new electronic technology, projected over the next five or ten years to improve the operation of the General Electric Company—not just data processing, but communications, TV, facsimile, video recording, and whatever is likely to come along during this period. I'll give you a budget to allow you to bring together a small group of experts, and I can arrange office and laboratory space for you at the Lynn River works. You'll still be a GE employee during this period so the company will take care of moving you and your family to the Boston area. Give me a good final report at the end of the study, and we'll give you a separation bonus to help you make your transition to whatever new career you decide upon."

Oldfield was amazed by LaPierre's offer, but he was quick to accept. He knew it would be far better to do his job hunting if he were still employed by GE rather than being out of a job. Besides, the study program would give him a chance to explore the latest advances in electronic technology. He'd gather together a few people like Bill Edson from Stanford and Fred Best from MIT's Draper Laboratory and give them an opportunity to brainstorm the future.

Harold Strickland was surprised at LaPierre's offer, not realizing it was calculated to keep Oldfield in the family, so to speak, during the Computer Department's management transition.

"Barney has recommended Clair Lasher to succeed him as general manager of the Computer Department. I think you know Clair from his part in the Metcalf Report. He has a good record in the Industrial Electronics Division, both in marketing and in managing the Technical Equipment Department's Special Products Section, and he's been the manager of marketing for the Computer Department almost from the beginning. My normal preference would be to appoint someone with much more management experience, but Barney has persuaded me that it would be risky to put anyone with no computer experience in the job."

"It's your call, Harold," said LaPierre.

"Okay, we'll appoint Lasher acting general manager so we can evaluate him for a six-month period before making a firm appointment."

At the end of 1958, Oldfield left for Massachusetts. He completed the study program for LaPierre and immediately joined Raytheon as General Manager of the Equipment Division. Meanwhile, Lasher had taken over the reins of the Computer Department. Oldfield was not to regain contact with the organization for thirty-two years, at which time he discovered the Bank of America had attempted (in vain) to locate him to participate in the 1992 celebration of the birth of ERMA.[41]

PART III

Era of the Big Look
December 1958
to
February 1963

Dramatis Personae

ALEXANDER BOTTS. Principal in a series of short stories run by *The Saturday Evening Post* during the 1930s. A field salesman with the Earthwork Tractor Company, he was continually feuding with his own front office, but was always successful in his unorthodox sales campaigns.

DICK PORTER. A senior member of 570's Engineering Services group, reporting to Clarence Linder.

CLARENCE LINDER. GE's vice president of engineering.

DICK BARNES. Manager of product planning and market research for the Computer Department.

ALAN BENSON. Manager of the Computer Center at Arizona State University, succeeding Herb Grosch who returned to IBM at the end of 1957.

CHUCK PROPSTER. Computer engineer recruited from RCA by Spielberg. Worked closely with Spielberg in the design of the GE 312 Process Control Computer and GE 200 series computers.

JEAN TROTTER. Wife of George Trotter.

ROY JORDAN. Lasher's manager of advertising and sales promotion.

RAY SHANAHAN and BOB CLARKE. Jordan's experts on press releases and visual aids.

GENE CLEVELAND. GE's western commercial vice president.

RONALD REAGAN. "Mr. GE" to the radio and TV networks. Future U.S. president.

SUZANNE LASHER. Wife of Clair Lasher.

MARY JOHNSON. Wife of Bob Johnson.

PAT BARCLAY. Wife of Ray Barclay.

MARY McCOMBS. Wife of Ken McCombs.

JOHN LOCKTON. GE treasurer and one of the few Computer Department supporters at 570.

VIC CASEBOLT. Sales engineer out of the Detroit sales office.

ART CRITCHLOW. Project engineer for the ill-fated MOSAIC line of advanced computers.

LACY GOOSETREE. Manager of marketing of the Computer Department, replacing Lasher when he became general manager.

DAVID SARNOFF. Chairman and CEO of RCA.

GERALD PHILLIPI. GE vice president for finance.

BOB SHEELEY. Goosetree's manager of sales.

KEN FISHER, JIM POMPA, TOM O'ROURKE, CLINT DE GABRIELLE, VERN SCHATZ, CURT HARE, WARREN PRINCE, LEO MOTT, RAY NOORDA, and JACK LORENZ. GE Computer Department sales managers and salesmen who were brought together by Goosetree to develop an outstanding sales force and who had long and successful careers in the computer industry.

BILL DUSTER. Manager of marketing personnel development. A sales training expert.

CHUCK RIEGER. GE vice president for marketing.

BILL BRIDGE. Manager of special systems engineering and inventor of the Datanet 30, the world's first communications computer.

WERNHER VON BRAUN. The German rocket scientist in charge of the army's rocket development program at Huntsville, Alabama.

DICK MAHEW. The Computer Department's district sales manager in Huntsville.

JIM RUDE. EDP manager at Pillsbury Corporation.

CHRIS KRYGSMAN. Product planner for the Datanet 30.

BEN FRANKLIN. Communications manager of Chrysler Corporation.

JOHN KEMENY and THOMAS KURTZ of Dartmouth College, developers of the BASIC computer language.

JOHN COULEUR. Project engineer of the M236 computer used in the MISTRAM system developed by the Heavy Military Equipment Department in Syracuse.

DON SHELL. Head of the Mathematics Department of GE's General Engineering Laboratory in Schenectady. He favored the M236 to replace the MOSAIC computer within the Computer Department.

ART VINSON. Group vice president and Harold Strickland's boss.

HELMET SASSENFIELD. Manager of the ASU Computer Center at the time.

CHAPTER 16
PLANNING FOR THE FUTURE

Clair Lasher, unlike Oldfield, came directly to GE after graduating from college, became a test engineer, and spent much of World War II in GE's Government Division where he became heavily involved in the development and sale of airborne radar. He remained in the government sales area for some years after the end of the war, and was a member of Oldfield's staff when Oldfield became sales manager. Lasher had expected to be appointed to the position, and there was some initial friction between the two. This had disappeared with time as they discovered their skills to be complementary.

When Oldfield went to Palo Alto to form the GE Microwave Laboratory at Stanford University, Lasher transferred to Bill Morlock's Industrial Equipment Department, a part of George Metcalf's Commercial and Government Equipment Division. There he was assigned to participate in a study program that resulted in the so-called Metcalf Report forecasting the future of the electronics industry and recommending participation in selected segments on the part of GE. The section on electronic computers was authored by Clair Lasher, and it forecast that electronic computers would become commercially feasible and would emerge as the fastest growing segment of the electronics market.

The report was issued in 1954. Many portions of the report were accepted and acted upon. The recommendation concerning the computer business was rejected by President Ralph Cordiner, much to the dismay of Doc Baker, vice president and general manager of the Electronics Division.

Despite the turn-down from Cordiner, Clair Lasher was given an OK to spend much of 1955 developing a business plan aimed at launching GE into the computer business. This proposal was submitted to Mr. Cordiner at about the same time that Barney Oldfield was authorized by Baker to submit a bid on the ERMA program.

Cordiner's abrupt rejection of the proposal came as a bitter disappointment to Lasher and appeared to put an end to the possibility that GE would become active in this rapidly developing electronics market. Contrary to all expectations, Oldfield soon flew into Syracuse with a letter contract for over $30 million of ERMA computer systems. On the face of it, this was a direct and blatant defiance of the mandate set down by the president of the company, though Oldfield was blissfully unaware of the recent declaration. (Some years later, when Oldfield wrote Cordiner for a letter of recommendation, he discovered that Cordiner had a long memory. He received a blistering reply that convinced him that ERMA had been a complete fiasco. He was wrong.)

Lasher expected the wrath of Cordiner to fall upon Baker and Oldfield, and he initially distanced himself from the project. However, he underestimated the power of a large order from the country's largest bank. It simply couldn't be refused; besides, Cordiner had evidently made a side agreement with Baker that, if he should obtain the ERMA contract, he could establish a Computer Department to implement the program and proceed in parallel with process control computers. Baker, in turn, was said to have agreed to abandon all efforts to enter the commercial computer market if he failed to win the ERMA competition. There is no written record of this agreement, but it was a plausible explanation of the apparent reversal in corporate policy that permitted the contract to be accepted.

Within General Electric, the Marketing Section of most operating departments contained a number of functions such as sales, market research and product planning, advertising and sales promotion, marketing administration, and (surprisingly) application engineering and product service. Inclusion of these latter two technical functions recognized GE's philosophy that selling and customer service were two parts of the same function. Clair Lasher had served in many of these roles. By nature, and by training, he tended toward the approach of detailed market study and product planning before committing to a new product line. In this respect, he differed from Alexander Botts of Earthworm Tractor[42] fame who relied on intuition and familiarity with human nature to guide his sales strategy. He deplored the fact that Ralph Cordiner had accepted the fait accompli of Oldfield, while his own reasoned approach, with its in-depth planning of alternate strategies, had failed to move the stubborn GE executive from his preconceived position. However, he accepted the inevitable in good grace and joined the fledgling organization as manager of marketing.

Lasher's first action after being appointed acting general manager was to contact Harold Strickland to determine what his initial objectives would be for his stewardship of the Computer Department. The reply from Strickland was succinct and to the point.

"I want you to concentrate on four things. First, be sure the ERMA system stays on course. Our reputation will be mud if we fail to complete this project on schedule or if the system doesn't meet the bank's needs. In connection with new projects, you are to concentrate on industrial process control—the one area that has been blessed by Harold Smiddy. Try to keep the cash drain down by obtaining government sponsorship wherever possible. And, finally, avoid head-on competition with IBM. This may be difficult, but the mandate comes directly from Mr. Cordiner."

Clair masked his disappointment with a wry smile. He had anticipated a more ambitious directive from on-high. In particular, he had hoped for some indication he would be permitted to market the ERMA computer for applications beyond the banking field. Deciding the time was not ripe to get involved in anything controversial, he accepted the marching orders without comment, except to note that the problem of obtaining government sponsorship would require some resolution of the

Product Charter with the company's military divisions, which considered any government computer business, except for commercial products and logistical computers, to belong to them.

Both Lasher and Strickland were aware of the MISTRAM (missile tracking and monitoring) program of GE's Heavy Military Equipment Department in Syracuse. This was a highly classified tracking system for the Atlas missile established at Cape Canaveral under contract with the U.S. Air Force. They were aware also that under the umbrella of this huge contract there were millions available for the design of advanced data-processing equipment. A less-decentralized company than GE would have channeled these dollars to that part of the organization dedicated to computers, but because each department general manager was judged by his dollar profit performance, it was extremely unlikely the Computer Department would receive any portion of this financing.

"At the moment," said Lasher, "the only government sponsorship we can count on is the data-processing work at the Army Ballistic Missile Center at Huntsville, Alabama. It hasn't produced any profits so far, but at least our work for Von Braun's group is under army sponsorship rather than the air force and of little interest to the boys from Syracuse. There's a lot of potential business at Huntsville for on-line data logging in connection with static testing of the large rocket motors. According to Arnold Spielberg it's a glorified version of process control techniques, so we'd really be following Mr. Cordiner's instructions 200 percent if we assigned a sales engineer to the Huntsville area to investigate the product opportunities."

"Good thinking, Clair. I'm sure Mr. Cordiner will be pleased. Now how about ERMA? Dick Porter from Mr. Linder's Engineering Services group has just returned from a trip to the ERMA engineering lab in Palo Alto and he reports that all sorts of problems have cropped up in matching the system to the bank's schedule for processing checks and preparing customer statements. What's the story?"

"The system at San Jose is working fine," said Lasher, hiding his irritation at the fact that Porter had reported his findings to New York rather than discussing them with local management first. "There is an operational problem involved in reconciling all checks rapidly enough to meet the daily schedule, and it looks as if it will require a larger third shift to solve the problem. Bob Johnson and A1 Zipf have started a joint project to bring the system up to speed by mid-June of this year, which will keep the project on schedule. We may have to furnish a bit of extra equipment to make up for the fact that the third shift will be larger than specified in the contract, but that's a drop in the bucket."

"Well, keep me up to date on progress. I don't want any premature publicity releases or advertising in trade magazines until the system is doing the job the way it was intended and the Bank of America is willing to proclaim the system operational."

"I'll do the best I can to keep the lid on Harold, but you'll have to realize the San Jose ERMA system is already serving customers though not yet at the design capacity. Actually the Bank of America is very happy with our progress, and they're already inviting members of the America Bankers Association to visit the installation to show off the automated character reading. The San Jose system is expected to be fully up to speed in June, and we're already starting to install the second system in Los Angeles. By November we should be delivering systems at the rate of one a month with the last one scheduled for early 1961. I'm sure the bank will want to make a big splash no later than this fall, but they've agreed not to make a release without GE's concurrence."

"Okay, Clair, but remember this is one decision not delegated to you. A mistake here and we'd both be out on our rears."

When Lasher returned to Phoenix he convened a weekend planning session to be attended by his key section heads and top technical people. He chose the quietly sumptuous Camelback Inn for the meeting, a rather rich setting for a fledgling organization—Lasher was a firm believer in maintaining an aura of success. Each attendee had a private room for Saturday night, and all meals and drinks would be on the house.

The first session was held in the large meeting room set aside for board meetings. To the side of the long conference table was a substantial bar on which soft drinks, coffee, and Danish were displayed. It would be opened briefly for more potent drinks at the conclusion of the day's business.

Lasher sat at the head of the conference table, dapper as ever in gabardine slacks, open-neck shirt, and string tie. His attitude was casual, but his glance was piercing as he surveyed the scene. He was aware that he faced a difficult task in maintaining high morale in view of Harold Strickland's rather restrictive instructions.

To Lasher's left was Audrey White, efficient executive secretary, stenographic notebook in hand. To his right was Bob Johnson, project engineer for ERMA, down from Palo Alto for the occasion. Lasher was acutely conscious that the youthful Ph.D. held the immediate future of the Computer Department in his hands. Next to Bob sat George Trotter, an unhappy manager of sales whose plans for professional advancement had been thrown out of whack when Barney Oldfield left the organization. George approached selling as if it were a chess game in which one probed for weaknesses in the competition and sought out the key moves to make to influence the customer's decision-making process. Clair relied on detailed market research, careful product planning, and a well-structured regional sales force to do the job. With Barney gone as a balance wheel between the two, it had become a thorny relationship, and both men knew they'd have to face up to it soon.

Next to Trotter sat Ken Geiser, manager of engineering. Ken also represented a potential problem because Bob Johnson was emerging rapidly as the technical leader in the Computer Department and would almost certainly deserve the top position as well. Ken had come to Phoenix from the company's General Engineering Laboratory in Schenectady. An experienced engineering manager with a background in analog computers, he had made an important contribution to staffing and organizing the engineering activity in Phoenix. Admittedly not a digital engineer, he would need a lateral transfer to a position of similar responsibility when Bob Johnson moved to Phoenix at the conclusion of the ERMA engineering program.

Ray Barclay, manager of manufacturing, was at Ken's right. Ray was an unsung hero of both the ERMA and the NCR 304 programs, having quietly and competently built up a computer manufacturing organization from scratch, using all the techniques he had acquired from GE's Advanced Manufacturing Program and applied to a variety of electronics manufacturing applications elsewhere in the Electronics Division. He had delivered the first ERMA computer exactly on schedule—the first fully transistorized computer to be installed in a commercial application—and would soon begin regular deliveries to the Bank of America at a rate of one a month. Clair had implicit faith in Ray's ability to enlarge the Computer Department's manufacturing capability to whatever heights might be necessary as the business expanded.

George Snively, manager of credits and collections, sat at the foot of the conference table studying an accounting spreadsheet. He was representing Ken McCombs, manager of finance, who was in Schenectady attending an accounting forum. George had been the accountant of the Electronics Laboratory in Syracuse and had been involved in preparing many of the forecasts and appropriation requests on which the Computer Department's programs were based. Lasher valued the talents of this young and ambitious financial man.

Sitting next to Audrey White on the left-hand side of the conference table was Arnold Spielberg, manager of process control computers. Arnold had been recruited from RCA's ambitious BIZMAC computer program and had been responsible for development of the GE 312 Process Control Computer, the first transistorized computer installed in steel mills for monitoring the manufacturing of sheet steel. Considered a "comer," he was one of the few Phoenix engineers who could argue with Bob Johnson and John Paivinen at their own technical level. Lasher always paid close attention to Arnold's opinions.

Spielberg was in the process of delivering one of his opinions to Dick Barnes, at his left. Dick was manager of product planning and market research, considered by Lasher to be perhaps the most important function in the marketing organization. He didn't have the salesman's knack of influencing a customer, but his analytical and technical skills were badly needed in developing a compatible series of products necessary to meet the market demands of the next five years.

Last in line was Alan Benson who had succeeded Herb Grosch as manager of the Computer Center, located at Arizona State University. The service bureau activity had picked up during the past few months, but it still represented a drain, primarily because of the high monthly rent of the IBM 704 computer. Lasher was looking forward to the day when a GE Computer Department machine could be substituted for the 704. He was optimistic concerning the market for computer services but could see no point in helping IBM achieve a dominant position.

Clair opened the staff meeting by describing his meeting with Strickland. "Well, that's the sad story," he said at the conclusion. "We're to put maximum effort on completing ERMA and the NCR 304 programs, which of course you already know. We're to push process control, and we're to go after government contracts, and we're to avoid any head-to-head contact with IBM."

"How about an aggressive program to market ERMA systems to banks?" said George Trotter. "IBM doesn't have an ERMA system to sell, so that wouldn't be a head-to-head confrontation. We've already signed several contingent contracts with banks in Arizona and California and have quotations outstanding with a number of others."

"We'll be allowed to honor any commitments already made, but Strickland won't authorize any further outside quotes until he's convinced the system is completely acceptable."

"That's ridiculous, Clair. We're getting more requests from banks every day, and they're willing to pay a premium to be close to the top of the list after the Bank of America. Before he left, Barney got approval from Howard Lief to make quotations to other banks so long as they didn't interfere with the bank's installation schedule. We can tailor our quotes with flexible schedules and performance specifications, with the final price subject to review of the user's system requirements."

"Suppose the B of A doesn't find the system acceptable?"

"Not possible," broke in Bob Johnson. "The system's rock solid. Sure, the bank's having normal teething problems, but they're pleased as punch with the equipment and totally committed. Al Zipf expects to have the procedures under control by June, and the bank expects to make a major announcement by the end of the summer. I'm sure you know IBM starts taking orders for new products even before they start development. If they don't get enough orders they don't do the development. We're in a new ball game, and we'd better learn how to play it."

"I'm sorry, Bob and George, but my orders from Strickland are specific. When you work for Cordiner, you do what he says, or else.[43] Look what happened to Doc Baker."

"Let's change the subject," he continued, turning to Ray Barclay. "How're we coming along with the move to the new Deer Valley plant?"

"The ERMA production line and services such as QC (quality control), incoming inspection, planning, and so on, are completely installed, leaving only 130 employees in the Peoria Avenue Plant devoted to process control and analog computers. The engineers have all vacated the lab space at ASU and are moving into Deer Valley this weekend. We'll be ready to move you and the KTAR headquarters group the next week. By the end of March, the move should be complete, with the only remote facilities being Palo Alto, Peoria Avenue, the ASU Computer Center, and the contract operation at Redstone Arsenal. So far, our only delinquent delivery items are the telephone switchboard and some cafeteria equipment. We'll have to make do without them for another few weeks."

"Thanks, Ray. You and your guys have done a terrific job. We're all happy to be moving into our permanent home. Let's see what's next. Process control, I guess. Arnold, what's the status of the J&L Tin Line Logging System?"

"The only real problem we've had since it's been installed," said Spielberg, "has been that the sensors turned out to be located at different locations than indicated on the customer's drawing. They forgot to tell us about the changes, and, of course, the delays we had programmed no longer matched their location. We had to rewire the logic to match their location, and then the system worked like a charm. J&L is very happy with the system and is making a big thing about it."

"What's the story with the McClouth Hot Steel Mill control system? I understand their top management is pressing 570 to put more emphasis on the program."

"That one's turning out to be a real beast. We've been struggling with roller hysteresis and are finding it difficult to measure thickness due to scab on the steel ingot. We've finally found a way around the problem, but we're a couple of months away from implementing it because we need to speed up the feedback process. Then I believe we'll be able to roll steel exactly to spec. You'll recall that our proposed budget for the program was cut by 570, so we've had to reduce engineering manpower."

"Consider your original budget restored," said Lasher, "and give me a report as soon as the program's on schedule. You'll make Mr. Cordiner happy, but I worry how this business can ever be profitable if all the applications are one-of-a-kind."

Dick Barnes had been waiting to get a word in edgewise. "We product planners have been working with Arnold on that problem, and we've developed specs for a basic process control computer that can be adapted to a large number of applications. It will be a stored-program computer so software changes rather than wiring changes can be used to meet different requirements."

"Chuck Propster and I are laying out the logic already," enthused Arnold. "We're using NOR logic with Resistor NOR gates, with never more than a three-input NOR logic element. The node of the NOR network will drive a low beta transistor whose range—"

"Whoa, please, Arnold. You're getting a bit too technical for most of us," said Lasher. "I'm satisfied your program is under control, and I'm sure your budget for the project will be approved.

"Now I want to talk to you all about the big picture," he continued. "We're going to have to play it very carefully to keep Strickland and Cordiner off our necks, but at the same time we've got to organize ourselves to compete effectively with IBM if we expect to stay in the computer business. That means building up our product planning group and field sales force in particular while completing ERMA and the rest but refraining from making commitments in the banking market until the Bank of America stamps ERMA operational and we receive a nod from 570 to market the system."

"But, Clair," said an obviously agitated George Trotter. "We've already become involved with hundreds of banks, and they're anxious to make commitments. We'll never have a better time to be the industry leader and to establish a price level at a figure highly profitable to GE. Ray Barclay says he could double the ERMA delivery schedule given a few months lead time, so we could be delivering systems to other banks by next year. We're winning the big gamble, and we can't let 570 turn it into defeat."

Both Bob Johnson and Ray Barclay gave approving nods. Clearly exasperated, Lasher replied, "Let's you and I discuss it after the staff meeting." Turning to Ken Geiser, he asked, "What's new in your area?"

"Clair, you've mentioned a number of times that we really need something unique in our product line to capture a place in this overall business. I agree with Trotter that ERMA is unique, but the most unique part of it is the magnetic ink character reader, the first of what will certainly become a family of products to replace card readers as the basic input to computers. We have an important market lead, and there's no reason to confine our advantage solely to the banking application. To this date I don't think we've invested one dollar in this other than what was necessary for the ERMA contract.

"I propose that we establish a development program based around a refinement of the character reader to cover other applications where information on documents can be inputted directly into the computer, completely avoiding the expense and wasted time in transferring the data to punch cards and then reading the cards."[44]

"I agree in principle, but the problem is to find the necessary dollars," said Lasher. "Let's kick this one around after dinner. We'll convene the staff meeting at 8 p.m. sharp."

Turning to Trotter, Lasher said, "Let's find a quiet spot in the dining room where we can have a drink and a bite to eat."

The two men found a quiet table in an alcove shielding them from the babble of conversation created by the other diners. Lasher took a sip from his habitual scotch on the rocks and opened the conversation.

"George, I'd go along with your proposal if our boss were still Doc Baker. He'd ignore any details such as lack of approval from Ralph Cordiner, though you'll note his independence from 570 caught up with him in the end, and he now finds himself a powerless consultant. Harold Strickland was appointed in his place in part to put the brakes on what he thinks is a wild-eyed adventure by a bunch of young Turks who can't be trusted 2,000 miles away from the home office. I'm acting under direct orders from Strickland, and I have to play his game, at least until we've successfully completed ERMA. All we need at this point is for some bank official to ask Cordiner if he can expedite delivery of his new banking computer. I'd be out on my kazoo, and one of Cordiner's professional managers with no knowledge of the computer business would be in my place, probably with orders to phase out the business.

"Besides this fact of life," he went on, "I want to build up our business on a solid foundation of market research and product planning. This way we can control our own destiny over the long run rather than jumping at opportunities of the moment."

"But, Clair, we're way past this point as far as the banking market is concerned. We have the product all of the major banks want, and we've become virtually 'insiders' at the Bank of America. We're in a position to dominate this segment of the computer market instead of chasing IBM, but we can't do it by being timid. Somehow, we've just got to find a way around this situation."

"Your analysis may be right, George, but we're going to have to play it the GE way. I'm not Barney Oldfield, and Harold Strickland ain't Doc Baker. Let's face it.

It's apparent that our philosophies of operation don't quite meld. I know you expected to step into the manager of marketing position when I was promoted, but I don't think it would work. You're a real star as an individual salesman—much better than I could ever be—but I don't think you'd enjoy the routine of being a marketing manager in a complete sense, particularly with the existing corporate constraints. What do you think?"

"Well, Clair, I obviously don't agree with your assessment, and I'm sorry you won't follow my advice, but I have to agree we can't continue to work together much longer if you feel as you do. So what's next?"

"I'll be delighted if you'll agree to continue as manager of sales, but you'll have to realize I plan to bring in an experienced manager of marketing who'll be your next boss."

"I hate the thought of leaving the ERMA program just at the point where our gamble seems to be paying off," said Trotter, "but it's obvious there's no long-term future for me here. I'll stick around until ERMA's declared operational, but I'm obviously going to start looking."

Much relieved to have this encounter out of the way, Lasher said, "I appreciate your attitude, George. There are still a few messy details to be negotiated to firm up the final version of the ERMA contract, and it would help a lot if you would handle them. In exchange, I'll promise a bonus when you leave."

"What's bothering you tonight, honey?" asked Jean Trotter as she completed setting the dinner table. Her husband seemed like less than his normal ebullient self. "Has something happened?"

"What's happened, Jean, is that I'm not going to be manager of marketing of the Computer Department. I've seen this coming ever since Barney left. My position as sales manager is secure enough, but there's no hope of advancement. On top of all this, I'm not permitted to go after the banking market until old man Cordiner changes his mind. We're going to sit on our hands while everything we worked for slips away."

"What do you plan to do about it?"

"First, I'm going to make up a pitcher of martinis. I've agreed to stay on to complete the contract hassles with Al Zipf and Howard Lief, and in the meantime I'll start looking around. I have a lot of good contacts and a reputation in the trade for selling big-ticket items. But I sure don't relish starting over with a new organization."

"Why don't you give Barney a call. You two always worked well together, and he's already told you they need more marketing know-how at Raytheon. We've always loved the Boston area."

"I'll do just that, Jean. Maybe it'll lift my spirits."

CHAPTER 17
FINAL NEGOTIATIONS FOR ERMA

It was late March, 1959, when Bob Johnson and Al Zipf began to see the light at the end of the tunnel. The San Jose installation had been almost completely converted to ERMA operation and the number of accounts handled each day had reached 50,000—only ten percent shy of the targeted capacity. One additional check sorter and an extra printer would soon be put on line, and Johnson was confident this would bring capacity well over the required figure.

"There's still one problem," said Zipf. "In order to utilize the added equipment we have to add operators over and above the contract amount. The way our contract is written, GE will be theoretically in default. I'm sure you know the bank has spent a great deal of money on programming upgrades that have made much of the recent improvement—money which really should have been spent by GE. Howard Lief is going to insist on getting some of this back by sticking to the strict contract terms."

"You surprise me, Al, because we've both overlooked minor contract technicalities in order to make the system do the job as nearly perfect as possible. However, I'll relay the bad news back to Lasher along with the good news that ERMA is going to do the job we all hoped it would do three years ago."

Bob Johnson was surprised at the serious view Lasher took of what Bob considered a small contract technicality. He had been well protected from the political environment in which Lasher had to thread his way; however, he accepted Lasher's instruction not to discuss the problem with anyone until he heard further from Harold Strickland's office. Strickland, in turn, went to Jim LaPierre, group vice president, with the news that ERMA did not meet contract specifications.

"You realize, Harold, that Cordiner might use this as a reason to pull the plug on the computer venture," said LaPierre. "You'd better resolve this fast."

The panic traveled down the line until it reached Trotter. "I really don't think it's all that serious, Clair. I'll get together with Howard Lief if necessary, but let me first see what I can work out with Al Zipf."

"Okay, George. Take care of this one without giving away the store and your bonus is assured."

Trotter took a late afternoon flight to San Francisco and was in Bob Johnson's office early the next morning. The ERMA group had moved to a 10,000-square-foot facility on Commercial Street in Mountain View, providing an enlarged laboratory area as well as space for draftsmen and a small machine shop. Trotter wondered what would happen to the facility when ERMA was completed.

"I'm hoping," said Johnson, "that GE will be willing to maintain a computer research laboratory here, along with a field service office to handle maintenance of the ERMAs installed in northern California. It's to our advantage to stay close to the Bank of America so we can test new developments in a realistic banking environment and, among other things, ensure that, five or ten years from now, GE and not IBM or Burroughs, will furnish the successor to ERMA.

"Changing the subject," he continued, "Lasher called me last night to set up an appointment for you to get together with Al Zipf to negotiate a solution to the problem of excess third-shift staff. He'll be waiting for you in the San Jose office at 2 p.m. I'm going to keep out of the negotiation, but I'm at your disposal for the rest of the morning."

"I did some figuring on the plane, which I'd like to try out on you before I tackle Al. The contract calls for 30 ERMA systems, each capable of handling 55,000 checking accounts per day, which gives a total capacity of 1,650,000 accounts per day overall. Okay?"

Johnson nodded.

"Actually," Trotter went on, "there won't be 30 separate ERMA centers but a total of only 13 to handle the 465 branches of the Bank of America. A number of them will be multiple installations, such as Los Angeles with 4 ERMAs. In Al Zipf's November 14, 1958, memo to the bank's board of directors, he concluded that this grouping of systems would permit the bank to handle 2 million accounts a day, or an average of 60,000 accounts per day per ERMA. Okay so far?"

"Yes, George. I never thought about it that way."

"Now," said George. "Have you and Al figured out how many additional accounts can be handled per day by ERMA by adding one printer and a character reader-sorter combination."

"Yes. It looks like about 20,000 accounts."

"Aha! This means that in the Los Angeles center with 4 ERMAs, one printer and sorter would bring the average capacity up to spec. Do you have the plans for San Francisco, Oakland, and the rest?

"Yes, and I see what you're driving at. I'll get the file."

The two men spent the rest of the morning studying each installation and reaching agreement on the additional equipment needed at each ERMA center. It came to seven sorters and seven printers, a far cry from the number Johnson had feared.

"Now," said Johnson, "all you have to do is sell this to Al Zipf. Good luck!"

"Piece of cake," said George. "I'm going to settle on a quantity of ten rather than seven, with the argument that the increase in capacity will ensure his 2 million account target and completely repay the bank for the added third-shift employees. We'll make up the difference in increased service charges over the life of the system."

It was late that afternoon when Trotter and Zipf initialed a memo of agreement incorporating the proposed equipment configuration.[45]

"I think you can tell your boss that the last barrier to a joint release and ceremony announcing ERMA as fully operational has been eliminated. I know the bank will want to make a big splash."

The next day, after passing on the news to Lasher, George placed a call to Barney Oldfield in Waltham. "I'm ready to come east for an interview whenever you say the word."

CHAPTER 18
ERMA'S PUBLIC DEBUT

The press release went out from Los Angeles on Monday, September 14, 1959, announcing that the Bank of America and the General Electric Company's Computer Department had that day stamped "operational" the nation's first completely automated banking system using magnetic character reading. The new system was hailed by both the Bank of America and General Electric as "the greatest advance in bookkeeping in the history of banking," and as "the end of the paperwork bottleneck in banks."

The announcement, the closed-circuit telecast to receiving sites at San Francisco, Chicago, and New York, and the ceremony attended by Bank and GE notables, was the product of three months of planning and negotiation necessary to adjust and reconcile the schedules of the executive officers of both organizations.

When Clair Lasher heard the word from Bob Johnson in Palo Alto that the bank had accepted the large Los Angeles installation as well as the San Jose system, he immediately got on the phone to Harold Strickland in New York.

"We're in, Harold! Al Zipf has signed the acceptance papers and has authorized us to go ahead with planning a high-level publicity bash to celebrate the event. Clark Beise, president and CEO of the Bank of America will attend the ceremony along with his top staff and assumes GE will wish to do the same."

"Congratulations, Clair; that's a load off my mind. However, I doubt if Ralph Cordiner will agree to attend in view of his opposition to being in the business machine industry. It would be a tacit admission of his support for your ambitious program. I'll check his schedule for the next few months and give you some possible dates, but don't get your hopes up."

Undeterred by this lukewarm response to the news, Lasher immediately summoned Roy Jordan, his manager of advertising and sales promotion. "Roy, gather your fellows together for a meeting in my office as soon as possible. We've a publicity event to organize."

"Coming right up, Clair."

Roy Jordan was a GE veteran from Electronics Park who had made the long move to Arizona in order to alleviate his wife's bronchial problems. The move had been successful and had provided Lasher with a highly professional representative to the public as well as to the customer community. Curtailed from an active program to the banking industry by corporate dictate, Roy was eagerly awaiting the decision to break loose. He was in Lasher's office within minutes, accompanied by Ray Shanahan, his specialist of press releases and Bob Clarke, specialist on visual aids and photography.

Lasher offered coffee and cigarettes all around while recounting his news from Bob Johnson as well as Strickland's reaction.

Roy was excited. "You don't need to worry about Cordiner attending. I'm sure Gene Cleveland, GE's Western Commercial vice president in San Francisco, will get on the band wagon the moment he gets the news. It will automatically get on Cordiner's visit schedule. Cordiner won't dare offend the mighty Apparatus Sales Division."

"Terrific," said Lasher. "Any other thoughts?"

Roy turned to his staff. "Okay, guys. You've been waiting for this chance to show your stuff. How about it?"

Bob Clarke said, "I think something this big would make a good showcase for Ron Reagan. People know him as the host of the "GE Theater of the Air," and we might work out some sort of a network event around the ceremony. Remember, he's an adopted Californian."

"Yeah," said Lasher. "That should help. How do we get in touch with Reagan?"

"I'll contact the 'GE Theater of the Air' as soon as this meeting is over," said Bob Clarke.

"I'll alert the major newspapers, business magazines, and trade papers as soon as we have a definite date, and of course I'll start right away to put together a draft of a basic press release. We'll need a number of variants to cover different business interests and, of course, a special edition of the GE Computer Department Newsletter for the employees. This should be a big boost for morale." Ray Shanahan was excited. "Do you think this will be the big breakthrough with 570?"

Lasher grinned. "We'll see."

September 14, D day, arrived. Lasher and his section heads had deserted Phoenix for the ceremony and the various demonstrations of the ERMA system. The dignitaries were in place in the huge Los Angeles branch of the Bank of America where four complete ERMA systems were located, capable of processing over 220,000 customer accounts for approximately 60 branch banks in the far-flung Los Angeles area. The ceremonies were being broadcast over a closed TV network to stations in San Francisco, Chicago, and New York, where major banks had been invited to witness the demonstrations, and the banking press had been provided with two-way communications to permit a limited number of interviews of the participants.

The day's events went off without a hitch. President Beise was lavish in praise of General Electric, Ronald Reagan followed exactly the script prepared by Roy Jordan, and Ralph Cordiner cordially acknowledged Beise's kind words, noting that General Electric, industry's largest user of digital computers in its own businesses, welcomed the Bank of America as the data-processing pioneer in the banking field.

A good time was had by all!

At the end of the meeting, Cordiner turned to Harold Strickland. "I have to leave now for a dinner date with Gene Cleveland. I'll see you and your key people after breakfast tomorrow. Let's make it 9 a.m. in my hotel suite."

George Snively from the Accounting Section was one of the few left in a very quiet Deer Valley plant the day after the Bank of America dedication. He had been expecting his boss, Ken McCombs, to return the following day. He was surprised when, in mid-afternoon, Clair Lasher and Ken McCombs came rushing in a day ahead of time.

"Drop everything," said McCombs, "and come into Lasher's office."

Curious and mildly alarmed at the note of panic, Snively complied. Armed with his pad of accounting paper and a sharp pencil, he joined Lasher and McCombs at the long conference table.

"George, I'm going to swear you to a vow of secrecy concerning our present discussion. Any leak about the substance of this meeting and you're out on your a__. Comprende?" George nodded his acceptance of Lasher's dictate, wondering what could possibly have happened.

"Briefly, George, the dedication was a big success and the demonstrations were flawless, but Cordiner outfoxed us. Instead of giving an implied commitment to the expanded marketing plan, he recognized that the ERMA computer and its various peripherals constituted a 'business machine.' He was in a towering rage when he summoned us to his suite, and we've been directed to prepare a new five-year forecast based on completing the ERMA and NCR 304 contracts and growing a process control computer business to $25 million in five years. We can fulfill any other orders already on the books, but the instruction is definitely to phase out of the 'business machine' business."[46]

"Why the secrecy?" asked Snively.

"Because we aren't going to pass it on to the rest of the organization, at least for now. Ken agrees with me that we'd lose our best people in a flash. We'll give the boss the forecast he wants and then we'll work like hell to develop a good business plan we can submit at next year's June review. It'll have to be a holding operation until then but with a couple of exceptions. We'll go after ERMA orders aggressively—God, I wish now I'd let Trotter loose six months ago; the man could really sell banking systems—and we'll use this along with process control to build up the field sales and product service staffs. If we're challenged, we'll just have to say they had been previously committed by George Trotter. And we'll also give Bob Johnson a green light to initiate his plan for the series of compatible computers to cover a selected portion of the general purpose market. I'm sure they'd be applicable to process control as well."

Two weeks later, Lasher received a surprising telephone call from Harold Strickland. "Ralph has received so many calls from banking friends congratulating him on his success in scooping the industry with the ERMA system that he's rescinded the order to completely abandon the general purpose computer field. You can go ahead and quote ERMA systems to the banking community and can study other applications so long as you don't go head-to-head with IBM."

"Doesn't he realize IBM is everywhere?" asked Lasher.

"Of course he realizes it, but he doesn't want GE to be over committed to a market he can't understand. Just keep things on an even keel and make your 1960 business review a good one—and, for God's sake, come in with a favorable financial variance for the next six months. This means more at 570 than any other accomplishments."

"I hear you loud and clear, Harold," said Lasher, much relieved at the evidence of a possible change in Cordiner's policy. He had not enjoyed the brief period when he had defied Cordiner's order, but now he could forget the artificial process control forecast and concentrate on the planning he loved best.

CHAPTER 19
IBM's DARK SHADOW

Clair and Suzanne Lasher, while in Syracuse, had been accustomed to a lively and lavish social life, and they decided to set a similar tone for the fledgling organization in Phoenix. For example, Clair insisted that all section managers should join the exclusive Paradise Valley Racquet Club, a focal point of local society and an ideal place for entertaining visiting dignitaries and customers. Many took to this with relish; others, like Ray Barclay, who did not play and chose not to watch tennis, claimed to his wife, Pat, that the Computer Department was becoming a social club.[47]

The cocktail parties grew more frequent as the 1959 Christmas season approached. The Christmas dinner dance was a must-dress occasion. The Christmas party committee had arranged to lease the Thunderbird Room atop the Westward Ho Hotel, and invitations had gone out to all employees. Attendance was virtually mandatory for everyone at subsection level or above, and there was a frantic scurrying around to the clothing rental outfits of Phoenix and Mesa as men accustomed to open shirt collars and string ties sought white dinner jackets and cummerbunds. It was a festive and successful party, even including the mandatory roaring drunk who organized a chaotic sing-along at the shank of the evening.

Late in 1959 Bob Johnson and his wife Mary moved from Palo Alto to Phoenix. Bob ascended to the position of manager of engineering of the Computer Department as a whole; Ken Geiser was moved sideways to become manager of the business planning operation. Lasher was happily surprised when the change was accepted without undue complaint from anyone. The Johnsons quickly established their position in the social scene by initiating what became the annual New Year's Day brunch—with Bloody Marys to alleviate any New Year's Eve hangovers.[48]

As time went on, the open houses during the holidays became quite fancy. In addition, it soon became necessary to ensure the right mix of invited guests. A complicated protocol developed among the wives, ensuring that couples who detested one another were never paired and that certain wayward husbands or wives were not exposed to temptation in public. It was much like the social life on a pre-war army post—often isolated from the civilian world, married couples and bachelors thrown together, usually for a three-year period as governed by the army's rotation policy, would form a miniature society of their own, which revolved around parties, open houses, golf, and tennis. So it was in Phoenix, compounded by the fact that they

On February 26, 1959, Arizona Governor Fannin snipped the ribbon opening the GE Computer Department plant in Deer Valley, Phoenix. Left to right are Ray Barclay; Clair Lasher; Linda Gosslin, Phoenix Rodeo Queen; Fannin; and Mayor Jack Williams.

were all involved in a business venture far more risky and exciting than anything they had encountered in Syracuse or Schenectady.

Competition was rife among the wives of the top echelon of management. Ray Barclay was away on a trip when his new office at the Deer Valley plant was ready for furnishing, and his wife, Pat, was asked to go in and attend to the details for him. This caused quite a stir. Mary McCombs, not to be left out, decided to do Ken's office when it was ready. The piece de resistance of the office furnishing competition was an exquisite bullwhip that Suzanne Lasher hung on the wall of her husband's office. No one dared top that.

For the most part, the goings on during the Lasher regime were healthy reactions to the pressures exerted by the GE corporate staff. It was not that the entire corporate organization was against the entry of GE into the commercial computer business; the ERMA announcement by the Bank of America intrigued such as John Lockton, GE treasurer, who had a major influence in the banking community and recognized the importance of the accomplishment. But there was an abiding fear of IBM, based on their ten-year lead and their importance as a customer for GE components. This fear was reflected down the line, causing a feeling on the part of employees and spouses that they were embarked on a dangerous mission indeed. The "eat, drink, and be merry" attitude was a natural consequence of this pressure, less so on the engineers and programmers who had specific technical problems to deal with, but more so on the managers and sales personnel attempting to gear up to grapple with what was considered the world's best marketing organization—Big Blue.

There was good reason to be concerned about IBM. Few people were aware of it but, in the 1950s and 1960s, IBM was essentially selling to itself.[49] The company had deliberately trained many more data-processing managers than were required for its internal operations, and their paths of advancement were to be placed in a better assignment with a substantial user of IBM equipment. Their loyalties were really more to IBM than to the company that employed them. Herb Grosch had been an example of this unique dual loyalty, and there were many more in the large departments of General Electric and the other large industrial concerns, the major users of digital computers at the time.

IBM assisted their Trojan Horses by having most of the big companies pass corporate resolutions forbidding the purchase of computers (for all the old familiar arguments, including the fear of obsolescence), thus eliminating the need for the data-processing managers to bother with cumbersome appropriation requests, and forcing a leasing environment that raised the cost of entry to would-be competitors. IBM also persuaded upper management that purchasing departments were incapable of making procurement decisions in regard to computers. Only the data-processing managers were capable of this. As a result, this was a very difficult market to crack, particularly when these tactics were not understood, and marketing strategies had not been developed to counter them.

These IBM tactics bred a certain degree of arrogance within IBM, and they created maverick customers with the courage to jump the IBM tracks. One of these mavericks was, of course, the Bank of America. Their award of the ERMA contract to General Electric sent shivers throughout the IBM organization because GE was considered the one company with the financial strength and depth of technology to mount a serious long-term challenge. IBM very effectively kept 570 informed of every problem encountered by the Computer Department in implementing the ERMA contract, and this was to continue in the future as a matter of IBM corporate strategy. In contrast, the data-processing managers and IBM would enter into a conspiracy of silence if an IBM product was late or failed to perform. No wonder Ralph Cordiner was frightened.

CHAPTER 20
THE GE 225 COMPUTER IS CONCEIVED

During the winter of 1959, Clair Lasher pondered at length over the business plan he was developing to submit to 570 at the June, 1960, business review. The backbone of the plan was to be the so-called Mosaic line of compatible computers that would cover the price range from $50,000 to $2.5 million. The problem was that the Mosaic line didn't as yet exist, and the first in the series would not be available for at least two years. There was no general-purpose product to fill the gap between completion of the ERMA and NCR 304 programs and the start of the Mosaic deliveries.

While Lasher was struggling with his business plan, Arnold Spielberg and Chuck Propster (another engineer recruited by Arnold from RCA's BIZMAC project) were struggling with the design of the GE 312 Process Control Computer, which was to become a standard product of the Computer Department.[50] The design used resistance coupled logic with the gates driving a single transistor. The problem, which had come to the surface as the computer went into manufacture, was the random appearance of spikes in the output. This defect had not arisen in the initial engineering models, and it was giving Spielberg fits. They struggled with the problem for months and had finally designed an experiment that they hoped would uncover the culprit.

Focusing his gaze on an oscilloscope face, Arnold said, "Okay, Chuck, substitute transistor number one, and give it a shot." There was no spike.

"Number two, please." Still no spike.

"Now, number three."

"Bingo," said Arnold, as a large vertical spike appeared on the face of the oscilloscope. "Let's keep going, to make sure the trend continues." They continued to substitute transistors with various values of beta, and the results were conclusive.

"Eureka," said Arnold. "We're out of the woods so long as we use transistors with beta values no greater than 70, and we can finally issue a change order to manufacturing. Incoming Inspection won't be too happy, but we'll cobble up a go/no-go chassis that will reject all transistors with betas above 70."

A week later, after having delivered the special piece of test equipment to manufacturing, Spielberg and Propster fell into a discussion of the Computer Department's chances of "making it."

"You know, Arnold, I wonder what the hell is going to happen to us over the next year. The market for process control computers is too small to support a computer business, and Bob Johnson's Mosaic program won't have anything to offer for two years or more. All the Computer Department has to sell is the 210 version of ERMA for banks, and it's too expensive for the general-purpose market. Of course, we also have the 304, but the design belongs to NCR, and we can't sell it outside of GE."

"Yeah. I've been worrying about the same thing, and I've been wondering whether our process control computer could be the basis of a general purpose machine to compete with the likes of the IBM 1401 and 650. That's the big-volume portion of the market, in the $200 to $500 range. The 312 is cheap and fast, and most of the development cost has already been written off. T'sai Lee has developed a good operating system, and Vito Damuchi has given us a fast core memory, so all we need is a card-reader interface to adapt it to the general-purpose computer market. What do you think, Chuck?"

"I think you've got a hell of an idea, Arnold, but how are you going to sell it to Bob Johnson and the product planners? Remember, it's a 20-bit machine, and Mosaic is supposed to be a 24-bit line of compatible computers."

"I've thought of that, but I don't think there will ever be a Mosaic product line unless we can buy Bob the two years he needs to develop it. Our only chance is to go directly to Lasher. He's trying to put together a business plan to sell Cordiner on letting us go after selected portions of the general-purpose market, and his biggest problem is that he hasn't a product except ERMA to plug this gap. We could release this baby to production by mid-year if we get a go-ahead now. There's no time for product planning, and no need because the design already exists except for peripherals."

Chuck Propster was sold. Eyes gleaming with anticipation, he said, "Let's call Lasher right now." Spielberg nodded and reached for the telephone. He dialed Lasher's private line.

"Good afternoon, Audrey. I have an urgent need to have an hour of the boss's time. Do you think he could fit Chuck Propster and me in today?"

"He's in a meeting with Ray Barclay and Art Newman at the Peoria plant. I think you know that the IBEW and the IUE are attempting to unionize as much of the factory as possible. They have both petitioned the National Labor Relations Board to represent the employees, and there will eventually be an election that will be between the IUE, the IBEW, and no union. In the meantime there's a lot of strategy to develop and a lot of answers to be given to the employees. Mr. Strickland is getting a lot of pressure from Mr. Cordiner, and he's passing it down the line. Anyway, I don't think he can see you today, but I'll page him and call you right back."

The phone rang a few minutes later. "He can't interrupt this afternoon's meeting, but you can see him at home tonight if you like, about nine o'clock."

"Thanks, Audrey. We'll be there."

Spielberg and Propster were at the door of Lasher's Scottsdale home promptly at 9 p.m. They were greeted by the attractive Suzanne Lasher, who smiled and said, "Come right in, gentlemen. Lash is in his study, waiting for you." She looked at the rolls of drafting paper under their arms. "I see you came loaded for b'ar. Can I bring you some refreshments—coffee, beer, or something stronger?"

"Some coffee would be nice, strong and black for me," said Spielberg. Propster nodded his agreement.

Two hours later, and after three refills of black coffee all around, the meeting broke up. Spielberg and Propster were hoarse after going over their proposal time and again and after answering Lasher's pointed questions.

"I'm sure you realize it's against all my principles to authorize a venture of this sort without approval from the manager of engineering and the manager of product planning, but I've got a t__ caught in the wringer, and this project might just help me pull it out. You can go ahead, but be sure to charge the engineering and model shop time to process control."

Elated, Spielberg and Propster gathered up their logic diagrams and circuit layouts and prepared to leave. As Lasher let them out the front door, his last words were, "Remember, Arnold, if you screw me up, I'll really have your a__."[51]

Five months later, the first production prototype rolled off Ray Barclay's line, christened the GE 225. It was a 20-bit binary machine with three registers in hardware and a separate box for floating point. It was a fast machine in terms of competitive offerings of the day, with an 18-microsecond cycle time. It was announced to the industry as less costly than the IBM 1401, with far more "bang for the buck."

In describing the 225 to the Computer Department sales force, Arnold Spielberg stated that emphasis had been put on low cost and relatively "snappy" performance in a wide variety of both business and scientific applications. Both objectives had been met. "For example," he said "we decided on a serial card reader to simplify and cost-reduce the electronics associated with reading cards in parallel. We were able to locate an inexpensive serial card reader made by Elliot Brothers in England; its innards are a bit fragile, but Ken Manning's peripheral group is working up some mechanical and electronic fixes. I think it'll do if we give it the proper level of preventive maintenance. Otherwise, the 225 is a pretty solid machine that you can sell to anyone for any purpose."

"How about the banking application?" asked John Hogg, the manager of marketing administration. "Once we've saturated the large bank market with 210s, we'll need a smaller, less-expensive system for the smaller banks."

"That's a management decision for Lasher and Johnson, but there's no reason why we can't design a controller to interface with the character reader and check sorter. That's one application where we don't need a card reader."

"How soon can we deliver?"

"I believe Lasher plans to announce the 225 to the trade by June 1, with delivery within six months."

The GE 225 was once described by Vic Casebolt of the Computer Department's Detroit sales office as "undoubtedly the most clumsy-to-use computer ever sold for commercial applications."[52] True, but once applied, the machine did a yeomanlike job in a surprising number of applications. The reason for its success was that it was both cheap and fast. It could undersell the IBM 1401 while giving more "bang for the buck." Several hundred were sold over the next few years and at a good profit despite the expenses involved in servicing the Elliot card reader.

CHAPTER 21
THE "BIG LOOK" IS APPROVED, SORT OF

The successful development of the GE 225 had breathed new life into Lasher's fragile business plan.[53] He could now put together a reasonable-looking forecast that covered both the near term and the remainder of the decade and was not completely dependent on inventions not yet made. Never mind that the GE 225 was not compatible with the Mosaic line; it would be phased out as Mosaic reached fruition.

Mosaic, sometimes termed the W,X,Y,Z line, was conceived as a family of compatible 24-bit computers covering the price range from $30,000 to about $2.5 million, which was the entire range covered by IBM except for the $10 million STRETCH computer. Initial emphasis was to be put on the Y model to compete with the IBM 7070 and 705 machines either planned or being installed by many General Electric Operating Departments. The hope was that the savings in lease payments developed by returning the leased systems to IBM would pay for most of the cost of developing the new machines. Art Critchlow, a computer engineer with a number of advanced concepts, was Bob Johnson's project engineer for the Y machine, and he was confident that it could be brought on-line within two years. Following closely on the heels would be the W machine, based on Y techniques but with more modest performance objectives. The cost of these developments would be substantial, but, having conquered ERMA, the technical staff were confident they could deliver.

Lacy Goosetree had become manager of marketing in early 1960. He and Lasher had been closeted with George Snively during most of April and May putting together the charts and tables necessary for the presentation to the executive office on June 22 in New York City. Lacy was an old hand at executive office presentations, and his presence in Phoenix at that point was quite reassuring. Snively had put together the financial analyses necessary to support Lasher's proposal to be cut loose to implement what they had decided to call the Big Look, and the three men spent most of their waking hours critiquing and polishing the business plan.

Late one evening, George Snively took a break from the Big Look numbers and went down to the company cafeteria for some coffee. Picking up a copy of the Wall Street Journal, he saw a reference to a talk by David Sarnoff of RCA claiming that RCA was going to be number two in the computer industry in five years, doing a billion a year in sales. Intrigued, he went back to his office and grabbed a copy of Moody's to look up RCA's financial position. There was no way Sarnoff could back

131

up his claim. RCA was in default on the interest on $50 million in debentures, had minimal earnings, and an indifferent balance sheet. The stock price was down and it was certainly no time for them to go to the market. He couldn't do it! This led George to analyze the other competitors. His analysis showed that none of the competitors except GE had the cash flow necessary to participate in the leasing-dominated business as the number two to IBM. He stayed up most of the night making the analyses and showed them to Lasher and Goosetree the next morning.

The analyses were converted to charts that graphically demonstrated the tremendous cash requirements necessary to participate in a continuously expanding leasing market. At first Lasher was dubious at highlighting the large cash requirement for GE.

"There's really no way we can avoid this particular issue," said Lacy, "and presenting it as a positive competitive factor is smart as hell."

"Okay, we'll redo the business plan to feature the Snively analyses, but make sure they're approved by Ken McCombs. We need the seal of approval from accounting so they can share the blame if the whole thing boomerangs."[54]

It was June 22, 1960, when Clair Lasher, Lacy Goosetree, and Ken McCombs, chaperoned by Harold Strickland, entered the large conference room of GE headquarters at 570 Lexington Avenue. Strickland was apprehensive; the business plan was based on the assumption that Cordiner would depart from his stricture about competing with IBM, based on the performance of the Computer Department in meeting its budgeted performance to date.

Lasher was scheduled to make the presentation while Lacy would man the slide projector. The two men, veterans of many presentations, quickly adjusted the projector, checked that the slides were in order and properly focused, and awaited the entry of the audience. Finally, towing his staff behind him like a prestigious physician doing grand rounds, Ralph Cordiner swept into the conference room. He shook hands with Strickland, nodded curtly at Lasher, and took his seat at the head of the conference table.

"Okay, gentlemen, let's hear your story."

Lasher took a deep breath and began. "Gentlemen, the purpose of our meeting here is to present a new plan for the Computer Department to secure additional volume and growth in its assigned industry. The department is doing well compared to previous plans and the market and competitive situation indicate the timing is right. I would like to pause to say that the computer business is a combination of sales and leases. In order to simplify this presentation, all the figures you will see, except at the end, will be based on a shipping-value basis. At the end, the totals will be converted to a sale-and-lease basis, and we will draw some important conclusions and recommendations from these data."

Lasher then went into a detailed presentation of the Computer Department's products, their relationship to the product of competition, and their future promise. He covered the banking field rather quickly, noting that the ERMA system had given

GE a launching pad into this particular market, and he projected continuing participation in the banking field. He stated that the Computer Department was the volume leader in the industrial and process control computer field, while noting that this particular market was relatively small compared with the general-purpose computer market. Most of his presentation related to the general-purpose computer market for which he believed the Computer Department had an excellent business plan.[55]

"The GE 225, derived from our process control program, has shown itself capable of achieving a workhorse position in the industrial business and scientific field. It will be a major contender in the $200,000 to $500,000 range pending introduction of the Mosaic line of compatible machines that will cover the entire range from $30,000 to about $3 million in shipping value. To date, we have attempted to avoid competition on a head-to-head basis with IBM, but we find IBM is everywhere, including process control, banking, and military. Consequently, our strategy, to which we hope you will agree, is to concentrate on specific market areas where we have an advantage. For the moment, these include banking, process control, internal GE, computer communications, and the army's ballistic missile program at Huntsville, Alabama.

"Up to now, all of the projections have been on a shipping-value basis. As you know, ours is a leasing business with substantial amounts of income deferred to the future and, correspondingly, reduced sales and income in the present. For example, shipping value for 1961 is projected at $50 million, while sales on a sale-lease basis are projected at $23 million. This chart shows 1965 to be the break-even year but with unrealized lease income reaching just over $122 million.

"The implications of this type of financial structure are significant when one analyzes the cash position of RCA, Control Data, CDC, Burroughs, and Honeywell, our major competitors for the position of number two in the industry. As you'll see from the chart, only GE has the cash flow necessary to grow effectively in the leasing market in an industry that is expanding at an exponential rate. You'll note that RCA, our most serious competitor in the race for number two, can't possibly finance such a program without giving up its main business, which is television."

Cordiner appeared apathetic during most of Lasher's presentation, but Clair had finally struck a responsive chord by setting forth RCA, rather than IBM, as the main competitor.

"Lasher, I want Lockton and Phillipi to hear this story. We'll take a brief coffee break while we round them up."

John Lockton, GE's treasurer, was the company's acknowledged expert on cash generation and absorption. Gerald Phillipi was the company's financial vice president. Between the two, they controlled the company's monetary strategy. Lasher knew the success or failure of his proposal would depend on their appraisal of George Snively's competitive analyses rather than on technical or marketing considerations.

Both men complimented Ken McCombs on the financial analyses. He accepted their praise just as he would have taken their criticism if any flaws had been found.

"Well, gentlemen, do you believe GE can finance the venture?" said Cordiner.

Phillipi was cautiously optimistic. "We have three major new ventures underway in the company: atomic power, jet engines, and computers. All three require massive investments.[56] If I had to pick just one, I'd probably pick atomic power as being closest to GE's traditional interests, but I'd certainly pick electronic computers next. I think we can swing it."

Lockton, who thought GE could finance the world, if necessary, said, "I'd give this an unqualified yes, Ralph."

Cordiner asked a few more questions and finally said, "Up until now I saw no reason for GE to be in the computer business because we had no unique contributions to make. It is essentially an assembly business, not manufacturing, so we can't capitalize on those skills, we have no unique technology because the engineers are freely exchanged, and we would be up against reputedly the world's greatest marketing organization. However, I now see it as a table stakes game and we have the stakes."

Turning to Strickland, Cordiner said, "Harold, the business plan of the Computer Department is approved. Get with it!"

On the TWA Constellation heading back to Phoenix, Lasher and his two colleagues toasted one another with champagne and indulged in the airline's free cigarettes. They were euphoric over their success in bringing Cordiner aboard their Big Look program even though, as Lacy remarked, "You know, what Cordiner said didn't make much sense."

"We'll take it," said Lasher.

CHAPTER 22
POW-WOW AT APACHE JUNCTION

C lair Lasher was a planner. His first inclination after approval of the Big Look was to recognize that it was out of date and to start re-planning. Emotionally exhausted after the strain of the previous months, he tended to leave the implementation of the plan to others. Fortunately, Lacy Goosetree, as manager of marketing, and Bob Sheeley, as national sales manager, were implementers of the highest order. Between them, they assembled a national sales organization second to none in quality if not in quantity. It included the likes of Ken Fisher (later of Prime Computer), Jim Pompa (to become a Honeywell vice president), Tom O'Rourke (founder of TYMSHARE), Vic Casebolt (later vice president of International Paper), Clint De Gabrielle (to become the czar of computing of the state of Washington), Vern Schatz (chairman, National Cache Card Co.–SMART Cards), Curt Hare (president, TERAK), Ray Noorda (president, Novell), Warren Prince (VP for Data Services, TYMSHARE), Leo Mott (president, Univ. Computers), Jack Lorenz (president, United Computing), and a host of others with outstanding careers in the computer field.

Few of these men came to the party as experienced computer salesmen, and it was necessary to implement a crash program to provide them with the marketing techniques, product knowledge, and presentation skills required to represent the Computer Department effectively in the field. Bill Duster, who joined the organization with a background in training, was made manager of marketing personnel development in early 1960. At that point in history, NASA's space program was constantly in the news, so Duster established what he called the Astronaut program in which groups of 20 or more astronauts were channeled through intensive training cycles lasting two to three months. All told, over 140 men and 1 woman were processed through this training regimen before being returned to the field. These salespeople constituted the nucleus of the 25 district offices created during the 1960 to 1961 period as a part of the Big Look.

One problem caused by this rapid expansion of the sales organization was that most of the sales force had been recruited from other companies and knew little or nothing about General Electric. The intensive specialization of the Astronaut program left little room for exposing the trainees to the details of this very complex business enterprise. Lasher recognized the need to educate the sales organization in the ways of GE so they could work smoothly with other parts of the company and, hopefully, become inculcated with some degree of company loyalty. He gave

135

Goosetree and Sheely the go-ahead to plan and develop a national sales meeting to be held at the Superstition Hotel in Apache Junction. The purpose was both to put the GE brand on the group and to introduce them to the Computer Department's product line.

The national sales meeting was convened on May 15, 1961.[57] The host group included the section and subsection managers from each of the Computer Department's major functions: marketing, manufacturing, engineering, programming, research, finance, legal, and employee relations—each with a part to play and a presentation to make. Also on the program were selected executives and personalities from corporate headquarters, including such as Ronald Reagan (toastmaster), Chuck Rieger (GE vice president for marketing), and Harold Strickland (GE vice president and general manager, Industrial Electronics Division).

The visitors swarmed into Apache Junction from every point of the compass: branch managers, district office managers, sales engineers, product specialists, and sales trainees. As they arrived, they were given western string ties, cowboy hats, and color-coded name badges pinned on by attractive cowgirls. The atmosphere was informal, but the business programs were rigorous and comprehensive, covering every aspect of General Electric's business, organization, and philosophy. The evening events contained their usual quota of horseplay aimed at developing a sense of comradeship—by and large successful, although the cowgirls had long since left the Superstition Hotel for the safety of their families.

The national sales meeting marked the official launching of the Big Look as far as the corporate executives were concerned. Their presence at the meeting, and their enthusiasm at the scope and nature of the Computer Department's plans, convinced the newcomers and Phoenix veterans alike that General Electric had indeed made the decision to enter the commercial computer market in a big way.

Harold Strickland, in a speech extolling the fact that GE had set its sights on being number two in the computer industry within five years, stated that process control had been split out as a separate section (not a part of the Computer Department) in order to free the organization to concentrate on its main objectives in the general-purpose computer market. The Process Control Section would be located at the Peoria Avenue plant, soon to be phased out in favor of additional manufacturing space planned at Deer Valley. This was a distinct victory for Lasher, who had long considered process control an unprofitable diversion. Arnold Spielberg, manager of process control engineering, had declined the opportunity to be manager of the new section in favor of becoming manager of small computer engineering.

Many others from engineering attended the national sales meeting, some to make presentations and demonstrations and others to form relationships within the sales organization. One of these was Bill Bridge, manager of special systems engineering. Bill had come to the Computer Department from the National Bureau of Standards where he worked on the SEAC computer, the world's fastest, fully operational computer as of 1950. He joined the Computer Department in 1957, working on the NCR 304 program under Bob Wooley. At the conclusion of the project, he was made man-

The 1961 National Sales Meeting at Apache Junction, Arizona.

ager of special projects engineering, a group that handled customer applications requiring integration of the computer with other functions such as communications.

During the sales meeting Bridge had occasion to compare notes with Clint DeGabrielle, manager of the Special System Sales Section. Clint came to the Computer Department from GE's Communications Equipment Department where he had been a sales engineer in the Microwave Systems Sales Section. There he had been involved with three major projects requiring a marriage between communications and data processing. He and Bridge spent many hours discussing possible projects for the Computer Department—discussions that would eventually have a significant impact on the future of the Computer Department.

As the national sales meeting ended, all participants felt a sense of accomplishment in terms of jelling the young organization behind an ambitious and challenging philosophy.

CHAPTER 23
BIRTH OF THE DATANET 30

One of the special customers of the GE Computer Department was the Army Ballistic Missile Center in Huntsville, Alabama. The Computer Department had a facilities contract to operate the ABMA Computer Center—an arrangement originally negotiated by Herb Grosch in an attempt to obtain financing for the Computer Center at ASU. The GE military departments, committed in a major way to the air force missile programs, left Von Braun's Huntsville activities to the Computer Department.

Dick Mayhew was the Computer Department's district sales manager in Huntsville. A pretty good engineer himself, he had developed an "in" with Von Braun's people doing the engineering of the propulsion vehicle they were developing for the space program. They needed a way to do "tied down" testing of the powerful rocket vehicles they were developing. Von Braun was almost fanatical in his insistence on extensive testing of his space vehicles before they were put on a launching pad, and the engineers were seeking a method to measure, in real time, the stress, strain, and vibration of a rocket when fired tied down to a test stand.

Dick Mayhew and Clint DeGabrielle spent many hours in the private club of Huntsville's Holiday Inn brainstorming the problem.

"What we have now," said Mayhew, "is a test stand and a rocket with strain gages, transducers, and pressure valves all producing analog signals of the rocket under test, and all the engineers can do is watch the meters on the test boards and read the charts after the fact. What we need are analog-to-digital converters and some means of collecting output and feeding it to a computer where it can be stored and analyzed."

"The analog-to-digital converters are no problem," said DeGabrielle. "I'm pretty sure the converters Arnold Spielberg developed for process control can be modified to be used here. The toughest problem is that there're about 100 different points to monitor, each producing a stream of data, and there has to be some scheme for collecting and storing the data bits so they can be assembled into characters and words for processing in real time with the 225. I'll write this up and give it to Bill Bridge and Spielberg when I get home. Hopefully, they'll have a solution."

When DeGabrielle returned to Phoenix, he set up a meeting with Bridge and Spielberg. What emerged some weeks later was a rack of equipment christened by Bridge as a "bit buffer," which took the data streams and stored the bits until they could be assembled and inputted to the 225. It remained only to develop computer programs that would predict what stress, strains, and vibrations should be according to theory; these were accomplished by the Huntsville group. The result was a powerful system that not only speeded up the rocket-testing process but was also a means of checking the engineers' calculations and improving their design techniques.

The test system never had a name or product number, but it was so successful at Huntsville that the army purchased over 20 GE 225s and a dozen GE 215s. Wernher von Braun paid tribute to the GE Computer Department for making the Saturn rocket a success. Not a single Saturn ever failed or had a malfunction during the entire Saturn program. Von Braun attributed this to the severe test-stand tie-down tests made possible by the GE on-line computer system.[58]

DeGabrielle began to consider what other applications the bit buffer could be used for. He knew the buffer performed a unique and potentially important function in interfacing a computer with a stream of incoming bits, storing the bits and releasing them to core as called for by the program. Even more important, the buffer could operate in reverse, taking commands from the computer at data-processing speed, storing them, and releasing the data at communications line speed.

One of DeGabrielle's major projects while with the Communications Equipment Department had been the cross-country microwave system GE had designed and installed for Western Union, carrying teletype, telex, and ticker-tape traffic. An important and expensive part of the Western Union network was the complex of switching centers that guided the teletype traffic from the originating point to the desired destination. The traffic would come into the switching center in the form of punched paper tape. There it would be collected by hand, the destination address was read visually, and then hand fed into a paper tape reader on the desired outgoing circuit. The Western Union New York switching center filled two floors, and operators on roller skates rushed tapes from circuit to circuit.

This seemed to be a logical application of the bit buffer, thought Clint. He went to Bill Bridge with his idea. "Would it be possible, Bill, to pack the bit buffer with enough logic to turn it into a communications processor that could automate the "torn tape" method of teletype switching? Most of the big companies—Pillsbury, Weyerhauser, Chrysler, Owens Corning, Bank of America, and all of the industrial-military complex—have in-house torn-tape switching centers to handle the teletype traffic with their field offices, vendors, distributors, and factories. This process, which is followed all over the world, is hopelessly clumsy and very costly. If we could automate it, we'd make a bundle for Generous Electric."

"Tell me, Clint, exactly what do you want this gadget to do?"

"That's easy, Bill. We want to buffer the input so the gadget can handle a lot of teletype grade lines simultaneously, and we want to buffer the output to allow the data streams to be channeled to the desired addresses. In between, the only logic we need besides error detection and correction is the capability to read the address on the incoming message and attach it to the outputted data stream."

"Easier said than done, but get me a teletype to play with and a maintenance manual, and I'll take a crack at it. By the way, what should we call this device?"

"I think the word datanet is pretty descriptive of the function," said DeGabrielle. Today's October 30. Why don't we call the product 'Datanet 30?'" They didn't know it at the time, but Datanet 30's packet switching technique would be an important step toward time-sharing.

DeGabrielle found the concept of the Datanet 30 hard to sell to the industrial customers he approached. Many of them had leased GE 225 computers, so they knew the Computer Department, but the people who bought and used computers were not the ones who ran the teletype networks. The computer people were not particularly interested in saving money for the communications people, and vice versa. In addition, the switching center managers were suspicious of any new system that would eliminate most of their staffs, even though they were impressed by the concept of the Datanet 30.

DeGabrielle's first order came from Pillsbury where the vice president in charge of computers, Jim Rude—a real company man who thought anything good for Pillsbury was good for Jim—gave Clint the costs of running the company's switching center. Armed with this inside information, he put some numbers together with Bill Bridge, called Jim, and invited him to visit Phoenix with the Pillsbury communications manager "to hear about a way to save a bundle of money for Pillsbury."

Bridge had put together a mock-up of a three-line chassis to illustrate the concept and made a blackboard explanation of the operation of the Datanet 30 as he conceived it. Clint made a detailed presentation covering the cost savings and handed Jim an order form with a price for the Datanet 30, a price for maintenance, and a ten-month delivery promise. Rude picked up the phone, talked briefly with his boss, and signed the contract.

The Pillsbury order was only the beginning. DeGabrielle reported what he had done to Bob Sheely, his boss.

"You realize, Clint," said Sheely, "that you've perpetrated a terrible sin by committing the Computer Department to deliver a product that we not only don't have but that also lacks any approval from product planning. I have faith in your judgment, but you'd better get this into the system fast, before anyone else knows about the order."

DeGabrielle, with support of Bridge and Spielberg, got hold of Chris Krygsman in product planning and asked him to develop a New Product Review Sheet for the Datanet 30. Chris, sharing their enthusiasm, completed the complex product review document in three days and (without mentioning to Lasher that they already had one order) submitted it for approval.

"I'll approve this as an engineering investigation," said Lasher, "but no production will be authorized until you receive five orders."

Based on this lukewarm approval, Bill Bridge went to work to complete the engineering, and Clint DeGabrielle hit the road to sell four more machines. He first spent two days at GE corporate communications in Schenectady, only to be rebuffed with the story that Western Union had promised to develop an automated switch—

after all, that was their business. Then, with the help of Vic Casebolt of the Detroit sales office, he was put in contact with Bob Franklin, Chrysler's aggressive communications manager, who was tired of waiting for Western Union to come up with a solution. He placed an order after a demonstration of the Phoenix breadboard, insisting that he wanted to be the first in the automobile industry. This was an easy demand to meet, because both Ford and General Motors had declined. With some help from Jim Rude of Pillsbury, both Clark Equipment and Weyerhauser placed firm orders, leaving one to go to reach the quota of five. DeGabrielle, figuring he had it made, then went to Al Zipf of the Bank of America. Zipf was anxious to help, but there was a bad scene in which the communications manager curtly told Zipf to stay out of his area.

As a last resort, DeGabrielle called Dick Mayhew in Huntsville. "Look, Dick, you helped get us started along this line. All we need is one more order and we'll have a product line. Do you think Huntsville will give us one?"

"I don't know, Clint. The Huntsville switching center is run by the army, completely separate from the rocket research center. I'll see what I can do, but don't be too hopeful."

A week passed, and Mahew called back. "I contacted all of the managers, and one of them has a little money left over. He'll give you an order, but only with a verbal promise to give him full credit if he can't find a use for it."

"I'll take it," was the answer from the jubilant DeGabrielle.

With this order, and a contingent order from Eastman Kodak, Lasher gave the production go-ahead, and the Datanet 30 program was off and running. The GE Computer Department time-sharing program was one step closer to reality.

Incidentally, while the Datanet 30 turned out to be a roaring success, one was never delivered to Huntsville. Instead, the Computer Department furnished another 215, invoiced "incorrectly" as a Datanet 30. Over 1,000 Datanet 30s would eventually be sold.[59]

Meanwhile, back at Dartmouth College, Professor John G. Kemeny and Professor Thomas E. Kurtz had initiated a research program to apply computers to the educational process. Their first project involved experiments with small individual computers such as the IBM 1620 and the LPG-30 installed in 1959. The experiments were encouraging but indicated the need to furnish terminals on a broad basis to the student body as a whole. In 1962, the college received a $300,000 grant from the National Science Foundation for the development of equipment to implement the concept of a shared computer network to serve Dartmouth College. Like the Bank of America, they requested bids from the computer industry, and this time General Electric was on the bidders' list.

Kemeny received proposals from IBM, NCR, GE, and Bendix. IBM proposed a two-computer system, with the 7044 as the CPU and another machine as the communications interface. It was rejected as being too clumsy and far too expensive, even with their 60-percent educational discount. NCR's offering lacked floating-point capability, a must for a research environment. The Bendix proposal was far too expensive, although it did have the attraction that a similar machine was being used at Carnegie Mellon University.

The GE Computer Department's proposal using the Datanet 30 and the GE 225 had floating-point hardware, was fully buffered (input and output), and included an 18-megabyte random access disc storage unit with dual ports permitting access from two computers. It also allowed 16 terminals to time share the computer simultaneously. By a fortunate coincidence, it was just what the doctor ordered.

After a visit to Phoenix by Kemeny and Kurtz, the deal was sealed, and the GE Computer Department and Dartmouth College entered into a productive, long-term partnership.[60] This resulted in the development and introduction of interactive, time-shared computing and networking—precursor of today's information super highway.

The project was so successful that it thrust John Kemeny into position of prominence in academic circles and was partly responsible for his selection as president of Dartmouth. It served also to create a new product line within GE's Computer Department—one that would ultimately throw a scare into mighty IBM.

CHAPTER 24
TEETHING PROBLEMS

1962 was a year of ups and downs for Clair Lasher and the GE Computer Department.[61] On the positive side, the Datanet 30 was a distinct success in its application of automating the teletype switching centers—although there was not a great deal of management enthusiasm about the joint program with Dartmouth College to expand the function to computer time sharing. The GE 225 was in full production; its versatility for both business and scientific data processing made it attractive to a number of smaller GE departments and similar-sized businesses. The GE 210 (ERMA) computer had been installed in banks outside the Bank of America, and had been well accepted. Arnold Spielberg was well advanced in the development of the GE 235—to be compatible with the GE 225 but three times as fast with a five-microsecond memory. (The following year, the GE 215 would be introduced, operating at one-third the speed of the GE 225, to create the first product line of compatible computers.)

Another favorable development was the success of the program to operate the Huntsville Computer Center on a contract basis. Originally, the intent had been to use this as a means of bleeding off work for the IBM 704-equipped Computer Center at ASU. As time went on, it became obvious that this strategy was faulty. The IBM 704 was replaced by a GE 304B (the in-house version of the NCR 304), and the Huntsville contract grew to a profitable $3.8 million-a-year operation.

On the negative side, the development program for the Mosaic product line had fallen several months behind schedule and was already over-expended. A decision was made to reduce the budget for field service in order to allocate additional funds to Mosaic, and this in turn had caused problems in the field. These problems were exacerbated by defects in peripheral equipment, particularly the Elliott card reader and the Computer Department version of the Pitney-Bowes check sorter. Several software programs were also behind schedule.

Most of these were inevitable "teething" problems typical of the still-immature computer industry, but they'd not been provided for in Lasher's Big Look budget; he was continuously apologizing to Harold Strickland for changes in the mandatory three-month financial forecast, and each time he did so he could sense that his credibility was deteriorating. It seemed that no sooner had a project been firmly scheduled and budgeted than some technical glitch or competitive move would cause a delay and an over-expenditure. The subsequent pressure from above to

143

Arnold Spielberg sits at the control panel of his GE 312 industrial process computer, the forerunner of the GE 215, 225, and 235 line of medium size business and scientific computers.

reduce expenditures usually triggered a reduction in field-service personnel, advertising commitments, and field salesmen—all steps harmful in the long run.

The lion's share of product development funds went into the Mosaic family plan—computers W, X, Y, and Z, which would cover the range from small computers to supercomputers. Initial emphasis had been placed on Y (the large machine) and W (changed to S because the product planners didn't want confusion with Westinghouse—but causing confusion for GE management even more). It was intended that each member of the family would be software compatible and utilize many common circuit packages. The Y project was both more costly and more important; it was intended to meet the needs of all of the large GE Operating Departments as well as other businesses of similar size.

As 1962 rolled along, it became increasingly apparent that the Y project was in deep trouble. Engineering costs had gone up, schedules had slipped, predicted performance on completion had deteriorated, and probable cost to manufacture had greatly increased. Delivery, previously planned for 1964, had slipped to 1966. To add to the tale of woe, the Y computer lacked program compatibility with the S computer, and an intermediate-level compiler to bridge the compatibility gap had not been feasible. All these negative factors came to a head during the preparation of the program for the 1962 annual business review when accounting informed Lasher that

The GE Computer Center on the campus of Arizona State University was based initially around an IBM 704. In 1962 the 704 was removed and replaced by the GE 304, a large general-purpose machine developed by the GE Computer Department for NCR.

engineering had requested $4 million to cover the cost of Y computer development during 1963.

"How can we justify this sort of thing?" said Lasher in a meeting with Bob Johnson. "We promised an aggressive Big Look approach to secure a solid position as number two to IBM, and now we have to go back and say we can't deliver on the key project. Maybe we should have put more emphasis on time sharing and communications."

"I'm sorry, Clair, but we both agreed to bring in Art Critchlow from IBM to take over the Y project. He's used to working with an open-ended budget to accomplish an ambitious objective, and he feels he can still be successful. I'll admit he is pushing the technology a little too hard. Ray Barclay's people say the Y computer just can't be built the way he's designed it. I'm sorry to say Ray might be right."

Lasher, visibly upset, lit another cigarette and blurted out, "My God, Bob, we've already spent millions on this project. Strickland will have a fit if we have to admit we can't hack it."

"My own reputation is on the line, too," said Johnson, "but I think there's a way out. A great deal of our expenditure on Mosaic has involved the development of an overall systems concept involving a family of compatible peripheral controllers, a common operating system, and other basic system-design concepts. We've done this so far in developing the Y data-processing system even though the computer portion is in trouble. I think it will be possible to utilize the Y system design and concept but using the higher speed version of the S as the computer element of the system.

This way we can retain the Y memory, central switching exchange, and input-output systems, permitting us to handle the largest commercial data-processing jobs. In parallel, we should initiate planning for a fast, simple scientific computer that can be plugged into the system complex. I realize this means a two-year delay as far as the scientific version of the Y is concerned, but it preserves the compatible feature that is all-important for the future."

"How soon can we pull the plug on the Y computer?"

"Immediately, if you wish. Art Critchlow will be heartbroken, but I think he's already expecting the worst. It's too bad. He's a fine engineer with plenty of imagination, perhaps too much in this case."

"How about the engineers and technicians?"

"I think most of them will be relieved. There's been a good deal of controversy within the group, and I've had to intercede a couple of times. Some of the group can be absorbed immediately into the S program, and Arnold has been screaming for more engineers to expedite the GE 235 development. I know he's anxious to get his hands on Jerry Wiener and Larry Hittle in particular."

"Yeah, and the elimination of the Y computer will save a lot of money in the short term and make our P&L look a bit better when we hit the annual business review. Okay, Bob, let's do it."

And so the Y computer was abandoned. It would be a few more years before the Computer Department would be in a position to offer a large machine capable of handling scientific and engineering calculations.

CHAPTER 25
FAILURE OF THE MOSAIC PROGRAM

Back at Electronics Park in Syracuse, the Heavy Military Equipment Department was engaged in the development of the missile tracking system for the air force's Atlas missile. The system, called MISTRAM, contained a data-processing unit that had grown from a vacuum-tube processor designed in 1959 to a solid-state computer called the M2360.* John Couleur, the project engineer, had headed up a group that visited Phoenix in July of 1962 to describe the features of the M2360 as a possible substitute for the Computer Department's Y computer. Aware of the problems with the Y machine, Charles Thompson of product planning (later to become senior vice president of Motorola) was an advocate of the M2360. Sadly, it was rejected, based on a lack of "advanced features and advanced technology," as well as the fact that its 36-bit word would not be compatible with the rest of the planned Mosaic family of computers.

Don Shell, head of the Mathematics Department of GE's General Engineering Lab, had been involved in the development of the FORTRAN compiler for the M2360, and he was quite impressed with the architecture of the machine. A member of GE's Large Computer Users Group (consisting of EDP managers of departments with large computers), Don had considerable influence at corporate level. He promoted the M2360 vigorously and was responsible for pressure being brought to bear on Lasher and Johnson.[62] This pressure evidently had a negative effect in Phoenix despite the failure of the Y computer. Couleur and his group visited Phoenix a number of times at the instigation of Art Vinson, group vice president (Harold Strickland's boss), to make proposals and presentations. Vinson favored the M2360 and hoped the Computer Department would agree to join in a joint design effort to make it a successful commercial product. However, he did not go to the extreme of demanding that the Computer Department acquiesce.

Lasher and Johnson were firm in their conviction that the introduction of a non-compatible machine into the picture would permanently disrupt their plan to create a compatible product line. Their conviction was based on a realization that IBM, embarked on its ambitious 360 development program, was in the process of establishing a way of life in the computer business that they believed must be followed by any company hoping to compete effectively. Digital Equipment Corp. would prove them wrong.

---

* The designation M236 was originally applied to the military version. The designation M2360 was used to describe the same computer if used commercially.

The annual business review was scheduled to take place at 570 Lexington Avenue on December 5, 1962.[63] Charts and graphs were drawn and redrawn as Lasher and his staff prepared for what they knew would be a crucial meeting with Ralph Cordiner and the New York corporate contingent of staff specialists and top executives. It was the first full-blown business review since the Big Look was approved, and Lasher knew the house would be packed.

Just getting to New York was a struggle that winter. The team of Lasher, McCombs, Johnson, Goosetree, and Helmet Sassenfield (Herb Grosch's replacement) had arrived very late the night before after a four-hour weather delay in Nashville. Struggling through the snow and slush the next morning, weighed down with flip charts, slides, and pamphlets, they straggled into the General Electric building and up the elevator to the board room. To Lasher's dismay, Ralph Cordiner and his staff had already arrived. Piling their soggy overcoats on an empty chair, they managed to get their displays together and the slide projector focused.

Lasher led off the presentation with a review of the past seven years, beginning with the ERMA system and the NCR 304, both successful programs in terms of customer acceptance and adherence (within a reasonable tolerance for start-up) to budget forecasts. He then commented on financial performance, indicating that sales of computers and services in the past year had been $9 million better than budget, due mainly to 225 sales to Huntsville and Datanet 30 sales to industrial customers; but annual rental income had been $4 million less than budgeted due to a number of problems that would be discussed. Nothing was particularly disturbing about this information, but the financial picture began to unravel when McCombs gave a more detailed explanation of the numbers. It became increasingly evident that the forecast of rental income, as opposed to outright sales, would not meet the projections made for the Big Look.

Lasher took over again at that point to outline the problems encountered during 1962.

"The Department has had problems this year that have resulted in program deferrals of approximately six months. Much progress has been made toward resolving these problems, but some still remain. Problems with mechanical peripherals—mostly the Elliott card readers and our own check sorter—have reduced sales by $1.6 million and annual rental created by $4.4 million. Delays in completing the GECOM software package have affected both our orders and sales budgets materially. We have reduced our level of maintenance in order to improve profitability, and neither we nor our customers are happy with the performance of our equipment in the field. We have been trying to expand too fast, and have undergone an agonizing reappraisal to develop a more orderly approach to these and other problem areas. We have made a great deal of progress in the last few months, and we are confident in our ability to eliminate these problems during 1963."

Lasher was visibly sweating as he continued. "In the new product area, we have encountered schedule delays, shop cost increases, and performance degradations in our planned large computer system. These problems are such that we are planning

GE President Cordiner pays a rare visit to the Computer Department.

major changes in both the Mosaic program and its leadership. These plans will be presented by Bob Johnson during his discussion of future products.

"So far, I've concentrated on problem areas. On the positive side, the GE 225 is being well accepted as a small to medium-size computer, the only one in the field capable of both business and scientific data processing. This product is particularly attractive because of its low shop cost and reliability in the field. The order rate is increasing despite the problems with the Elliott card reader. We're interfacing the GE 225 with the check sorter for sale to small banks that do not need the capacity of the GE 210. In addition, we are developing a higher speed version of the GE 225, which we call the GE 235, and a lower speed version we'll call the GE 215. They will both be released to the market next spring."

At that point, Chuck Rieger, vice president for marketing services raised his hand. "Clair, your charts show the GE 215, 225, and 235 covering an increasing price range and performance range. Are they program compatible?"

"Yes, Chuck. They're all three basically the same computer, with different cycle speeds and plus or minus a few circuits such as floating point. However, being binary machines with only a 21-bit word length, they are not expandable further."

Rieger had touched on a sore point that Lasher didn't want to explore at that meeting. Actually, Arnold Spielberg had suggested a scheme to grow the GE 235 into a 48-bit GE 245. The 48-bit word would require some software massage and upgraded instructions to be used in a higher performance operating system. No action was taken on the proposal, due primarily to budgetary restrictions.

Continuing, Lasher introduced the subject of data communications, which he cited as being one of the most important new developments in the computer field. "This year," he said, "we've received $2.5 million in orders for this new product line. We're forecasting that between 50 and 70 percent of all computer systems will require data communications by 1970. We're in on the ground floor—to tell you about it, Dr. Johnson."

"We got into this market on an opportunistic shoestring," said Johnson, "but the products we already have are unique and technically leading. Basically, we've learned how to make computers talk to other computers and with humans over long-distance telephone lines and even via satellites. The importance of—"

At that point an imperious voice from the audience expressed total skepticism about Johnson's claim. "I don't like being snowed with science-fiction claims," said Ralph Cordiner. "On what basis can you make such a forecast?"

Johnson was aghast. How could he tell the president of General Electric that he didn't have any perception of what was going on in the computer field?

"I'll admit it sounds kind of wild," he said, "but Bill Bridge's Datanet 30 just recently sent computer data from Phoenix to Paris via satellite. We do think we have the technology to play a leading part in this kind of development."

"I'm sorry, Johnson, but I just don't buy such nonsense as computers talking to each other over the telephone. It doesn't make business sense."[64]

Sensing he should avoid arguing with the boss, but disheartened, Johnson decided he'd better change the subject. He went on with a complicated but necessary discussion of the Mosaic family, including the reasoning behind abandoning the Y computer after having expended so much money and engineering effort. He could sense that his plan to "grow" the Computer Department's large computer by incorporating many features of the Y architecture into the S computer and dropping in a high-speed scientific computer at a later date was not really understood by most of the audience, but he continued to provide the technical details.

Lasher had expected one of Cordiner's staff to come up with the question "Why don't you accept the proposal of the Heavy Military Equipment Department to contribute the M2360 and to join the Computer Department in a joint program to make this your large machine?" It wasn't a question he particularly wanted to deal with, in part because he wasn't completely convinced that the opposition on the part of his engineering staff was not tinged with a bit of NIH (not invented here) attitude. In any event, the question didn't come up during the course of the business review.

The business review was concluded by Lasher with the statement, "Despite the problem areas, the department has grown rapidly in the last three years—60 percent per year on an all-sold basis, and it is profitable on this basis in 1962. However, the books show a net loss—McCombs terms this 'profit deferred.' The cumulative unrealized income from future lease payments will offset booked losses by the end of

1964 and will be creating future income at a rate of 18 cents per share in 1965. This indicates the department is on the verge of profitability if the effect of renting is factored in and after very substantial investment for the future—$12 million in 1963."

Lasher closed with the up-beat statement, "With these thoughts in mind, the department undertakes with confidence to meet its two key objectives: to achieve second place in the industry and to make money."[65]

There was surprisingly little discussion at the conclusion of the presentation. The subject of data communications was avoided because of Cordiner's outburst, which was unfortunate because it was the most important accomplishment of the Computer Department since the Big Look was initiated. Most of the subject matter had to do with the implications of leasing versus outright selling of computers. Many veteran GE executives could not understand why the product could not be sold outright, blind to the fact that the computer market, created by IBM, belonged only to those with the financial resources and long-term commitment to struggle with ten-year negative cash flows.

Cordiner got to his feet and left the meeting, bringing an abrupt close to the discussion. The visitors from Phoenix, not very happy about the tone of the meeting, packed up their exhibits and returned to their hotel.

"Well, fellows, what do you think?" Lasher drew deeply on his cigarette, blew a smoke ring, and stirred his scotch and soda. The five men were seated at a small table in the spacious Biltmore bar, surrounded by well-dressed men and women whose small talk created an atmosphere of intimacy.

"What I think is that the blonde at the second table from us looks bored with her present company and is smiling in my direction," said Ken McCombs. "I *like* this city."

"Well, I don't like it," said Bob Johnson. "That man at 570 just doesn't understand the computer business and doesn't seem to want to learn. I think we're in trouble."

"Let's have a few more drinks and worry about it in the morning," said Lacy Goosetree. "I think our presentation was pretty good despite Cordiner's dumb remarks. There's not much use trying to figure out what he's going to do at this point, so why bother?"

Back at 570, Cordiner was closeted with Jim LaPierre, senior vice president, Defense and Electronics Group, and Harold Strickland, Clair Lasher's immediate superior.

Cordiner was at his most acerbic. "I let Lasher sell me on his Big Look a year and a half ago, and now look at the mess he and that crew of kids have made of things. We've spent too much money to back out now—you two better get on top of this organization in a hurry."

"Now calm down, Ralph," said LaPierre. "I hear a number of good things about the Computer Department from my friends in the business. Remember, they're playing catch-up after GE made a very late start in the commercial computer market. I'll admit my disappointment with Lasher when he turned down the opportunity to adopt Heavy Military's M2360 as the Computer Department's large computer, but it still may not be too late to turn this situation around. What do you think, Harold?"

Strickland was ingrained in the GE management philosophy, promoted by Harold Smiddy and enthusiastically implemented by Ralph Cordiner, which held that a general manager's performance could be measured accurately by his achievement in meeting forecast objectives in terms of return on sales, return on investment, and other related numerical standards. This technique was valid in GE's traditional businesses such as motors, generators, light bulbs, transformers, and electrical appliances where a good general manager could optimize all elements of expense and investment to achieve maximum dollar per share of stock, but Strickland had learned enough about the commercial computer business, with its emphasis on leasing and technological change, to realize that the traditional measurements did not apply. He also knew it was hopeless to argue the matter with Cordiner.

"I've been following the situation closely for some time," he said, "and I've been assessing possible candidates to replace Lasher. I have the man in mind, but I haven't talked to him yet. I'll have a recommendation to submit to Jim and you within a week."

PART IV

Time Sharing
February 1963
to
December 1965

DRAMATIS PERSONAE

CHARLIE THOMPSON. Manager of product planning under Goosetree.

JOHN WEIL. Manager of the GE 600 program.

ED VANCE. Chief programmer for the GE 600 program.

FRED BORCH. New GE president and CEO, replacing Cordiner.

HERSHNER CROSS. New group executive and Strickland's boss.

VERN COOPER. Cross's son-in-law, brought in to replace Goosetree.

CHARLES DE GAULLE. French Prime Minister.

HAL GENEEN. Ambitious CEO of ITT.

GERALD PHILLIPE. GE chairman.

BRAINARD FANCHER. Manager of GE's Apollo Support Division, picked by Rader to be general manager of GE Bull.

HENRI DESBRUERES. Former chairman of Air France, selected to be president of GE Bull.

DON KLEE. Denver district sales manager.

JOHN HOPKO. EDP manager for Martin-Marietta

CLIFF SINK. Former IBM eastern regional manager. Head of GE 600 sales team for Martin-Marietta.

GENE SCOTT. Headquarters sales manager for the GE 600.

BUCK ROGERS. IBM West Coast regional manager and IBM star salesman.

PAUL SHAPIRO. Los Angeles district office salesman for GE 600.

BUCK CLEVEN. EDP manager for Hughes Aircraft Corporation.

DON BENSCOTTER. Independent leasing specialist.

CURT HARE. Manager of Seattle district office.

JIM RICHTER. EDP manager of GE's Gas Turbine Department. Later joined GE Computer Department in Phoenix.

BOB CLAUSSEN. Computer Department engineer.

GREG WILLIAMS. Computer Department programmer.

LOU WENGERT. Successor to Van Aken as general manager of the Computer Department.

ART ASCHAUER. Sheeley's replacement as manager of sales.

CHARLIE LIGHTHAUSER. Executive vice president of Martin-Marietta.

CHUCK ETTINGER. Computer Department product service manager.

"ELECTRIC" CHARLIE WILSON. Former GE president and wartime director of the War Production Board.

DON KNIGHT. Manager of advanced system planning. Promoted time-sharing services.

TOM O'ROURKE. Western regional manager. Left GE and founded TYMSHARE.

VANCE SCOTT, DICK ROJYKO, STAN JOSEPHSON, ZIGY QUAESTER, and KEN McDONALD. Members of Don Knight's team in developing time-share business concept within General Electric.

HELMET SASSENFELD. Manager of computer services for Computer Department.

WARREN SINBACK. Succeeded Sassenfeld as manager of computer services.

BOB CURRY. Lawyer for Lou Rader.

CHAPTER 26
A TOUGH NEW GENERAL MANAGER

Harrison Van Aken was a veteran of 26 years with GE. An accountant by education, he had passed through the many GE courses in professional management and had performed well in a number of successively more responsible positions, including the most recent assignment as general manager of the Communications Equipment Department in Lynchburg, Virginia. He was respected as a hard-driving, no-nonsense executive who got results. Humorless and meticulous, he appealed to Strickland as just what the doctor ordered after seven years of management under gung ho disciples of Doc Baker.

Van Aken's family life had not been as happy as his professional life. His wife was an alcoholic who grew increasingly more difficult to live with as time went on, and this, no doubt, increased his desire to create a well-ordered and disciplined workplace. The death of his son after a long illness, each parent blaming the other, brought the bitter relationship to an end under circumstances where a change in scene was indicated.

It was late 1962 when Van Aken received two offers to become general manager of two completely dissimilar departments within GE. One was a large government-oriented operation—a part of the Electronics Park complex in Syracuse. The other was the GE Computer Department in Phoenix. He weighed the two opportunities carefully and opted finally for the Computer Department.[66]

"You've made a good choice," said Harold Strickland prior to Van Aken's departure for the Valley of the Sun. "The Computer Department has some of the best technical people in the company, and what it needs most is tight business management and a good dose of financial accountability. I'm counting on you to do the same sort of job you've done with the Communications Equipment Department but on a much broader scale."

"I'm looking forward to it," responded Van Aken.

"Good. On the business side, I've made a collection of business plans and appropriation requests from time zero, and I've consolidated the personnel files of all the key people. I understand you're planning to stay over tomorrow, and I've set up an office for you to use while you're here. I expect you'll have to feel your way among the many projects when you arrive, but there's one very important one where you'll have to take the lead at once. I think you know that Heavy Military at Electronics Park has developed a high-performance computer, the M2360, for the MISTRAM missile program. The army has declassified it, and it's the consensus of the Research

Laboratory and the GE Large Users Group that the M2360, with some added software, can be the answer to the Computer Department's desperate need for a large computer to fill out their product line. Lasher turned down the offer because the M2360 wasn't compatible with his planned Mosaic family. I'm not saying your appointment is based on the assumption that you'll reverse this decision, but it's very important that you look into it right away with an open mind."

"Say no more," said Van Aken. "By the way, have you talked about all this with Lasher?"

"Yes. I've offered him an appointment as manager of offshore operations, with the job of studying the international market in detail and recommending our course of action in Europe in particular. He's pretty unhappy, but he's accepted with the understanding that his headquarters can remain in Phoenix until he finds a permanent position. I haven't yet told him you're taking his place, but I'll call him this afternoon and break the news. I want all this accomplished and you out there by mid-February. Can you move that fast?"

"The sooner the better, Harold. My successor is chomping at the bit, and I'm naturally anxious to get into the swing of things before the rumor mill gets going."

The announcement, issued to the employees and the press on February 13, 1963, was worded in typical General Electric fashion, which made every traumatic management change seem like another step in expansion of General Electric's computer business, pointing up the company's increasing emphasis on its computer business and the importance of the offshore computer market. He (Strickland) said establishment of the new computer offshore operation will put the company's most experienced computer manager in a key position to mobilize General Electric's computer effort outside the United States."[67]

CHAPTER 27
THE M2360 COMPUTER IS ACCEPTED

Van Aken came into Phoenix roaring like a lion. He established his authority at his first staff meeting, which he called for eight o'clock on the first Monday after his arrival. Exactly at eight he closed his office door and called the staff meeting to order. A few minutes later Lacy Goosetree and Ken Geiser were heard walking down the hall. Van Aken ceremoniously opened the door and ushered in the two laggards.

"If you came for the eight o'clock staff meeting, you've almost missed it." Van Aken's voice contained a hint of menace. "From now on, I expect all our staff meetings to start exactly on time. My time is valuable. How about yours?"

The word of Van Aken's pronouncement quickly spread to the troops as he had intended, and the next morning Lacy Goosetree's faithful secretary, who religiously punched in three minutes early, arrived in tears fifteen minutes late. She had been caught in the biggest traffic jam the Black Canyon Highway had ever experienced — all 3,500 Computer Department employees struggled to get to work on time.[68]

Van Aken's management style was considered oppressive after the rather informal atmosphere created by Oldfield and Lasher. Van, as he was known, believed in running a taut organization rather than a happy one. By and large, he was successful. He believed implicitly in the chain of command, and he could be counted on to follow instructions from above to the letter. He expected his subordinates to do likewise, and he had an explosive temper that would show itself whenever he discovered his orders had been flouted or misdirected.

The Computer Department benefited in a number of ways from this tightening up of the organization. Personnel at all levels became more conscious of meeting deadlines and of carrying out instructions. Closer attention was paid to the control of expenses and to the need to be accountable for results. He was never to become a greatly loved boss, but he gained the respect of the majority of employees.

Van Aken's first project was to get up to date on the M2360 computer. He found Charlie Thompson, manager of product planning under Lacy Goosetree, to be the main adherent of the large high-speed computer. Thompson had attended the presentations made by John Couleur and his group, and he'd visited Syracuse several times to witness the computer in action. He was sold on the M2360.

158

"Couleur and his group have designed a high-performance mainframe-class computer with high reliability, and they apparently did so on schedule and at less than quoted cost. The performance of the M2360 far exceeds that of the IBM 7090, the solid-state version of the IBM 705 that is installed in most of GE's large Operating Departments.[69] Our stated reason for rejecting the design is that its 36-bit word length makes it incompatible with the Mosaic family, but this is absurd because there is no Mosaic family since the termination of the Y machine. The real reason for the rejection is that our own engineers didn't invent it."

"Why don't you contact Couleur and invite him to come into Phoenix for another presentation?"

"He'll be overjoyed," said Thompson.

It was not true that the Computer Department had abandoned the Y concept, though the set of hardware comprising the computer element of the system had been terminated. Bob Johnson had brought in John Weil from GE's Atomic Power Laboratory at San Jose to study the lab notebooks of Critchlow's engineering group and develop the specifications for the large computer that would be "dropped into" the S framework at a later date. The lower end of the Mosaic family, then, would make up the GE 400 series, and the high end would comprise the GE 600 series. The original plan had scheduled the first of the 400 family for introduction in early 1964—which still seemed doable—and the first of the 600 series a year later.[70] There was no solid forecast for the 600 series as a result of the termination of the Y computer.

John Weil, being new to the Computer Department, had no emotional attachment to the Y computer or to the Mosaic family. When John Couleur and his team visited Phoenix in late February 1963, Weil listened carefully to the presentation and was impressed with the potential of the M2360. He sensed that his boss, Bob Johnson, had little enthusiasm for the project, primarily because of its lack of compatibility with the GE 400, but he was impressed with the fact that the 36-bit word length was the same as that of the IBM 7090 and 7094, the large computers being used by most of the large GE Operating Departments.

Dr. Don Shell, director of the Mathematics Department of the General Engineering Laboratory, was a part of the delegation put together by John Couleur to sell the M2360 as the basis for the GE 600 series.

"Let's face it," he said, "the data-processing managers of all the company's Operating Departments and their programmers have mostly cut their teeth on IBM machines, and many worked for IBM before they came to work for GE. They feel comfortable with the IBM sales engineers and programmers, and most of them think our company is crazy to try to compete with IBM. If we're going to change this mind-set, the Computer Department has to produce a computer reasonably near the 7090 and 7094 in power and flexibility. On the positive side, the data-processing managers are all members of the SHARE group, which picks flaws in IBM's products. Should you succeed in installing a competitive mainframe within GE, you'd drive a wedge into the mainframe market."

John Couleur, sensing he had a receptive audience for once, said, "Let me make another point. We've made calculations showing the total cost of developing and producing a commercial version of the M2360 should be less than the lease payments being made by GE to IBM for the large computers. In other words, the program will pay for itself purely by replacing the IBM computers now under lease."

Couleur's "sales pitch" had impressed Van Aken. While he had no personal knowledge of computers, he liked the sound of the argument, and, of course, he had previously been told that corporate management was in favor of the project. A few days after the presentation, he gave the go-ahead. Bob Johnson was distressed, recognizing this move would kill the compatibles idea and subvert his influence as manager of engineering.

CHAPTER 28
MASSIVE REORGANIZATION

Van Aken's next project was to reorganize the Computer Department. He established the Special Projects Operation under John Weil, with responsibility for the GE 600 program. John Couleur was transferred from Electronics Park to head up the central system hardware development. Bob Johnson had previously brought in Ed Vance from the Nuclear Power Laboratory, and he was transferred to Weil to head software development for the 600. Bob Johnson was appointed manager of the advanced products operation, which included the Computer Laboratory in Palo Alto (the remnants of the ERMA technical group) and responsibility for design engineering and systems engineering for "advanced products," of which the GE 400 was the only example. This reduction in Bob's authority did not sit well with much of the technical staff and marked the beginning of what became a continuing series of personnel changes as Van Aken sought to create a superior organization.

Herm Green, Bob Johnson's manager of engineering administration, was appointed acting manager of the engineering operation, responsible for the 200 line, custom products, and data communications. This was a holding action until Van Aken could sort out the key personalities such as John Paivinen, Arnold Spielberg, and Bill Bridge. The marketing and manufacturing organizations were left unchanged by this initial reorganization, announced officially on April 8, 1963.[71]

Meanwhile, back at 570, major changes in corporate management were underway. Fred Borch ascended to the presidency, replacing Ralph Cordiner as CEO. Art Vinson, group vice president, died early in the year, and he was replaced by Hershner Cross, an MBA from Harvard Business School who had come up the financial chain in GE, becoming general manager of the Distribution Assemblies Department of the Industrial Power Components Division in 1954. He fit the mold of the proficient GE professional manager, though he had no technical background or experience in the computer field. As group vice president, he was Harold Strickland's direct superior, and as time went on his lack of knowledge of the computer market was to have an increasingly negative impact on GE's computer business.

Hersh Cross was intrigued by computers, and he was eager to make his mark in this fast-growing field. While at Harvard Business School many years before, he was exposed to the growing importance of the international market, and one of his first steps was to investigate the European market. Clair Lasher, manager of offshore operations for the Computer Department—one of two employees of this virtually fictional operation, the other being another employee temporarily assigned while seeking another position—had surveyed the market, augmented by visits by Ray Barclay, Bob Johnson, and Ken Geiser. They had identified a number of opportunities for GE as possible acquisitions or joint-venture partners, the two most likely being Machines Bull in France and Olivetti in Italy. Lasher had recommended that the offshore computer operation, whatever its mix of export sales and joint ventures, should report to the Computer Department in order to ensure uniformity of manufacturing procedures and compatibility of products. Cross didn't much care for the concept of having a complex European operation reporting to a bunch of salesmen and engineers in Arizona, and he decided to take over personally. During 1963 he made a number of visits to Europe, becoming increasingly enthused with the possibilities of an international computer empire.

Back in Phoenix, progress was being made despite grumblings about Van Aken's management technique. Arnold Spielberg and Chuck Propster, augmented by the cast-offs from the Y program, were putting the finishing touches on the GE 235 version of the 200-compatible series. With its five-microsecond memory developed by Vic DiMucci and its transistor-coupled circuits meticulously designed by Gerry Allard, the GE 235 had a safety margin 20 percent above "worst case" while operating three times as fast as the GE 225. Unlike the GE 225, which had been put together as a modified version of the GE 312 process control computer, the GE 235 logic was checked out and implemented so thoroughly that the system was up and running the day it was turned on and was essentially debugged in two days, including margin checks and test routines. It went into production smooth as glass, and it turned out to be a profitable product that extended the life of the 200 line by about two years.

Spielberg's accomplishments were not well rewarded by Van Aken. John Paivinen, who left GE after the completion of ERMA, had returned and was put in charge of the 200 line. He and Spielberg marched to different drummers, and Spielberg left the Computer Department in September 1963 to join IBM in San Jose.[72]

Another important development program, the Datanet 30, reached fruition in 1963. In parallel with its quantity production, Bill Bridge was finalizing details of data error detection for the marriage of the Datanet 30 with the GE 235 (the GE 265) for delivery to Dartmouth.[73]

At Dartmouth, where a GE 225 had already been installed, Professors Kemeny and Kurtz, along with a group of student programmers, were working on a compiler for the first version of BASIC, the programming language to be used with the time-sharing system. The objective was to create a system whereby students and faculty, at a number of different points on the campus, could use the computer

The GE 225 computer, launched in 1961, could handle both scientific and business data processing and was used in many diverse applications—from time sharing (with the Datanet 30) to banking (with MICR). It was followed by the higher speed GE 235 and the smaller GE 215. Many installations of this GE 200 family were in service ten years later.

simultaneously and, with BASIC, do the programming required for their differing projects using teletype terminals as input-output devices.[74] It was a revolutionary concept, destined to have an impact on the computer world in a major way, and all participants were excited about the possibilities. There were some skeptics in the Computer Department who considered it an experiment in education with little commercial value, but most were highly supportive.

The program receiving most of the attention in Phoenix was the GE 600. John Couleur moved a 20-man engineering group from Syracuse to Phoenix after committing himself to a one-year development cycle for turning the M2360 into a commercial computer. He had split the staff of his Heavy Military Equipment Department in two, leaving the remaining Syracuse organization under Walker Dix. This group would continue working on the military applications of the computer.

Ed Vance had cleverly put together a team of GE's large-scale computer users to write the specifications for a highly advanced operating system and software family. Most of the team members eventually joined the Computer Department; Vance filled the rest of the software organization with outside people. The operating system was known as GECOS, an acronym for General Electric comprehensive operating supervisor. The first version was called GECOS I and was intended to be the operating base of the GE 600 series product line. GECOS I was never shipped, and GECOS went through a number of changes, additions, and modifications before it would finally emerge as GECOS III some years later.[75]

The 1963 Christmas party was a somber affair in contrast with the light-hearted joviality of prior years. The absence of Arnold Spielberg and his wife Leah seemed an ominous foreboding of things to come. (Actually, 1963 had been a most productive year in terms of accomplishments. However, there had been rumblings about organizational shake-ups both at the corporate level and within the Computer Department.) The partying was subdued and conversations were guarded. Van Aken definitely set the tone—if he laughed, others laughed; if he talked, everyone listened respectfully. There were no really free exchanges or jokes made in a bantering way as had been the case before.[76]

Van Aken was not conscious of the change in mood of the Phoenix family. He was, he felt, achieving the corporate objective of whipping the Computer Department into a solid business enterprise.

CHAPTER 29
DIVERSIONS IN EUROPE

In February 1964, Bill Bridge supervised the final tests of the GE 265–the combination of the Datanet 30 with the GE 235–to be shipped to Kurtz at Dartmouth College. He and Ray Barclay stood on the loading dock of the Black Canyon Highway plant, paying critical attention to the packing and handling for the long trip to Dartmouth.

"If this system works as well as we think it will, and if the BASIC programming language is successful," said Bridge, "this may turn out to be the most important shipment yet made by the Computer Department. Congratulations on hitting the delivery schedule on the nose."

"Routine for us in the factory," said Ray. "You and Arnold deserve the kudos."

Two weeks later, both men were gone from the scene. As Bill Bridge put it, "My seven years with the Computer Department have been an invaluable experience. However, during my last year at GE, all levels of management between me and the shareholders have been replaced. Cordiner retired, Art Vinson died on the job, and was replaced by Hershner Cross. Strickland has been shifted aside by Cross who is micromanaging from atop the ivory tower. Clair Lasher has been replaced. Bob Johnson's engineering operations have been split into three separate sections. Custom systems and communications software have been split away from the hardware engineering. I've ended up in a good position on paper, with a larger staff and responsibility for all computer systems currently in production, including banking and the 200 line. This won't begin to provide me with the entrepreneurial technical and business experience I hoped for when I joined GE."[77]

So Van Aken lost his second golden goose! Ray Barclay's departure from the scene was more traumatic.[78] Immensely popular with the factory personnel at all levels, his open-door policy and style of holding staff meetings was much admired. Each man had five or ten minutes to talk about anything he felt like–sex, last night's party, the weather, or manufacturing problems. If late for a meeting, a fine; if not in attendance, a dollar. Then every fall the pot was used to have a bag of clams flown in from the East. The clambakes were hosted by Ray's pretty and popular wife, Pat, who threw open the Barclay house for the occasion, which included raw and steamed clams, salt potatoes, and shrimp, followed by a steak dinner. Everyone enjoyed Ray's style, and it paid off in terms of employee morale.

Barclay was not above having a drink or two, or more, except he never indulged at work. He dressed casually–some said sloppily–and his mannerisms were casual, though he was a dedicated professional in his approach to manufacturing. Van Aken, unhappy with Barclay's lack of executive presence, gave him a favorable performance review for 1963. However, he decided to replace him in early 1964.

One day in late February, Ray showed up at home much earlier than usual. "Let's go for a ride, Pat." His expression was wild-eyed.

Concerned that he might have been drinking, his wife got in the car. Barclay headed down Calle del Norte, opposite to the way they usually drove. "What's the matter?" she asked.

In answer he gunned the car down the street, finally blurting out, "I've been removed from the job, no longer manufacturing manager–that's what's wrong." Barclay was trying hard to hold back the tears.

"Do you mean fired, let out?" Pat had just moved her parents to Phoenix–her father was a diabetic with a time table–and Pat herself had been postponing a much-needed operation.

"No, I'm not being fired," he replied. "I'm still on the payroll, but I might as well be fired–it amounts to the same thing. I've staked my career on the Computer Department, and, until today, I thought I'd succeeded. Now I'll be put out to pasture somewhere."

At least, Pat thought, there'll be time to come up with a constructive plan for the family. "We'll make out."

Van Aken replaced Ray with Bill White, a personal protégé from the Communications Equipment Department. He was in turn replaced by Cy Statt, veteran manufacturing man from Electronics Park who had Barclay's respect.[79] Ray was placed on special assignment, a no-man's land created by GE to present a business-as-usual face to the outside world during times of organizational turmoil.

Once started, the management purge of 1964 spread like wildfire:[80] Vern Cooper, said to be Hersh Cross's son-in-law, was brought in to replace the popular Lacy Goosetree. Not well liked, Cooper was described by George Snively as articulate, imposing, vain, intimidating, incompetent, stupid, and naive; not the type one would normally choose to represent GE to the customer population. It was a catastrophic example of nepotism. John Weil was appointed systems and processors operation manager, encompassing all of the department's engineering sections, including the Palo Alto Laboratory. Bob Johnson, completely disillusioned with GE's top management policies, accepted an offer from Burroughs Corporation to become director of engineering. John Paivinen, equally bitter, left to become vice president and general manager of Advanced Scientific Instruments, Inc.

Van Aken was a strict practitioner of the concept of corporate discipline, so it was never possible to pin down the decision pattern responsible for many of the peculiar organizational changes. However, it was accepted by all concerned that the replacement of the highly respected Lacy Goosetree by Vern Cooper was directed by Hersh Cross. Lacy had been Van Aken's manager of marketing back at the Communications Equipment Department, and the two had worked together harmoniously for many years. The story goes that Van Aken announced the decision at a staff meeting while Lacy was out of town, apparently unable to face him directly with the bad news.[81] It did little to increase his popularity with his subordinates. In contrast, the resignations of Bob Johnson and John Paivinen could have been expected after the decision to abandon the Mosaic family.

While this turbulent series of events was taking place in Phoenix, Group Executive Hersh Cross was busy in Europe.[82] He had been intrigued by reports of surveys of the European computer market made by Ken Geiser, Clair Lasher, Bob Johnson, Ray Barclay, and others. They had identified a number of possible partners in Europe, but warned that there were problems associated with each. Brushing aside the cautionary words, Cross decided that an aggressive program in Europe would help expand the scope of GE's computer activity and improve chances of success.

GE already had a relationship with Olivetti in Italy. Olivetti had established the Olivetti Data Processing Division to develop and manufacture small computers. Cross had no difficulty persuading Fred Borch, GE's president, to pay $12 million for 75 percent ownership of the Olivetti Division. This seemed a bargain and whetted Cross's appetite for more.[83]

Compagnie Machines Bull was founded in 1931 to produce and sell punch-card equipment. The company stayed small, in the order of $7 million in sales a year, until 1950 when the owners decided to build a big computer, which they called Gamma 3. It was introduced in 1953, but it was a fiasco. In a desperate move, Bull negotiated a license agreement with RCA to sell and produce the RCA 301 computer. This venture also turned out badly because the 301 was itself plagued with technical problems. By early 1964, Machines Bull was facing bankruptcy.

Despite the company's profound problems, there were a few positive factors. Bull had over 5,000 tabulators in the field, all generating lease income. To service and sell these tabulating machines there was a substantial field sales organization with important contacts in a number of countries. Given a modern computer product line, Bull could be a major force in Europe.

Without analyzing the problems, and excited by the potential benefits, GE paid $45 million for a 50-percent interest in Bull. To satisfy French law, it was necessary to create two separate companies for the acquisition: Societe Industrielle GE, with 51-percent GE ownership, and Compagnie Bull General Electric, with 49-percent GE ownership. The companies would be under common management with a French figurehead president and a GE directeur general. GE had a management contract, or would have when the closing papers of the complex purchase had been signed. It was said that General de Gaulle was very unhappy about the negotiation, but his Parliament had refused to bail out Bull financially so he had to go along. It was said also that he vowed to hold GE's feet to the fire!

Hersh Cross assigned a team from Phoenix to study Bull's operations and develop a plan for integrating the French company with the GE Computer Department and with Olivetti. Ray Barclay, still on special assignment, was the leader of the manufacturing team. What he found brought Cross down to earth.[84]

Bull had three million square feet of manufacturing space in seven widely scattered plant locations. All but the plant at Angers were old mill-type structures. By GE manufacturing standards, less than one-half million square feet of space was actually required. Bull had 15,000 employees on the payroll, most of whom were represented by a variety of unions, all with different contract conditions. Barclay's calculations indicated that 2,500 of these employees were excess manufacturing workers. French law was a real problem, particularly with De Gaulle lurking in the background. It was necessary for central and local governments to approve any reduction of personnel or plant closings, a very lengthy process. Also, women could not work past 10 p.m., which virtually eliminated use of a second shift. The language barrier had not been considered when Cross negotiated the acquisition. Barclay found that few of the Bull workers outside of Paris spoke any English, including the manager of manufacturing.

Faced with these complications, Cross decided he needed an experienced executive to handle the problems involved in integrating the activities of Machines Bull and Olivetti Data Processing with those of the GE Computer Department. He went to President Borch and Chairman Phillipe for permission to go outside the company to find such a man.

"You know," said Fred Borch. "I've heard good things about Lou Rader, who left the company a few years ago and went to UNIVAC as president. He apparently turned the company around. I happen to know his wife is quite unhappy in Connecticut. He might be approachable."

Dr. Lou Rader had joined the General Electric Company in 1938 on completion of his doctorate in electrical engineering at California Institute of Technology. He left GE briefly at the end of World War II to become chairman of the Department of Electrical Engineering at Illinois Institute of Technology and returned to GE in 1947 as an engineering manager. In 1953 he became general manager of the Specialty Control Department, then a part of the company's Apparatus Division. In 1959, frustrated by the appointment of Harold Strickland as vice president and general manager of the Industrial Electronics Division—a position which logic dictated should have gone to Rader—he left GE a second time to become vice president and member of the board of directors of International Telephone and Telegraph Company. Alarmed at some of the legally risky actions of ITT chairman Hal Geneen, he left to become president of the UNIVAC Division of Sperry Rand Corporation. Over a two-year period he had succeeded in bringing UNIVAC out of the red; this accomplishment was pretty well known around the New York business community.

While Rader's career was blossoming at UNIVAC, his personal and family life were suffering. His home in Darien, Connecticut, was in an upscale town with a population of wealthy, society conscious, hard-drinking, and generally high-rolling executives and their families. The atmosphere was not a healthy one for the Rader children, and both parents were unhappy with the corporate lifestyle.[85]

One day Rader received a telephone call from Hersh Cross. "How are you finding life at UNIVAC?"

"First rate," said Rader. "It's a fine company, and we've made real progress pulling it out of the red."

"Great. And how's the family?"

"Fine. Though we all miss our old home in Virginia."

"Well," said Cross, "we wondered if you might be interested in discussing a possible return to GE."

"I'm always willing to talk," said Rader.

"Then how about getting together for dinner Wednesday with Phillipe, Borch, and myself?"

"Fine. Just let me check my calendar." Wednesday's just two days away, mused Rader, and Cross is bringing the chairman and president into the act. They must be in a big hurry. "Yes, I can make it," he said.

The four men met for dinner in a private dining room at Borch's club. After the amenities had been attended to, and during the second martini, Cross made his proposal.

"We'd like you to return to GE as vice president and general manager of the Industrial Electronics Division. I've been acting as general manager ever since Harold Strickland decided to leave the company to join General Signal. I've since enlarged the division to include two important acquisitions in Europe, so we badly need an experienced computer executive to integrate the businesses. The position is yours if you want it."

"I'm willing to listen," replied Rader.

The conversation then turned into a series of negotiations concerning salary, bonuses, stock options, moving expenses, executive prerogatives, and the like. Rader, who had complete authority to plan and fire and hire at UNIVAC, asked if he would have the same authority at GE.

"No problem," said Cross. "Of course there's the usual group-level oversight, but you'll have no problem with me if you meet your business plan." Borch and Phillipe nodded agreement.

"I have one condition I must insist on if I'm to return to GE," said Rader. "I must have my office in Virginia."

"That's fine," said Phillipe. "Name a city."

"I'll pick Charlottesville for my office and Waynesboro for my home."

"It's a deal," said Cross. "By the way, there's some urgency because we're very close to signing the final papers for the Machines Bull and Olivetti acquisitions. The business plan's all set, but I'm sure you'll want to review the situation firsthand before signing the contracts."

They shook hands all around, but nothing was reduced to paper. Rader was later to regret this omission.[86]

In Paris to sign the final papers for the acquisition, Rader found he was expected to produce his "management team" as promised by Hersh Cross. In particular, the new companies lacked a president (who had to be French for legal reasons, though without any real authority) and a direceur general who would actually run the company in accordance with GE's management contract. Rader was also met with the news that 35 percent of Bull's output had traditionally been for the French government but De Gaulle had abruptly shut this off because of his dislike of Americans.

Rader, believing he had been "had" by Cross, returned to Charlottesville quite upset but determined to resolve the immediate Bull dilemma. It took three months to find a technically qualified general manager who knew the GE way of doing things, but Rader finally decided on Brainard Fancher, manager of GE's Apollo Support Division. Rader was unable to get constructive help from 570, so he finally went to an outside consulting company (McKinsey & Co.) to find a French executive for president and to advise him on the subject of appropriate salary and other benefits. This eventually resulted in the hiring of Henri Desbrueres, former chairman of Air France and president of SNECMA, the French jet-engine company. This turned out to be an excellent choice because Desbrueres—though not participating in the business—could interface with De Gaulle, the unions, and the network of French executives. Thus, in 1964, began the expensive saga of GE and Machines Bull.

The newsletter announcing the appointment of Lou Rader[87] as vice president and general manager of the Industrial Electronics Division was received with cautious optimism by the members of the Computer Department in Phoenix. Rader had a reputation as a top-grade technical man with a practical approach to the solution of business problems. Van Aken, in particular, hoped Hersh Cross would cease his habit of mandating personnel changes within the Computer Department. He considered Cross a fast-thinking, intelligent person, but compelled to show others how smart he was; he often belittled the intelligence of those reporting to him with demeaning and caustic remarks and, as a result, was not an effective manager. Van Aken recalled the time, a few months before, when Cross asked his opinion about implementing the possible Machines Bull acquisition. Van Aken had replied that GE should not do so because the company didn't have the products, manpower, or experience to coordinate this type of endeavor.

Cross replied, "Van Aken, I don't care what you think. I don't need your advice. This proposed acquisition is a great opportunity for General Electric."[88] Van Aken wondered whether Lou Rader would have any better luck in his dealings with Cross.

The GE 600 project had been underway for about a year when John Couleur developed what was to be known as the translation lookaside buffer (TLB),[89] the first practical method of implementing paged virtual memory. About a month later, the leaders of MIT's Project MAC swung through Phoenix on a search for a platform for the Project MAC time-sharing system (MULTICS). The group from MIT presented their ideas on a computer architecture for supporting time sharing, and it

GE-645 SYSTEM

The GE 645 computer replaced IBM equipment at MIT as the major element in the so-called MULTICS time-sharing network, a new generation in scientific time sharing. The 645, far more complex than the 625, contained a number of advanced features not required for the commercial computer market. It was produced in small quantities for MIT and Bell Telephone Lab and became a workhorse in the development of time-sharing concepts and techniques.

became apparent that the use of paging was the only way their concept could be made to work. Couleur showed them the TLB and explained how it would interact with their concept of segmentation. MIT liked the idea, and GE agreed to modify the 600 design to include paging and segmentation, with MIT/ARPA paying for the development. Bell Labs, MIT's other partner in Project MAC, liked the new system and ordered several. This version of the GE 600 series was known as the GE 645.

The news of GE's selection as the computer supplier for the prestigious Project MAC, and the purchase of several systems by Bell Labs, electrified the world of large-computer users.[90] This defection of two of IBM's most influential customers had a major impact on the market. Many of these organizations were unhappy with the 32-bit word length and other features of the recently announced but not yet delivered IBM 360 series. Before the first GE 600 had been shipped, GE received letters of intent from more than half of the IBM 7090 users in the United States.

It appeared that the gamble to proceed with the GE 600, regardless of incompatibility with the Mosaic family, had been a rousing success. The September 1964 issue of *Datamation* included the following paragraphs:

Of the announced machines, GE's 600 series looks like the hottest. We understand that 26 machines have been allocated on the basis of letters of intent, including

GENERAL ELECTRIC NEWS

PHOENIX, ARIZONA   February 9, 1968

More Than 100 Persons Using System Simultaneously

GE-625 Reaches Time-Sharing Milestone At Dartmouth

A significant milestone was reached recently at the Kiewit Computation Center on the Dartmouth College campus. More than 100 persons successfully used a GE-625 computer system simultaneously.

This is believed to be a world's record for time-sharing computers, Dartmouth College and GE. The number of simultaneous users exceeded 100 for a period of nearly an hour. Most requests received responses within 10 seconds, and the peak load for the GE-625 was 113.

At the peak time, the computer system was serving 47 Dartmouth faculty members and

students, 20 students from secondary schools in the northern New England region and 46 customers of the General Electric Information Service Department located in the Boston, New York and Washington, D. C., areas.

The computer is connected by ordinary telephone lines with GE computer terminals at the remote locations.

Dr. John G. Kemeny, Dartmouth mathmetics professor and a pioneer in the time-sharing development, described the event as "a major breakthrough which opens up an exciting future for the educational use of computers."

He said that this accomplishment "gave dramatic testimony to the mutually beneficial results which can be achieved through cooperation between a major industry and an educational institution."

Each user was able to type a program into his individual terminal (a teletypewriter) and have his request for data processing serviced almost instantly by the GE-625 on the Dartmouth campus.

Dr. Kemeny noted that Dartmouth's time-sharing network now enables 50 students to use the computer at the same time. He expects this to grow to 200

or more users as a result of developments now under way.

Moreover, the students learn quickly, he reported. They "start writing their own computer programs in a simple language called BASIC after just two one-hour lectures." BASIC is an easy-to-understand computer language developed at Dartmouth to enable almost everyone to learn to use a computer, he stated. Professor Kemeny added that routine class exercises at Dartmouth include the use of a computer in such problems as plotting a rocket's course to the moon.

GE's 225 computer, combined with the GE Datanet 30 communications processor, was combined with Dartmouth's BASIC computer language to launch the world's first interactive time-sharing net work. The GE 625, some years later, provided a major expansion of this capability.

Project MAC (see below). Other systems seem headed for ASEA, a Swedish organization, and several GE departments. Martin, NASA, and a couple of other big scientific users are leaning toward 600s; one company is thinking of ordering 8 of them. One tentative GE order knocked a man out of the SHARE presidential race, won, incidentally, by Jim Babcock of RAND.

At Project MAC, king of the time-sharing research efforts, a decision has been reached on the next round of gear. The winner and new champion—despite stiff IBM in-fighting—GE, with a modified 635, which will include two processors, 131K of core, beaucoup communication lines (for initial configuration of 64 on-line consoles), plus disk files and drums.

At IBM headquarters, IBM brass were so shaken by the Project MAC loss that they slashed 360 prices and rushed the development of associative memory for communications, multiprogramming, and multiprocessing. For the first time, IBM was forced to bring out a product before IBM wanted to.

Another important high point was also reached in 1964. The November issue of the *Dartmouth Alumni Magazine* announced that a new breakthrough in computer technology, "time sharing," combined with the BASIC computer language, had ushered in a new era in which computers could serve the needs of many users simultaneously regardless of their physical locations. As many as 20 students and faculty members were using the GE 265 time-shared computer simultaneously from different points on the campus, and there was no practical limit seen for the time-sharing technique.

In some ways, this was a more significant event than the GE 600 because it launched the computer time-sharing industry, on-line database services, and many related corporate and service bureau applications. (The 25th anniversary issue of *IEEE Spectrum*, the official organ of the Institute of Electrical and Electronic Engineers, listed the most salient events, inventions, discoveries, successes, and triumphs of man over matter during the quarter century; there, sharing space with coverage of the transistor, the satellite, and the integrated circuit was the story of Dartmouth, Datanet 30 and GE 235, and GE's pioneering commercial time-sharing service.) But GE's management, excited by the apparent success of the GE 600, was slow to exploit the technical and marketing lead that had been created in the commercial time-sharing market by the more modest GE 265.

CHAPTER 30
TIME SHARING—CHALLENGE TO IBM

GE's advances in time sharing, combined with the vote of confidence from MIT and Bell Labs, opened up new market opportunities within the booming aerospace industry—dominated almost exclusively by IBM computers. One key customer in this category was Martin-Marietta, with headquarters in Baltimore and major facilities in Denver (devoted primarily to the huge Titan missile program).

Since 1961, Don Klee had been the GE Computer Department representative in Denver. He graduated magna cum laude with a degree in accounting from Notre Dame and joined GE after World War II, assigned to the company's Business Training Program, which he later headed up. Like George Snively, he had been located at Electronics Park where he was given a number of assignments, including one in which he worked closely with Bob Sheeley, who, some years later, was to become manager of sales of the Computer Department.

It happened that GE's Hotpoint Division had a position open as operations manager in Denver, a very desirable location from Klee's point of view. He transferred to Hotpoint in 1958, only to discover at a later date that Hotpoint planned to phase out this particular facility. This discovery coincided with an advertisement in the Wall Street Journal to the effect that the GE Computer Department planned to establish ten new district offices and was looking for candidates. When he saw the ad, Klee immediately put in a call to Sheeley in Phoenix.

"Hi, Bob, this is Don Klee. How's life in the desert?"

"Love it, Don. This is really God's country. How's life with you?"

"I love Denver, but Hotpoint is closing down here. I just saw your ad in the Wall Street Journal. Is Denver on your list?"

"It sure is," said Sheeley, "and you're the new district manager! We've already sold an ERMA system to the First National Bank of Denver. It's basically the same as the systems we have in the Bank of America, but we call it the GE 210. It's a slick installation that would give you something to demonstrate to prospective customers. Are you interested in the job?"

"Bob, I haven't seen you in three years; you don't know if I can hack it."

"Baloney, Don. I check you out every time I visit 570. Your timing couldn't be better. We've developed a new sales training course that starts up the first of the year. We call the trainees astronauts to jazz up the program. If you can be on board on time, you can be a member of the first astronaut contingent. It's a good way to get up to date on our new product line, including the GE 225, and to learn the ground rules of the computer leasing business. I'll get you and your family an apartment here where the astronauts stay. How about it?"

"We'll be there with bells on and whistles blowing."

The Klee family ended up spending a year in Phoenix, where Don finished the training and then worked for Vern Schatz in headquarters sales. In 1961, Klee returned to Denver as district manager. He had one big account, the First National Bank of Denver, and his sights were set on Martin-Marietta, the biggest computer user in the area. He decided to start as near the top as possible and made an appointment with John Hopko, manager of data processing.

Klee explained that he had just taken over as the representative of the GE Computer Department in the Denver area and was hopeful of obtaining some of Martin-Marietta's business.[91]

Hopko's smile was on the condescending side. "I'm sorry, Mr. Klee, but we're quite satisfied with IBM equipment and service. We have a tremendous investment in programming, both for business data processing in accounting and scientific calculations in engineering, so the prospect of changing vendors is pretty remote. Bud Feely, who runs the engineering computers, is out of town, but you can leave a note with his secretary if you like."

Hopko's reaction was not surprising. The man was obviously an IBM convert who thought GE should stick to its light bulbs and motors. "They tell me GE is the largest computer user in the country," he remarked, "and it's practically all IBM. Come back and see me when your own company switches to GE computers."

Hopko's remark was heard over and over by every GE salesman in every part of the country—almost word for word.

Not discouraged, Klee finally made contact with Feely in engineering.[92] Feely had three IBM 7094s and four IBM 1401s in his large data-processing center. Klee discovered that the mainframes in both accounting and engineering produced magtape output that was then processed to printers using the 1401s. Here was a possible application for the GE 225. He knew the 1401s were on the verge of obsolescence, particularly in terms of processing speed, and he was pretty sure one 225 could handle the load of three 1401s. After consulting with Arnold Spielberg and Bill Bridge, he developed a proposal to replace three 1401s with one 225 at GE's normal rental rate.

Klee was overjoyed to get a foot in the door and to find someone in a position of authority who was not wedded to IBM. As it happened, the GE 225 worked out fine both in terms of performance and reliability. As time went on, Martin-Marietta's data-processing load increased, and, by 1964, a GE 415 was installed to replace the 225 in the Engineering Department. The door had opened a bit wider.

As 1964 went on, Martin-Marietta's Titan program generated an ever-increasing data-processing load. Dick Webber, director of administration, had planned on replacing the large IBM mainframes with the promised IBM System/360, with its higher speed and greater capacity. IBM had previously announced six months for delivery but ran into serious hardware and software problems. Suddenly the delivery promise shot up to 24 months, causing a panic within the aerospace industry and opening up the Martin-Marietta window a little wider still. Faced with a computer crisis, Webber had no choice but to obtain additional 7094 capacity, a distasteful solution because of the 7094's approaching obsolescence.

While in Phoenix in 1964 testing their new programs for the GE 415, the Martin-Marietta group was approached by Gene Scott of headquarters sales on behalf of the new GE 600. A presentation was arranged, attended by Scott, Don Klee, Ed Vance, and John Couleur, and the visitors came away from the meeting and subsequent meetings extremely impressed with the concept. The Martin-Marietta Denver Division then proceeded to try to win over the Orlando and Baltimore divisions of their company to the GE 600.

With the Martin-Marietta Denver Division apparently sold on the GE 600, the possibility of the first sale of the GE 600, a breakthrough into the large (and wealthy) aerospace industry, and the possibility of unfastening IBM's stranglehold in the industry, it seemed to Klee that everyone at the GE Computer Department wanted to get involved. This could (and did) become the largest order since ERMA, and the commissions were potentially enormous.

It was at this time, in early 1965, that the GE Computer Department was reeling from the replacement of Lacy Goosetree as marketing manager, Bob Sheeley as sales manager, and (ultimately) the replacement of three of the four regional sales managers and 15 of the 19 district sales managers. Vern Cooper established a Martin-Marietta national sales team headed by Cliff Sink, the ex-IBM eastern regional sales manager. Klee was partially bypassed by this move, and it was to have serious repercussions in the future.

Despite these internal problems, the development of a leasing proposal for Martin-Marietta went steadily forward. There were still a number of hardware bugs to overcome, but John Couleur was confident they could be cleaned up within 18 months. The main concern was the new GECOS software being developed by a GE team headed by Ed Vance. This new and potentially powerful operating system was essential to permitting the GE 600 to provide simultaneous processing of both administrative and scientific data.[93]

When Vance was questioned by Klee concerning the status of GECOS, his answer was not comforting. "Well, we had to abandon GECOS I. We tried to hang too many applications on it, and it grew too cumbersome to use in the real world. We're now working on GECOS II, and it should be available in about 18 months."

"What happens if GECOS is delayed even further?" asked Klee. "We can't deliver computers to Martin-Marietta without an operating system."

"No sweat," said Vance. "We've already developed a simulator that, with a little tweaking, can run all the 7094 programs on the 600. It obviously won't have all the features of GECOS, but it should accomplish Martin-Marietta's present mission of increasing speed and accuracy."

"Hey, that's great. That's exactly what they need. Feely's been worrying about the cost and time involved in converting his existing programs to fit a different operating system. This way he can put the 600 in operation the minute it's installed and convert to GECOS at his leisure."

Feely was pleased with the proposal ultimately submitted by GE. "Your proposal's the only one with a 7094 simulator," he told Klee. "and the Engineering Department is definitely in your corner. I'll have to warn you, though, that our company is full of IBM people, and the details of your proposal will almost certainly be leaked to IBM. They won't take this lying down."

Sure enough, IBM came back a few days later with a 17-month delivery promise for the System/360, down miraculously from 24 months. At this point the Computer Department sales group took over the negotiation, thus beginning an almost unbelievable series of concessions to Martin-Marietta on the part of both IBM and GE. Both parties were aware this was a make-or-break occasion in terms of GE's attempt to invade IBM's mainframe territory. Ultimately, Vern Cooper and Van Aken agreed to a delivery schedule of 7 months!

Klee shuddered when he heard the news. There was no conceivable way the schedule could be met, and he was told by Feely that Martin-Marietta had negotiated severe financial penalties if the equipment didn't work as specified. He knew he'd be the fall guy.

There were also pitched battles within Martin-Marietta before a final decision was reached in favor of GE. The IBM faction predicted disaster if a new and untried supplier of mainframes should be introduced into the complex workings of Martin-Marietta. Bud Feely countered by outlining the excellent experience he had with the GE 225 and GE 415. Feely finally won the day, and a lease contract was negotiated with General Electric.

Soon after this, a story was published in a *Los Angeles* trade paper revealing IBM's delivery schedule juggling. One early morning, Dick Webber received a call from Buck Rogers, IBM's West Coast regional manager and star salesman.[94]

"Yes, Mr. Rogers."

"I have to tell you that IBM will never again do business with Martin-Marietta if your company can't keep our confidential information private!"

Feely later discussed this incident with Klee. "You know, Don, I came close to losing my job over this. The funny thing is that IBM hasn't taken any equipment out. They're not about to give up any rental income while waiting for the GE 600s to arrive."

The prospective loss of Martin-Marietta's business sent waves throughout IBM. For the first time, Big Blue faced a real threat from the one company with the financial and technical strength to challenge their domination of the computer industry. The word went out from headquarters, "Don't let it happen again."

The Los Angeles area spawned the country's largest concentration of what were called aerospace companies. One group consisted of pre-war aircraft companies, such as Douglas, Lockheed, Northrop, and Ryan—greatly enlarged due to meeting World War II production volumes and actively seeking large system contracts for advanced aircraft, guided missiles, and satellites. Another group consisted of electronics companies such as Thompson Ramo Wooldridge (TRW), General Dynamics, and Hughes Aircraft (an aircraft company in name only). These companies, as well as their suppliers, were prodigious computer users.

One of the GE Computer Department salesmen beating at the doors of this complex group of potential customers was Paul Shapiro of the Los Angeles office. He joined GE in 1969 after receiving his bachelor's degree in marketing management and went directly into GE's Marketing Training Course. After a number of assignments he was assigned to the Computer Department as a member of the first astronaut training course, which he helped to organize. In 1961 he was transferred to the Los Angeles district office to sell computers to the aerospace industry.[95] Shapiro's most important and potentially most difficult target was Hughes Aircraft, looming like a giant over Inglewood—world leader in military electronics.

Like Martin-Marietta, Hughes was strictly an IBM shop, both on the business side and on the engineering-scientific side. When Shapiro first approached Hughes, he was told that the company had never had any computers but those from Big Blue. Hughes was the showplace for IBM in the Los Angeles area, and practically every piece of equipment made by IBM was to be found somewhere in the sprawling Inglewood facility.[96]

Despite the unpromising reception, Shapiro continued to call upon Hughes at regular intervals and to furnish technical bulletin and sales literature. He found little apparent interest in the GE 225, and even the novel time-sharing version using the Datanet 30 failed to interest the EDP people of Hughes. Shapiro had identified a couple of good applications for the time-sharing version, but the absence of the IBM logo on the equipment appeared to be an insuperable barrier.

Two events took place in 1964 that signaled a possible breakthrough at Hughes. First, Hughes hired a retired air force officer by the name of Dr. Gale (Buck) Cleven.[97] An astrophysicist by education, Cleven's last military post had been the Pentagon where he was responsible for the entire EDP operation of this massive facility. Most of the computer equipment at the Pentagon was IBM, so no one expected any fireworks when he took over at Hughes. In fact, his first step was to investigate the $12 million in annual rental for IBM equipment, to cancel pending orders for another $2 million, and to return excess equipment with some $4 million in annual rental. This did not endear him to Big Blue.

At that time, Hughes had two of IBM's biggest and fastest computers—two 7094s to be upgraded to 360s when available. The GE 635 was calculated to have the data-processing capacity of at least two 7094s as well as the time-sharing capability. Paul Shapiro and the rest of the local GE team, supplemented by such as John Couleur from Phoenix, had made presentations to every level in Hughes, aided by Buck Cleven who sensed the opportunity to "make a difference at Hughes."[98] IBM made light of the GE claims at the beginning, but, as 1964 drew to a close, the local office of IBM realized they were in a real dog fight.

In the spring of 1965, Cleven called for both IBM and GE to submit formal proposals for replacing all existing equipment and upgrading the capability of the company's EDP network. His plan was to conduct a 24-month competition between the 635 and the 360, at the end of which time the loser would withdraw all equipment. During the time it took to deliver the competing systems and bring them fully on line, Hughes would continue to lease the 7094s. The 360, during the trial period, would be located in financial data processing, and the 635 would be assigned to engineering and scientific data processing.

Paul Shapiro was delighted with the prospect of a head-to-head match between IBM's 360 and GE's 635, but he could not offer a long-term lease to Hughes if the equipment might be returned at the end of 24 months. He knew GE's conservative accounting system would never countenance a monthly rental-use agreement for a computer of this magnitude, particularly in view of the high-risk nature of the competition. At his wit's end, he called George Snively in Phoenix.[99]

"George, we've got IBM on the run for once. Hughes is ready to run a two-year competition between our 635 and a version of the 360 that IBM has advertised but really doesn't exist. We have a good chance to displace them if we can come up with a responsive proposal for the test program. It doesn't fit the standard GE pattern, and I really need your help."

"You've got it, Paul. I'm tied up tomorrow, but I'll be on your doorstep by noon the next day if you can set up a meeting with Dr. Cleven."

True to his word, Snively showed up at the Computer Department's Los Angeles office two days later. The subsequent meeting with Cleven persuaded him he'd have to structure something unusual to meet Hughes' requirements.

"It's a toughie," he told Shapiro, "but I have the glimmerings of a plan. I'll get back to you in a couple of days, after I've had a chance to talk over the situation with Don Benscotter."

Don Benscotter was a leasing specialist, a principal in Lease Financing Corporation, an organization that had provided third-party leases to a number of customers of the GE Computer Department—leases at rates and with conditions not possible under GE's conservative policies. Benscotter had an uncanny ability to move a transaction up through an organization. He would often meet, as planned, with the manager of finance in the morning and by afternoon would be taken to meet the treasurer, the president, and others. This capability was to prove quite important at Hughes Aircraft. He had previously helped out Snively by negotiating an arrangement whereby Hughes was able to exercise the purchase option on one of the 7094s and arrange for future disposition on a profitable basis. In the process, he had gotten close to John Couterie, Hughes' treasurer, and had gone on to finance a number of other transactions. He was a powerful ally.

Snively put in a call to Benscotter and explained the nature of the 360-635 competition and the problem presented by the possible cancellation. "My plan, Don, is to propose a sale with an option to rent. We'll sell the 635 to Hughes with an option to return it, if we lose the contest, during the 24th to 27th month. If they exercise the option, we'll refund the purchase price plus the monthly maintenance paid less the rental that would have been charged during the period. Do you think LFC could handle such a thing as a termination provision in a lease?"

"I'm sure we could," said Benscotter. "Tell you what, George. I'm having dinner with Doc Cleven tomorrow night. He's always after me to figure out how Hughes can get the Investment Tax Credit on some of these large deals, and I'll mention the type of plan you're suggesting."

"Terrific. Don't tell him the plan came from me. Maybe if you tell him you don't know whether GE will go along with it, he'll be particularly receptive."

"You've got it, George."

The next day, Snively received a call from Doc Cleven urging him to come to Los Angeles as soon as possible. He caught the 11 a.m. flight the next day and was met at the airport by Cleven. At lunch, Cleven was noncommital but did say, "You'll find out when we get to the office, and I'm paying for lunch today—I'm selling *you* this time!" Snively got the drift.

One wall of Cleven's office was covered by a schoolroom-size blackboard that was soon covered with numbers as he proceeded to sell "his idea": Hughes Aircraft was to get the Investment Tax Credit and a reduced rental during the initial 24 months and for the following five years of a seven-year net lease should they elect to keep the 635.

"Even if GE should lose out and the equipment is returned, GE would have had use of the purchase monies for the two years," said Cleven, "we would have paid the personal property tax and insurance, and GE would have received 24 months rental."

"This is a pretty wild idea, but it's beginning to make sense to me," said Snively. "I'll do my best to sell it to my boss."

Snively returned to Phoenix, knowing in advance that his own proposal would be approved. However, he waited two days before calling Cleven, telling him he had obtained management approval except that GE couldn't grant the option without some value being received for it. He suggested that 1 percent of the purchase price be added to the rent, which, spread over seven years, would cause an almost negligible increase in rental rate. After some initial grousing, Cleven agreed and the deal was closed.[100]

From that point on, the main subject of concern was the competitive evaluation between IBM and GE.[101] Toward the end, word leaked out that Hughes was definitely leaning in GE's favor. Buck Rogers, at this point IBM's top marketing executive, roared into Hughes with flags flying and guns blazing. He accused Cleven of taking bribes from GE and kickbacks from Lease Financing Corporation and numerous other sins.[102]

Cleven was well prepared, thanks to conversations he had had with Howard Hall, an attorney who appeared on no organizational charts but reported directly to Howard Hughes. Hall had supplied Cleven with specific language to relay to Buck Rogers concerning his notes on IBM's activities and transactions and his contemplation of possible legal action against IBM for defamation of character and a number of other charges. (The meeting between Cleven and Buck Rogers became the subject of legend within Hughes and would reverberate around the corridors of GE and IBM for years to come—long after Rogers had ascended to the presidency of IBM.)

The two men started out on friendly terms, but soon degenerated into accusations and counter-accusations.

Finally, Rogers slammed a fist on the conference table. "Look here, Mr. Cleven. I don't give a damn about General Electric. They don't know a thing about the computer business. There's only one company capable of handling the computer load of an outfit like Hughes Aircraft, and that's IBM. I'll take this all the way to Howard Hughes if I have to, and don't be surprised if this mess costs you your job."

Cleven smiled and pushed a button on his intercom. "Security," was the immediate response.

"Code 1," said Cleven. Shortly two large men in security police uniforms entered the office.

"Please escort Mr. Rogers off Hughes Aircraft property," said Cleven.

Rogers, red faced and blustering, found himself lifted gently but firmly from his chair and hurried out of the building in front of an amused group of employees. GE's Paul Shapiro was a happy observer.[103]

Shortly thereafter, Hughes Aircraft announced the award to GE of a long-term lease contract for two GE 635 computer systems to replace the existing IBM equipment.

The victory at Hughes was the result of a concerted team effort in which the resources of GE and its leasing consultant were brought to bear to defeat IBM. Employed properly, they could be, and were, awesome. Unfortunately, computers still seemed to be only a side issue at higher levels of GE. As Curt Hare, Seattle district manager would discover, GE top management often withheld these resources from its Computer Department.[104]

Hare, while a member of the Los Angeles district office, was the account manager who had sold a dual processor GE 635 system to Space Technology Laboratories (a spinoff of TRW). This accomplishment was responsible for his promotion to manager of the Seattle district. There, he and his team did quite well in selling Weyerhauser, the local banks, and several other accounts, but they were unable to break into Boeing, the most important computer user in the area. Hare finally decided to call for executive help in arranging a channel to Boeing executives. He sent a request letter up through the formal chain of command as required by GE policy. Not getting an answer after a long period of waiting, he kept wondering when, if ever, he was going to get an executive visit.

One day a friend, the district manager for the Industrial Products Division, who sold millions of dollars of products to Boeing every year, invited Hare to a meeting. After making him take a vow of secrecy, his friend showed Hare a copy of his request letter on which several handwritten notes had been scribbled as it passed up and down the chain of command. They essentially said, "We do not want to foul up our excellent relations and business volume at Boeing by helping those computer guys sell their equipment."[105]

The situation at Boeing was not an isolated incident. Many of GE's very large customers—utilities, aircraft, government, automobile, construction, and so on—made purchases in the $100 million range. GE's decentralization policy, combined with its procedure of rating department general managers on the basis of departmental financial performance, was not calculated to assist one of the company's new businesses to penetrate a customer area in which one of the mature businesses held a dominant position. It was "sink or swim, but don't make waves in my pond." As a typical example, the Computer Department was told, "Hands off Florida Light and Power Company lest computer sales efforts screw up an impending $50 million turbine offer!"

Most Computer Department managers and technical people recognized these problems as a fact of life at General Electric, and it was generally agreed the advantages outweighed the disadvantages. The GE operating components were probably the best in the world with respect to the application of computers in industrial information systems and engineering computations. Many of the application system packages available to the Computer Department came from internal GE operations. For example, the Integrated Data Store system (IDS) came from Large Transformer in Pittsfield and was the mainstay database management system for the GE 200, 400, and 600 computers. Also, conversion tools between these incompatible computer series often came from operating groups and associated computing centers. There were problems in establishing bridges between GE users and the Computer Department, and, to the extent such bridges were established, they had a substantial impact on sales. It was always an advantage to take a customer to a site that had a problem similar to his own and show him there were ways of reaching a solution and that generic tools would be available to him.

Often people at the working level within GE were more willing to help the Computer Department than were their superiors who had been imbued with the philosophy of Harold Smiddy that every component was an independent business and basically had no responsibility for the welfare of other components. A prime example was the Aircraft Gas Turbine Department (AGT) in Evendale, Ohio, which operated large Computer Centers both in Evendale and in its Lynn Works. Actually, the first replacement of a large IBM computer by a GE 600 had taken place in Lynn. Jim Richter, in charge of computer services for AGT, had supervised the development of FORTRAN for the GE 600 and, together with Bob Claussen of the Computer Department, had developed a thruput ratio that could be used to compare the 600 with IBM's 7094.[106] The test to establish the ratio (or "Richter" as it became known) consisted of running a full shift of actual IBM 7094 workload through the 600 and comparing the times to complete the process. A ratio, or "Richter," of 1.76 was established, which turned out to be an extremely useful selling tool. (It also turned out to be an Achilles' heel at Space Technologies Laboratory where a GE 635 was returned because the Richter ratio did not meet the 1.76 target in that company's application!)

AGT also contributed a number of key personnel to the Computer Department, including Jim Richter, who eventually moved to Phoenix. When he arrived in

Ray Barclay uses a scale model of the GE 400 computer to explain details of the system to representatives of GE Bull. The GE 400 and, later, the GE 600 would be manufactured at Bull's Angers plant for the European market.

Phoenix, the GE 400 was in serious software trouble. Its four operating systems (magtape, disk, time sharing, and direct access) were not completely developed, and the field perception of the 400 was that of unreliability and missed commitments. The French were particularly unhappy because the main thrust of Machines Bull at that time was the 400. Richter, together with Greg Williams (another transplant from AGT), were able to improve the software reliability to the point where even the French were satisfied. Eventually, with the help of Bob Bemer from Machines Bull, the 400 could do floating point work faster than the IBM 360/Mod 44 scientific system.

Despite these welcome occasions of support from the working level, there seemed to be no driving force at corporate level to make the computer business a resounding success. There was still a proliferation of IBM mainframes and IBM-trained EDP managers throughout the company. The wait-and-see attitude at corporate level was galling to those in Phoenix who recognized the window of opportunity opened by the GE 600. It was hoped that the new division vice president would effectively promote integration of the Computer Department's product line throughout General Electric while the window was still open.

CHAPTER 31
PROBLEMS AND TRIUMPHS

No sooner had Lou Rader established his office in Charlottesville and put some initial order into the Machines Bull program than he was approached by Hershner Cross. They met in late 1964.

"Lou," said Cross, "I've decided that, since the future of your division depends so much on solving problems of the Computer Department, you should move your headquarters to Phoenix and take over there. I'll put Lou Wengert in charge of specialty control, industry control, communications products, and Lynn Instruments."[107]

Rader was flabbergast. "I'm sorry, Hersh, but that's not the basis on which I agreed to return to GE. You'll recall that both Borch and Phillipe joined us in shaking hands on the deal."

"Don't tell me you're going to act like a company lawyer," grumbled Cross. "All they need out there is someone with some common sense to go out and solve their software problems."

"I wouldn't have the slightest idea how to solve any software problems," replied Rader. "What I do know how to do is to work with Van Aken and his people to make sure the fundamentals, such as product service, are being handled properly and that cost-reduction programs are being instituted to make the products profitable. The Computer Department has top-notch engineering, manufacturing, and marketing people, and I believe we need to leave them in their jobs long enough to understand the computer industry, which is unlike anything they teach in Crotonville. I plan to visit Phoenix frequently and give them all the help I can, but I can't and won't move to Phoenix and leave the rest of the division in the hands of a nice guy like Wengert who knows the motor business but never even heard of computers."

"Listen, Rader. I don't care what you ivory tower scientists say. Computers are nothing but products, and an experienced professional manager can make money from the business. I could do it myself if I had the time."

The argument raged for two hours, but Rader stood firm on his refusal to move to Phoenix. He knew he had made an enemy of his boss, though he had no inkling of the revenge that Cross would take to punish Rader for his refusal to submit to his will.

Cross was right about one thing. There were troubles aplenty in Phoenix during 1965; most of them related to the GE 600 program. Like all new computer system introductions of the day, hardware problems were inevitable. In addition, the

GECOS software was pushing the state of the art and had more severe problems. As it happened, the IBM 360 software was encountering similar problems. One customer, who had taken early delivery on five of the early systems, summed up the software status with the statement, "GECOS is much better than the IBM 360 operating system, and far ahead of the 360 operating system. You have problems, but you know what they are and how to fix them. You are coming out of the woods, and IBM is just beginning to find out what their software problems are."[108]

Despite these reassuring words, most of the large-system users kept the pressure on the Computer Department by making their needs and complaints at GE executive office level, as did IBM salesmen who had long-time relations with GE. Van Aken became increasingly upset, particularly when he heard of Computer Department problems from Hersh Cross's office before he heard from his own people.

The worst hardware problem with the 600 was the tape transport.[109] Van Aken had established a Peripheral Products Operation under Bob Wooley, a fine engineer who had been project manager for the NCR 304 computer. In parallel, a GE-owned plant in Oklahoma City had become surplus and would become the production facility for peripheral products: tape transports, printers, card readers, disk files, and the like. This was a highly desirable program because the cost of peripherals had become a significant portion of the overall cost of the computer system. In addition, there were not many independent suppliers of peripherals as of 1965, and the Computer Department needed to establish its own competence.

The tape transport used for the 600 was a design that had been bought from DECCA in England. Unfortunately, it turned out to be a disaster. It could not read tapes reliably and destroyed tapes in the process of reading and writing them. The Peripheral Products Operation insisted there was nothing wrong with the DECCA mechanism—that it only required a little tweaking from time to time. Unfortunately, the time between required "tweaks" was so short that the tape transports quickly became the Achilles' heel of the 600 program.

John Couleur was at his wit's end. He pleaded with Van Aken to purchase admittedly more expensive units from the outside, but the Peripheral Products Operation persuaded him to stick by their product. They won the internal policy battle, and for several months design engineers were diverted to customer locations where they forlornly tweaked away.

It was at times like this that the marketing organization showed its true mettle. One of IBM's secrets of success was the technique of holding the customer's hand through periods—often lengthy—when a new computer model was first installed. There were *always* problems at that stage of development of the computer industry, and most computer users accepted them as a matter of course. Lacy Goosetree and Bob Sheeley had become expert at this type of hand holding, and had developed a team approach with George Snively who was able to negotiate what they termed "non-green" dollar concessions such as delayed starts on net lease rentals. The team was broken up when Vern Cooper was brought in to replace Goosetree, and it was fractured further when Art Aschauer was brought in from UNIVAC to replace the popular Bob Sheeley. Aschauer was likable, easy going, and competent, but he was too mild-mannered to stand up to the aggressive Vern Cooper. Cooper was inclined to dominate any conversation in which he was involved and to use his position as manager of marketing to make arbitrary pronouncements and decisions. An embarrassment before customers, he was simply the wrong man in the wrong place at the wrong time.

It was at this point in the 1965 to 1966 period that the Computer Department paid the price for accepting an unrealistically short delivery to Martin-Marietta of the GE 600s. From the time the first system arrived in Denver, GE engineers were on site trying to solve a myriad of problems with tape drives, disk drives, and printers. Charlie Lighthauser, executive vice president of Martin-Marietta, quickly read the riot act to GE.

Cooper's reaction to the complaints from Martin-Marietta did little to ease Klee's concerns. At a sales meeting in Phoenix Cooper announced, "Klee proposes we let Martin-Marietta pay rental based on the percentage of system up-time, but I'm going to make them pay 100 percent of their monthly lease payments." Klee couldn't believe his ears. There was no way a customer would pay full rental for a computer that was running only 40 percent of the time.

Some weeks later, a Martin-Marietta group came to Phoenix to discuss the issue. Cooper made a cash offer of $1.2 million for the penalties included in the lease contract for non-performance of certain benchmark software programs, providing the equipment would go on rental the following month. Feeley agreed to the arrangement after contacting Lighthauser in Martin-Marietta's Baltimore headquarters. However, he did not commit Martin-Marietta to pay for computer time when the GE 600 was inoperable.

Some time after the Phoenix meeting, a three-day session was scheduled to take place in Baltimore. Lighthauser was still unhappy with GE's progress in correcting the faults in the GE 600, and he was anxious to hold the Computer Department's feet to the fire until he was confident the program was under control.[110] Chuck Ettinger, product service manager, had been given the assignment to dig into each problem and to develop a plan to salvage the account. In parallel, George Snively worked out a series of non-green concessions totaling $3 million—to be recouped over the term of the lease. Armed with these technical and financial proposals, a group of Computer Department representatives—headed up by Vern Cooper, descended on Martin-Marietta.

The first day of this fateful meeting was spent in fact finding and attempting to determine which complaints were the most important. Ettinger and Snively got the impression the customer was not unduly troubled or surprised by the problems with such a large machine at this point in the program; indeed, Martin-Marietta had been through this sort of thing before with IBM. They just wanted to know what GE's plans were to fix the problems and to lessen the financial impact on Martin-Marietta, which, after all, had to continue to make lease payments on the IBM 7094s and 7095s until the GE 600s could pick up the load.

The second day was spent in presenting and explaining what GE was planning to do to correct the problems. Cooper was unusually quiet, referring questions to others for the most part. The technical interchange had progressed reasonably well, and there was good reason to believe an agreement would be reached.

That night at the hotel, Cooper relaxed by imbibing a bit too freely. He cornered Snively and proceeded to unburden himself. "You know, George, my ambition in life is to emulate Secretary of Defense Robert McNamara. He's one of the most powerful men in the world.[111]

"That's interesting," said Snively. "Do you plan to go into politics?"

"I don't need to," responded Cooper as he signaled the waiter for a refill. "My plan is to use GE as a stepping stone to a Cabinet post just as 'Electric' Charlie Wilson did during World War II. The Vietnam War provides just the right environment.

"You know, George," continued Cooper, "characters like Lighthauser represent the main competition. He thinks he's so smart and tough and a captain of American industry, but I'll show him."

Snively went to bed that night with a sinking feeling. The man responsible for marketing the company's products to its most important customer to date considered the customer to be a competitor!

Lighthauser opened the next day's meeting by stating Martin-Marietta was reasonably satisfied with GE's proposal to solve the existing problems. "Now," he continued, "I'd like a better understanding of the concessions to make up for the delays we'll experience."

Snively and Ettinger began to detail the proposed financial arrangements and engaged in a question-and-answer session with Lighthauser. Suddenly Cooper rose to his feet with the words, "Mr. Lighthauser, you can take your $3 million and give me back my machines!"

The meeting came to an abrupt halt. Aghast, Snively blurted out, "But, Vern, the $3 million in concessions was already approved, and they're in consideration of Martin-Marietta keeping the machines. We'll recover it all over the lease term."

"Shut up," commanded Cooper. "I know what I'm doing."

Lighthauser looked at Snively and Ettinger, shrugged his shoulders, and said, "Mr. Cooper, your offer's one I can't refuse."

Upon his return to Phoenix, Cooper reported to Hershner Cross that he had managed to get the 600s out of Martin-Marietta without a big lawsuit—for which he was commended![112]

The return of the Martin-Marietta machines was a body blow not only to the GE 600 program but also to GE's future in the computer business. Reports of the fiasco spread quickly around the industry, causing potential customers to take a wait-and-see attitude. It was not so much that GE had encountered severe technical problems with the new system—these were part of the game—but that the company had committed the sin of giving up on a customer after signing a lease contract and installing a system. Time would show the GE 600 to be too good a machine to be killed by one bad event, but customer confidence in GE's commitment to computers would never be the same.

Meanwhile, Lou Rader and Brainard Fancher were finding the Machines Bull and Olivetti acquisitions to be a costly diversion.[113] As expected, the French government opposed moves to reduce employment and unnecessary plants. An equally serious problem was GE's inability to control the direction and extent of product development to produce product line compatibility. The worst example was the overlap between the Bull Gamma 140 and the Olivetti 115. They were both small machines, hopefully to fill out GE's lower end. Meetings were held over several months to reconcile these projects to produce a single "common market computer" to be built by both companies, but local pride made it impossible to combine the efforts or even to make the two software compatible. A year after the establishment of a common software committee it was discovered, almost by accident, the committee had never met. Sacre Bleu!

Brainard Fancher decided he would have to take drastic action. In late 1965 he stopped production of the unprofitable tab equipment manufacture and terminated the Gamma 140 project in favor of the Olivetti 115—a move not calculated to win any votes of confidence from the French government. In parallel, he instituted a number of GE financial controls that greatly curbed the tendency of Bull middle management to go around his instructions. The labor unions were in a frenzy and the French government was upset, but GE ultimately had the upper hand so long as the company was furnishing the cash to keep Machines Bull afloat. By that time, Bull had cost GE over $50 million in addition to the purchase price, and GE had increased its percentage of ownership from 51 percent to 66 percent.[114]

Ray Barclay had hoped his performance in setting up the Bull Angers plant to manufacture the GE 400 would warrant an advancement to a responsible management position in the European operation. However, this was not to be despite his excellent performance rating. Late in 1965 he left GE to become manager of the Mechanical Products Division of Gates Rubber Company.

Tom O'Rourke, a BSEE from the University of Washington, joined GE in 1948 as a test engineer. After that assignment he joined GE's Welding Department as an electronics control engineer. This turned out to be a poor choice because GE decided to get out of the welding business in 1957. Fortunately, GE decided to go into the computer business at about the same time, and Tom joined the Computer Department in a marketing assignment. By early 1965 he was western regional manager with a staff of 500 people (100 salesmen, 100 customer technical support, and 300 computer maintenance, of whom 75 were for the Bank of America alone). O'Rourke was doing exceedingly well; 20 percent ahead of budget for revenue and 10 percent under expense budget for the preceding four quarters.

Ottorino Beltrami, managing director, GE Information systems Italia, supervises tests of a GE 115 computer, designed and produced in Milan. This was the only computer developed in Europe and marketed in the United States by GE.

One day O'Rourke was called into Vern Cooper's office in Phoenix. "Tom, we're expanding so fast with the 400 and 600 lines that we've concluded we need a proven computer professional to run your region. We're bringing Ted Green in from UNI-VAC because of his experience in the large-computer field."[115]

"But Vern," said the puzzled O'Rourke. "You know I've exceeded my budget every quarter. Both you and Van gave me a superior rating a few months ago and scheduled me for Crotonville."

"I'm sorry, Tom, but the decision's a firm one. We do appreciate your good performance, but we're ramping up for a much faster growth rate. Why don't you look around the department and the rest of the company and see what's available. We'll give you four months to make a change."

O'Rourke was livid, but knew he needed the four months to make an adjustment. It was bad enough to be fired, but it was adding insult to injury to be fired by the man whose only claim to fame was that he moved more electrical conduit than anyone else in GE supply—great credentials to bring to the sophisticated world of mainframe computers.

In early 1964, O'Rourke had managed a study team to advise management on the desirability of GE entering the time-shared computer service field. He became fascinated by the concept and followed the Dartmouth program closely. In fact, he had converted his Regional Customer Support Center in San Francisco into a time-sharing system for regional use as well as for the use of his customers. He was impressed with how well it had been accepted, and he made a series of presentations to Phoenix management suggesting the Computer Department go into this as a means of making GE's struggling service bureaus business profitable. His proposal didn't fly, but the concept stuck with him when he resigned in the autumn of 1965. He would cash in his GE pension plan and invest his savings to become an independent time-sharing business.

George Snively, a good friend of O'Rourke and a believer in the future of time sharing, helped him prepare the business plan and five-year projection for the new company to be called TYMSHARE. The plan was based on use of a GE 235 and a Datanet 30 (later called the GE 265) as an expanded version of the Dartmouth system. O'Rourke immediately placed an order for the lease of the computer, with delivery the first quarter of 1966.

Snively helped also by introducing O'Rourke to Tim Clausen of the Bank of America who had an SBIC (Small Business Investment Corporation) under his control. Impressed by the business plan, Clausen authorized the SBIC to make an investment of $250,000 in TYMSHARE.

When the time came to ship the computer to O'Rourke's facility in San Francisco, Van Aken called him with the news that they could not lease the computer system to TYMSHARE for credit reasons.[116]

O'Rourke was beside himself. "But I have a previous confirmation of credit approval from George Snively."

"Impossible," said Van Aken, putting down the phone and buzzing Snively to come to his office.

Van Aken had no master when it came to "chewing" someone out, and Snively got the full treatment. In the midst of the tirade, Snively made the mistake of saying, "You mean the Bank of America is not good credit?" This led to another explosion in the midst of which Van Aken declared that it was a stupid business decision to lease GE 235s so near the end of the product life cycle and that they were only to be made available for cash sale.

"Does Tom have enough money to buy a 235 and a Datanet 30?"

Both men knew the answer was no. The rental contract was canceled.

Meanwhile, Arnold Spielberg had left the shelter of IBM and become vice president for engineering of Scientific Data Systems (SDS). As it happened, SDS was working with the University of California at Berkeley to develop a time-sharing system similar to what GE and Dartmouth were using. O'Rourke approached Spielberg, and the two worked out the specifications for a system to meet TYMSHARE's requirements. SDS agreed to lease the system to TYMSHARE, and this enabled O'Rourke to reestablish his venture capital funding with the Bank of America's SBIC.

O'Rourke's timing couldn't have been better. He was able to tap into a growing circle of technical zealots who had followed the time-sharing work at Berkeley, MIT, and Dartmouth. His business prospered and grew, and he was later to sell TYMSHARE to MCAUTO for $350 million dollars![117]

Don Knight joined the Computer Department in 1960 after spending several years in a variety of engineering assignments in the company's Apparatus Division. He badly wanted to get into computers, and one day he contacted Ken Geiser. Ken was no longer manager of engineering—he had become manager of business planning after Bob Johnson moved to Phoenix, and he was impressed by Knight's experience as a computer user rather than a computer designer.

Knight was assigned to a number of study programs aimed at identifying markets and applications of potential importance to the Computer Department. He ultimately became manager of advanced systems planning covering a variety of applications such as process control, inventory control, banking, and production control. One of the major projects of the group of systems analysts and programmers was BANKPAC, a combination of demand deposit accounting with other banking functions, so organized that the functions provided by ERMA could be accomplished on a service-bureau basis for banks that could not justify their own ERMA centers.

Dr. Helmet Sassenfield, who had taken over Herb Grosch's position as manager of applications, had established seven Information Processing Centers (IPCs) around the country intended to act as demonstration systems for the sales organization and, hopefully, to operate at a profit by selling computer services. By incorporating BANKPAC as one of those services it was possible to establish a steady flow of income from banks, though not enough to cover the cost of the computer and programming staff. There was plenty of computer time available for other customers because the checking-account processing didn't start until four or five o'clock in the afternoon and ended in the early morning when the statements and checks were returned to the banks. The problem was that the hardware salesmen demanded most of this available time and basically gave it away for the purpose of selling computers. It was time well spent in terms of support for the hardware selling effort, but of course Sassenfield got none of the credit. As far as management was concerned, the bottom line was that the IPCs were not profitable and Sassenfield's job was in jeopardy. Helmet was well respected by the advanced systems planning group, and they were desperate to figure out a way to make his IPCs profitable.

At this time—the summer of 1964—Don Knight received a call from Charlie Thompson, head of product planning. "Don, there's something wrong up at Dartmouth. Our computer's working fine, but the BASIC software programs developed by the students will only run for minutes, and then they crash. They're very worried about it because they've been invited to demo at the Joint Computer Conference and they don't want to be embarrassed."

"Sure, Chuck," replied Knight. "I'll go up there with a couple of my best programmers and take a look."

Knight and his programmers visited Hanover shortly after this conversation. The problem was evident immediately when the listings were inspected. The students, not being professional programmers, had created what Knight termed a "kludge" when they attempted to put together the two languages—the ALGOL compiler and the BASIC interpreter—with the GE 225 and the Datanet 30.

"It's a wonder it works at all," Knight reported to Charles Thompson of product planning. "The kids are really smart considering they've had no real training as programmers, but the listings need a complete cleaning up, right down to the code level. I don't think they can do it without some real help from us."

"Any ideas?"

"Well, Chuck, we need to get the student programmers together with some of our professional programmers long enough to clean up those listings. It can't be done while the students are in school, but maybe they'll be willing to devote their Christmas vacations to the project."

"You mean we should send a bunch of programmers to Dartmouth during the Christmas break? Van Aken would never stand for it."

"You're right. Suppose the student programmers came to Phoenix over vacation?"

And that's what happened during the 1964 to 1965 vacation season. Knight arranged to reserve four separate conference rooms at the Black Canyon plant, each one devoted to a particular listing. The GE programmers went through the listings line by line, asking questions such as, "Now, what were you trying to do here, test the register or set a flag, or what?" and the students would talk about it a bit, and the GE programmer would say, "Now here's how I would have done that." This sort of give-and-take of information went on for every line of code, and the four listings were cleaned up by the time vacation was over. The students went back to school, confident of their software, and the Computer Department had the beginning of what was called GE BASIC.[118]

Don Knight was still determined to save Helmet Sassenfield's job, and he believed passionately that the addition of the time sharing-capability to the IPCs would do the trick. During 1965, he and an informal organization, which actually operated outside the formal Computer Department organization barriers, worked to bring time-sharing services into the department. There was Vance Scott in software, Dick Rojyko in hardware engineering, Stan Josephson in product planning, Zigy Quastler in applications, and Ken McDonald in marketing. They managed to bootleg a written-off 235 and install it in the Phoenix IPC—away from the main plant and management oversight—and loaded it up to the hilt with time-sharing tasks, primarily of an engineering nature. They found that up to 80 customers could use the machine simultaneously, and they developed a pricing strategy that was programmed into the machine so the person using the computer could tell at any time how much money he'd spent and how much it would cost to solve various types of problems.

Knight even went so far as to bring the most knowledgeable people into Phoenix from all seven IPCs to help Snively develop an overall business plan for the Computer Department's time-sharing business. It involved a commitment of about $8 million in 1965 to equip each of the IPCs, put them in, train the people, and get them loaded up, and it projected the installation of 21 additional centers the second year. Even with the most conservative projections, the pay-out period for each IPC was forecast as being between three and six months.

Helmet Sassenfield had been kept up to date on progress and was enthusiastic about the business plan Knight handed him. As manager of computer services it was his job to take the proposal to Van Aken and persuade him to include it in the overall 1965–1966 Computer Department budget. He did so, but was rather rudely rebuffed.

"Look, Sassenfield," said Van Aken. "I inherited this computer service business from Lasher and Oldfield, and it's been a pain in the neck and a money loser ever since. We're in the business of building and selling computers, and I'm not interested in investing any more money in service bureaus. If you want to push this time-sharing business you'll have to get Lou Rader to authorize the expenditure."

That conversation turned out to be Sassenfield's swan song. Shortly afterward, he was removed from his job. Don Knight's hope of saving Sassenfield had vanished.

Warner Sinback from Syracuse replaced Sassenfield as manager of computer services. He was an experienced electronics engineering manager, though he knew nothing of the computer business and had never heard of time sharing. Don Knight took him in hand, stressing that the Computer Department had a tremendous opportunity to make history. His sales pitch was a success, and Sinback agreed to go with him to Charlottesville and help sell the business plan to Lou Rader.

As it happened, Rader had assigned his lawyer, Bob Curry, to the task of reviewing Knight's time-sharing business plan. Curry, an experienced businessman, had the reputation for being the toughest cross examiner in GE. He spent a solid week with Knight and Sinback, going over every conceivable weakness in the plan and making Knight justify every assumption. By the time the week was over, the $8 million budget expenditure had been approved, and GE was on its way to creating a time-sharing business.

Unfortunately for the Computer Department's profit and loss statement, 570 decided to split the time-sharing business off as a separate unit located in Bethesda, Maryland. To add to the insult, the new operation went through the chain of command and got a decision that made time sharing their proprietary product. This decision was to have far-reaching consequences. For example, the Computer Department had supported Ford in the development of a particularly useful software package to be used with the GE 265 and was furnished with a copy of the package. The Computer Department was forbidden to offer the software as a product. This pattern was repeated in the case of a number of other GE 200 users. The troops in Phoenix wondered, "Are they trying to tell us something?" They were indeed!

Time sharing was not the only new business to be incubated within the GE Computer Department and then spun off to grow and prosper elsewhere. An unlikely beneficiary was the ancient and honorable game of golf.

Karsten Solheim, who started life as an apprentice cobbler in his father's Seattle shoemaker's shop, had an affinity for tools of all kinds and became a self-educated mechanical engineer by the time World War II came along. He moved from Seattle to San Diego to work in the aircraft industry and remained there until 1953 when a newspaper ad caught his eye, inviting experienced mechanical engineers to be interviewed for an "exciting opportunity" at General Electric's Advanced Electronics Center at Cornell University in Ithaca, New York. Intrigued, Karsten applied for the position and was accepted. A month later, Solheim, his wife, Louise, and children moved to Ithaca, New York, in the shadow of Cornell University.

Solheim's job involved the design of an intricate, lightweight radar antenna. He was fascinated by the challenge, and he threw himself into the project with a will. Louise, knowing he needed some relaxation to take his mind off the project, suggested he join some of his fellow employees at the Cornell golf course. He reluctantly decided to follow her advice.

Solheim soon became a golf addict, but he was frustrated at the difficulty of persuading the little white ball to go into the cup. From that time on, most of his spare time was devoted to the development and refinement of golf clubs—especially the putter, which he considered the most important of all the golfing implements. The first putter he designed was a simple blade putter made of aluminum to which he welded weights at both the sole and the toe. Noticeably, he began reducing his handicap through better putting, an improvement remarked on by the club professional who suggested he make the putter commercially. That same day, Solheim drew up a design incorporating his heel-toe weighting theory and took it to a machine shop to be fabricated.

Solheim's GE career took him eventually to Phoenix as a member of the Computer Department. By this time, requests had begun rolling in from golf pro shops as far away as Florida, New York, and Wisconsin—all without any marketing effort or advertising other than the inspired creation of the word PING, referring to the unique sound the putter made when striking the ball. His garage could no longer contain the flourishing side business, and, in 1963, he decided to leave GE and strike out on his own.

Karsten Manufacturing Corporation was successful beyond its founder's dreams. Still a family business and still located in Phoenix, it produces a complete line of golfing equipment and accessories, marketed all over the world. The 1995 issue of *Forbes* listed Karsten Solheim as one of the 400 wealthiest men in the United States.[119]

The year 1965 had not been a good one for Harrison Van Aken. The euphoria surrounding the early market penetration of the GE 600 was dispelled virtually overnight by the return of the Martin-Marietta computers and the continuing problems with the DECCA tape transports. Complications requiring locating engineers at customer sites to handle these and other problems had delayed shipments and created a crisis atmosphere. Actually, this was not much different than the problems IBM was experiencing in its introduction of the 360 line, but the management of GE was not attuned to this fact of life that accompanied each major introduction in the computer environment

When Van Aken gave short shrift to the time-sharing proposal of Don Knight some months before, it was not that he lacked vision in this new technology. He knew, unfortunately, that any major program involving a substantial deterioration in short-range profit position would be counted against him as the general manager of

Karsten Solheim, former GE Computer Department engineer, demonstrates his computerized golfer to an amazed Walter Cronkite. Inventor of the PING putter while with General Electric, Solheim has become one of the largest producers of golf equipment in the United States.

the Computer Department, regardless of future business potential. General Electric management, at that point in history, committed its department general managers to long-term goals but held them to short-term financial objectives, which substantially negated the possibility of meeting these goals. They had done this with Clair Lasher, and Van Aken sensed a repetition in his case.

The 1965 business review for the executive office was a solemn affair in which Van Aken made a realistic presentation of the many problems and put forth a forecast less rosy than the year before.[120] Most of the discussion centered around the GE 600 and the steps being taken to correct the problems encountered in the field. Rader, who had been faced with equally worrisome situations at UNIVAC, was not too concerned. He knew the problems were soluble, and he decided to spend more time with the Computer Department in 1966.

Hersh Cross reacted differently to the forecast. He decided to reorganize the division by appointing four deputy division managers, all reporting to Rader on paper but, in fact with a dotted-line relationship directly to Cross. One of the purposes of this reorganization was to reduce the span of control of the local Phoenix management, a step that, in theory, would spread the workload and increase management effectiveness. It was typical of General Electric at that time to solve problems through changes in organization or management personnel rather that by dealing with the specific problem in hand, which, in this case, was the health and welfare of the GE 600 series of computers.[121]

On paper, it looked—or attempted to look—like a big promotion for Rader. The name of the operation was changed from Industrial Electronics Division to the Information Systems Division, though exactly the same departments as before made up the division. The announcement of Rader's appointment as vice president and general manager of the division read, "These changes are the result of the impressive successes in General Electric's data-processing business over the last year or so."[122]

It was true that the substantial growth of the business warranted changes in organizational structure, though the nature of the changes and the way they were brought about were to prove less than beneficial to the troops.

PART V

The Professional Managers
December 1965
to
January 1969

DRAMATIS PERSONAE

JEROME COE. Appointed by Cross as deputy division manager for electronic data processing and communications.

LEN MAIER. Appointed by Cross as deputy division manager for advanced development and components.

W.L. LURIE. Assistant to Lou Rader.

ERWIN KOERITZ. Manager, Computer Equipment Department, reporting to Wengert.

EUGENE WHITE. Manager of engineering, replacing Weil.

BOB SULLIVAN. Head of GE 600 Circuit Design Section.

STANFORD SMITH. GE vice president for marketing; appointed group vice president to replace Hershner Cross.

ART PELTASOLO. International vice president for Information Systems Group.

BILL SMART. Directeur general of GE Bull.

JEAN PIERRE BRULET. Directeur general adjoint for GE Bull.

PIERRE DAVOUS. Engineering and manufacturing manager for GE Bull.

OTTORINO BELTRAMI. President of GE Italia.

JOHN HAANSTRA. Former vice president for federal systems, IBM. Recruited into GE by Stanford Smith.

TOM VANDERSLICE. General manager, Information Devices Department.

BOB KETTLETY. Cape Canaveral sales representative.

ED PARKER. Lou Rader consultant.

JOHN BURLINGAME. General manager, Information Devices Department in Syracuse.

DICK SHUEY and ROBIN KERR. GE research laboratory scientists who developed software for the MULTICS program.

HILLIARD PAIGE. Group executive replacing Stanford Smith.

CHAPTER 32
MICROMANAGEMENT FROM CORPORATE HEADQUARTERS

Hersh Cross's organizational plan established three deputy division managers located in the New York office and one located in Phoenix. The Computer Department in Phoenix was renamed the Computer Equipment Department, but several of the functions that previously reported to the general manager in Phoenix would now report directly to one of the deputy division managers in New York. For example, marketing, field engineering, and information processing services—formerly a part of Van Aken's organization—though still located in Phoenix, would be responsible to someone located 2,000 miles away. This essentially destroyed the identity of the Computer Department as an integrated business entity.

Lou Rader and Harrison Van Aken considered the new organization a disaster in the making. To Rader, it seemed a calculated act to consolidate command of the computer business in New York. To Van Aken, the loss of responsibility for the marketing function had stripped him of one of the tools he needed to control the business. Cross had given Van Aken the choice of remaining in Phoenix in charge of the Computer Equipment Department or becoming deputy division manager for overseas operations. He chose the latter position in the belief that he would have more freedom of action in the international arena. This was reminiscent of Clair Lasher's departure from the Computer Department a few years before.

There is little record of what either Lasher or Van Aken did in connection with GE's international computer program. It was as if both men sailed away on a ghost ship that vanished in mid-ocean. Van Aken eventually tired of being relegated to the sidelines. He resigned to become president of Hallicrafters.

Succeeding Van Aken in Phoenix was Lou Wengert, deputy division manager of the Information Systems Division and acting general manager of the newly christened Computer Equipment Department. Wengert had graduated from the University of Iowa in 1936 with a degree in accounting. He joined General Electric after graduation and was accepted as a student in GE's Business Training Course. Upon completion, he was assigned to a number of different positions in corporate accounting before his first major task as manager of budgets and measurements in the GE X-ray Department. In 1952 he was made manager of finance of the Direct Current Motor and Generator Department, one of GE's highly profitable "core" businesses. There he rose to the position of general manager, which he held until 1966, when he was tapped by Cross to take over the Computer Equipment

Department. An intelligent and capable general manager, he was an obvious choice, thought Cross, to bring the maverick computer business under control. It mattered little that he had never been involved in the electronics business and that he came from a business environment where the typical product lifetime was 20 years or more.

Jerome Coe, an MIT graduate in chemical engineering, held a number of engineering and marketing positions in the company's Silicon Products Department before becoming head manager of marketing and public relations research in GE's Marketing and Public Relations Services in New York City. He was appointed deputy division manager for data processing and communications with headquarters in New York, and reporting directly to him were the Phoenix-based functions of marketing, field engineering, and computer services.

The final appointment was that of Len Maier, an MIT Ph.D. in solid-state physics, and formerly general manager of the Semiconductor Products Department. He was appointed deputy division general manager for advanced developments and components, and reporting to him were the Semiconductor Products Department and the newly invented Advanced Information Technology Operation with laboratories in Palo Alto, Phoenix, and Schenectady. As with Coe, Maier's office was located in New York.

Thus began an era in which most of the problems and opportunities were concentrated in Phoenix, but with much of the decision-making authority located remotely and split between New York and Charlottesville. Such an organization was clumsy at best, but it could have functioned reasonably well if the key individuals at each level had worked well together in the past and had shared a common understanding of the computer business and their mission in that business.

There was apparently little Lou Rader could do to assert his authority as division general manager. As group executive, Cross could (and did) isolate Rader from the president's office, and Rader was not the type to violate accepted organization channels. While he had done the right thing by his family in establishing his headquarters in Charlottesville, he had isolated himself from the men's rooms, elevators, and restaurants where relationships were cemented and high-level decisions made.

This was the situation when Rader was told to gather together the newly appointed group of deputy division managers to prepare the division's business plan for 1966. For the first time, computer services, time sharing, and integrated systems were presented in their proper perspective, and specific assignments were made to deal with specific problems. Then Rader presented a curve of cumulative profit and loss through 1972 that indicated a requirement for approximately $100 million of GE cash during 1966, including the European subsidiaries. The projection showed the entire GE investment being paid back by mid-1971.[123] There was grumbling in the executive office, and Rader was given three more months to develop a "better" profit projection.

Rader was pretty sure he was being set up by Cross because there was no way the job could be done properly without the amount of investment that he had carefully calculated. Indeed, as the months rolled by, the new management team found new ways to spend money, and the 1966 cash requirement jumped by an additional $20 million. The payback year leaped ahead to 1973.

In August, 1966, there was a presentation of these results to Cross and his staff in Phoenix. At the conclusion of this meeting Cross made an important organizational change that was announced in September. He split the non-computer parts of the Information Systems Division away from that division and created an Industrial Process Control Division consisting of the Specialty Control Department, the Communication Products Department, the Instrument Department, and the Process Computer Department. Lou Rader was appointed general manager of this division, while Hershner Cross established himself as acting general manager of the Information Systems Division. The organizational changes were, as usual, described as expansions of GE's worldwide missions in computers and process control, but GE insiders knew better.

Lou Rader was accepted by most of the people in Phoenix as an able professional who understood the computer business and would act as a sympathetic superior in the higher echelons of General Electric. He was also recognized within the industry as GE's senior representative in the computer field. It would not do to create a crisis atmosphere in removing him from a position of authority and responsibility for GE's computer business. Yet Hershner Cross was determined to accomplish just that.

At the conclusion of the Phoenix business review and Rader's return to Charlottesville, Cross had discussed his intentions with lawyers R.B. Curry and W.L. Lurie, two close advisors of Rader. The two men were horrified but—being realists—they realized it was a battle Lou could never win. Hoping to minimize the damage to Rader and to the company, Curry and Lurie sent a "strictly private" memo to Cross on August 15.[124] It read in part as follows:

> We believe that some external announcement is needed to prevent rumors that will be damaging to the company's best interests. The draft press release creates the impression that our growing business justifies two divisions. We have selected the title of Doc's new division to emphasize that it is also a computer division—which it is. This, we believe, is important to the marketplace to indicate that Doc, who probably has the best established GE computer image, has not been pulled out of the computer business. For emphasis, we have also elevated the Process Computer Business Section to department status. . . . The proposed release also subtly implies that the Virginia location (of Rader's headquarters) may have influenced Doc's choice of these two divisions. . . . The letter attempts to be stern but also flattering enough to clinch his cooperation."

Cross followed the advice given in the memo, and the switch was made without the press realizing the true significance of the move. It was a stunning demonstration of the GE philosophy of the time that a professional manager with Crotonville credentials could manage any business. Starting with Cross as group vice president and also as acting division general manager, and down through the four deputy division managers (excepting Van Aken, who was substantially out of the loop), there was no one in the chain of command who knew that COBOL was a programming language and not a rare gem stone. It was to be the acid test of the Drucker/Smiddy/Cordiner management religion.

One of the first steps taken by Lou Wengert, deputy division manager for information systems equipment and acting general manager of the Computer Equipment Department, was to opt out of the "acting" position and appoint Dr. Erwin M. Koeritz as general manager in his stead.[125] Dr. Koeritz had been manager of manufacturing for GE's Metallurgical Products Department in Detroit, and he had outstanding credentials in the cemented carbide business.

This influx of managers without computer experience was to continue. They were of two types. One category included management personnel from GE divisions that were being phased out or relocated. They were generally highly skilled in the technical fields in which they had spent most of their careers, but utterly lacking in computer technology or computer marketing experience required for the dynamic data-processing industry. Those in the second category were the more dangerous. They were individuals on the "fast track," usually with a sponsor at 570. They were often in the MBA category and were short on experience but long on industrial dynamics and management theory. The working-level people called them "the carpetbaggers."

Cross occasionally asked Lou Rader for advice, though he rarely followed it. One day Rader received a call from Cross. "John Weil, our manager of engineering in Phoenix, is leaving the department," said Cross. "Do you have any suggestions for a replacement?"

"I sure do," replied Rader. "This time pick someone who has designed a computer, preferably a successful one like ERMA or the GE 235.[126] John Couleur is the likely choice if you want someone from within. Whatever you do, don't put another professional manager without extensive computer background in the job. Technical judgment between alternate solutions is much more important than managerial dogma."

"I don't think that's necessary," said Cross, "but I'll pass on your comment to Wengert."

A few days later, Rader received a call from Wengert with the same question. He gave the same advice.

The November 15, 1966, issue of the *Computer Headliner* carried the story that Eugene R. White, formerly manager of engineering of the company's Direct Engineering Conversion Operation in Lynn, Massachusetts, had been appointed manager of engineering of the Computer Equipment Department. Once again, Cross had opted for a non-computer engineering manager.

The influx of professional managers was matched by a continuing exodus of key marketing people, distraught at the erratic pattern of Vern Cooper. Cooper was never in favor of the banking business on which a good part of the department's sales volume depended. He disbanded the headquarters market support group and shipped the specialists to the field where their special expertise was diluted. The very closely knit banking industry, which had a very active grapevine, always watched GE close-ly for any sign of wavering in the Computer Equipment Department's support. George Snively was at Pittsburgh National Bank negotiating the final documentation for the lease of two GE 400 systems the day this decision was announced to the banks. Pittsburgh National Bank decided to see what happened and delayed signing the contract. They ultimately signed with Burroughs.[127]

Warren Prince, Midwest regional sales manager, was dismayed at Cooper's action. His normally placid temperament was raised to the boiling point when he discovered that the engineering effort to interface the new GE 600 with the MICR sorter/reader had been cancelled and it had been decided also not to manufacture the full field proof encoder the engineers had developed in response to extreme customer interest. Prince called Cooper to protest, and was told to be in Phoenix the next day to discuss the matter. Prince took the night flight from Chicago, arriving in Phoenix bright and early the next morning. He waited in Cooper's outside office all that day and was eventually told to return to Chicago. On arriving at his Chicago office the next day, he received a message telling him to return to Phoenix Friday.[128]

Warren Prince was a loyal GE employee and a productive sales manager, but he'd had enough. He resigned in November 1966 and joined Harris Trust and Savings Bank as vice president of operations. He was later to make his fortune as vice president of data services of Tom O'Rourke's TYMSHARE.

Meanwhile, John Couleur was plugging away on the GE 600, determined to correct the problem areas that cropped up the minute another problem had been corrected. No sooner had the tape drives been brought under reasonable control than there was a crisis in connection with the DSU270 disk file. The DSU270 was intended as a replacement for the Data Products disk, which had been found both inadequate and costly. A number of severe technical problems had cropped up during the course of development, but most had been resolved with the assistance of the GE Research Laboratory in Schenectady. Controversy raged for many weeks as to whether to put the GE disk file into production or purchase a new fixed-head design Burroughs proposed to deliver. Couleur strongly favored the GE disk based on a technical comparison between the two, but Bill White was more conservative and recommended the Burroughs approach. Wengert accepted White's recommendation, disbanding the disk design group and laying off the personnel before the end of the year.[129]

The GE Research Laboratory group who had solved the technical problems of the DSU270 were so upset with the decision to kill it that they took the case to Fred Borch, GE's president at the time. Borch decided to support management, and it would be three years and several management changes before GE would have a competitive disk file.

Then the worst problem hit!

Starting with the 25th 600 system, the computers would not meet standards in the factory, and Cy Statt, manager of manufacturing, was tearing out his hair.[130] An investigation showed that purchasing had bought transistors from Motorola despite objections from engineering. Manufacturing claimed that the Motorola bid was $.10 per transistor below the price of the Fairchild transistors used in the first 24 systems and that Motorola had offered to perform 100-percent testing on the transistors. Incoming inspection discovered that a large percentage of the Motorola transistors did not meet specs, but nevertheless they had been built into computers. It developed into a typical engineering-manufacturing donnybrook, with each side pointing fingers at the other.

Several of the old-line Computer Department engineers had resented the decision to use John Couleur's M2360 computer as the basis for the GE 600 product line. Couleur and the group of engineers who had moved to Phoenix from Electronics Park—the "Syracuse Mafia"—had ruffled the feathers of the Phoenix group by their independent attitudes, and they received little sympathy when they ran into trouble. They were quick to tell management that the 600 circuit design was too dependent on transistor performance, that the system should be a 32-bit architecture like the IBM 360, and the 600 should be scrapped in favor of a new design.[131] Actually, the superior cost and performance of the 600 central system was due to a brilliant, unconventional circuit design done by Bob Sullivan, manager of the 600 circuit design unit. At the post mortem meeting, Sullivan explained.[132]

"The 600 delay calculation is based on statistical performance (that is, using average rather than worst-case performance to determine circuit delay) that can be expected from transistors in a long logic chair. The key to achieving the required average performance of the transistors is careful vendor selection and statistical sampling of production batches. The Motorola production and testing cycle isn't capable of producing transistors that meet the required performance range, and that's why we specified Fairchild transistors."

Sullivan's statement unleashed a lengthy discussion of average rather than worst-case transistor performance, most of which was over the heads of the local management who had never previously been required to referee such highly technical debates. The discussions escalated into battles between engineers, product planners, and quality-control specialists—battles that were often decided on the basis of managerial seniority rather than technical considerations. In the midst of the yelling, Wengert apparently panicked. He withdrew the GE 600 from the market and threatened to cancel the whole project. This action, combined with Martin-Marietta's defection, caused GE to lose credibility. Most of the GE 600 customers went back to IBM, having decided that while IBM might not always design the best computers, IBM at least knew how to run a computer business.[133]

In all fairness to Lou Wengert, nothing in his successful career up to that time had prepared him for the chaos of a high-tech product introduction. Nor was there anyone in the upward chain of command with the technical background necessary to deal with the crisis.

In January 1967, *Datamation* made the following statement:

GE Still Searching for Loss-Trimming Formula—Although GE announced in November that it was laying off 450 people in its Phoenix plant, many outsiders claim the number is more likely two to three times that, with more cuts due worldwide. Many of the Phoenix folks are being offered jobs elsewhere in the company, and bodysnatchers and other recruiting vultures invading Phoenix say only "deadwood" is available there. The company says it's not cutting back marketing, but admits "adjustments" in some sales offices. Also, the Computer Research Lab in Sunnyvale is no more, with the work there either terminated or transferred to other locations. The company is currently evaluating its peripherals, may stop making its own tape drives, is looking for a new small-disc source.

Not to be interpreted as a sign GE is bailing out, the cutbacks instead are an attempt to reduce the corporation's staggering EDP losses, estimated in some quarters as $400 million or more.

Meanwhile, the company continues to believe that a good GE-trained manager can manage anything and leaves the information systems division in the hands of management relatively new to the costly mysteries of the computer biz.

CHAPTER 33
DRASTIC MANAGEMENT CHANGES ACCELERATE

On Pearl Harbor Day, 1966, GE President Fred Borch invited J. Stanford Smith to lunch at his club on Park Avenue. Smith was a senior member of the executive office and vice president for marketing and public relations services. As GE's top marketing man, Smith had over 30 years of varied experience in marketing and operating management in GE. Prior to his appointment in the executive office, he had been general manager of GE's Outdoor Lighting Department where his performance had been outstanding.

"Stan," said Borch, as the two men lingered over their coffee and cigars, "We have a runaway business on our hands, and I need your help."

"I assume you're talking about the computer business," retorted Smith.

"Good guess. We probably made a mistake by taking over a couple of losing companies in Europe before the domestic business was well in hand, and the result has been one problem after another. We pissed away $100 million this year, and the projection for 1967 isn't much better. They keep telling me that much of the investment is for computers that are on lease, and that the payback will come in future lease payments, but the stockholders are reading articles in *Fortune* and *Forbes* pointing out our big losses in computers, and they don't like it.

"All this," Borch continued, "comes at a time when we're suffering one costly strike after another. Our cash flow is beginning to decrease, and we simply can't afford to finance too many new business ventures. Both atomic power and jet engines are asking for money to cover large projects in areas where we have a major market share, and they seem to be better bets than chasing after IBM."

"Why not get out of the business and cut our losses?"

"There are many who think that way," said Borch, "but we have thousands of computers out on lease between Phoenix, Bull, and Olivetti. The unrealized income is over $400 million, and we'd lose most of it if we went out of business. There's also the huge dent it would make in our reputation. Finally, Stan, there are many who believe, and I've always been one of them, that computers and computer services are basic to the future of our electronics businesses. What we need now, I think, is a prudent downsizing combined with a competent job of fitting the product line to the market; the kind of thing you did when you turned around the Outdoor Lighting Department."

"But, Freddie, I don't know anything about the computer business."

"Damn it all, Stan, you're as bad as Lou Rader. We have all the technical talent in the world. What's needed now is hard-headed professional management at the helm. I thought I'd get it from Hersh Cross, but he got fascinated with the European market and let things get away from him. If you'll take on the job, I'll go along with whatever technical talent you decide to hire."

"Will I still report directly to you?"

"Of course. . . . Oh, I see what you mean. Cross has been acting manager of the Information Systems Division as well as group executive, so he's been reporting to himself. If you have no objection, I'll initially announce you as vice president and general manager of the Information Systems Division, and I'll tell Hersh to let you have your way in reorganizing the division. I'll then put Hersh in charge of the Industrial Group, which will include Rader's Industrial Process Control Division, and we'll promote the Information Systems Division up to group level in parallel. I don't expect Lou Rader to be very happy about it—he and Hersh have never gotten along very well—but they're both big boys."

"How soon do you want me to start?"

"How about a month from now, to give you time to select your successor and study the computer business plans for the last couple of years?"

"Okay. I'd also appreciate a joint session with you and Hersh so that there'll be no question about our relationship during the interim period when I'll be reporting to him on paper. I'll want it clear that though I welcome his help during this period, I will make the decisions."

"Consider it done, Stan."

The management change was a bitter pill for Hershner Cross to swallow, particularly the planned elevation of the Information Systems Division to group status. Lou Rader had strongly recommended this step two years before in order that the decision-making authority for the computer business would be at the highest possible level in the company. Cross had refused to recommend the move because the division was not yet profitable, but Rader believed it was because Cross wanted to block Rader's access to the executive office. In any event, Borch's mandate would have to be obeyed.[134]

The January 10, 1967, issue of the *GE Computer Headliner* announced J. Stanford Smith's appointment as vice president and general manager of the Information Systems Division, "one of the fastest growing and most complex in the company." No other names or positions were included in the release.

On April 1, 1967, *Forbes* ran a feature article entitled, "GE's Edsel." In announcing Smith's appointment, it traced the history of the GE Computer Department and its affiliates in Europe. The article concluded as follows:

> If Smith can gradually stop the losses and make GE a strong No. 2, his already high
> stock will soar further at GE. If he cannot, then there will be some soul searching
> in GE's Manhattan executive offices. For Smith is one of the company's most

talented managers. But if Smith—a thoroughly accomplished generalist in the best GE tradition—fails in so technical a field as EDP, perhaps GE top brass will have to rethink some of its basic concepts.

Smith knew of the *Forbes* article when he was in the process of preparing his first annual business plan presentation to the board of directors.[135] The presentation was scheduled for April 24 giving him little time to deal with the implied criticism of GE's management philosophy, including the continuing appointment of non-computer people—such as himself—to key management positions. During his presentation to the board, he made the following statement:

"You may recall the *Forbes* article quoted one of our former domestic engineering managers (Bob Johnson) who left the company when one of his subordinates was promoted over his head. What he said is true. There are three functionally equivalent line printers (Bob Johnson had been sent to Europe as a part of a team to evaluate Bull and Olivetti and had noted the printer duplication as one example of the difficulty of creating a unified product line on an international level.) However, our ex-employee overlooked all of the complexities of a multiple product line, minority shareholders, and nationalistic considerations. This perhaps is understandable since he did not live through the period with us. *However, what is difficult to understand is the apparent lack of technical recognition that each device or peripheral requires for an individual controller to connect to a particular central processor*" [emphasis added].

This statement by Smith was not calculated to gain votes from Computer Department veterans who had lived through the complex ERMA program in which the coupling of peripherals—including the revolutionary MICR character reader and high-speed check sorter—represented a substantial part of this successful product development managed throughout by Johnson. The statement was probably authored by someone other than Smith, but it does serve to illuminate the vast gulf of misunderstanding existing between the managers of that time and those with the task of making things happen.

In a letter to a colleague, Johnson had said, "My decision to leave GE was based on two things. First, GE seemed to be in a major state of management instability; the mode was for the department to make proposals (annual plans to the executive office) such as were required of/for the business; for the executive office to replace the department general manager once he failed to meet those plans; for the division VP to be replaced after he failed to meet the plans submitted by his new general manager; and for the group executive to be replaced when his new division and department managers failed to meet their plans. These executive replacements cascaded on down the management tree every time a higher executive got replaced. It was clear to me that this was going on and that there was no stability possible.

"Second," continued Johnson, "Burroughs offered me a position leading to vice president of engineering (which I did become), and Burroughs struck me as a place that knew the computer business and the data-processing industry."[136]

Most of the other more creative people in the Phoenix organization were in agreement with Bob Johnson's sentiments. John Couleur, father of the GE 600, left as Smith came in, fed up with the proliferation of what he thought of as carpet-baggers. His comments had a slightly different slant than Bob Johnson's.

"I guess the secret of making 'professional management' work," said Coleur, "is that the managers plan, organize, integrate, and measure, while the troops do the work. As new managers come in, they get to know the troops and who they can and can't trust. In this way, the business is actually operated by competent people, managers and troops operating as a team.

"When so many new managers descended on Phoenix at one time," said Couleur, "the new organization destroyed the relationships that had made the business grow and that could have worked to find solutions to the problem. No one knew who to trust. The troops had no reputations with the new managers and, with that, lost their influence over the businesses they created. The control was taken by the new managers who made decisions on their newly granted authority rather than on their knowledge of the facts. That's when the chaos started."

Stan Smith had indeed inherited a business that was unstable, and one with low morale. He realized, wisely, that his management team lacked experience in the computer field, and he made it a point to look around the industry for a qualified general manager with the required background to put in charge in Phoenix. Lou Rader was the only possibility within GE, but he had made it plain he would not leave the Charlottesville area. Smith settled temporarily on the same group of deputy division managers as Cross had picked.

Because of his prior experience as GE's corporate vice president for marketing, Smith was more familiar with the European scene than with the domestic computer business. In 1966 he had assisted the English company De La Rue Bull (DLRB) in persuading Vic Casebolt,[137] then headquarters sales manager of the Computer Equipment Department, to join DLRB as managing director. DLRB was one of the Bull affiliates picked up as a result of GE's acquisition, and it had been established by Bull to provide an outlet for the company's products. The small English subsidiary had never been profitable, partially because of a lack of computer products to sell, and they were trying to sell one of the early GE 600s. Informed by Casebolt that the 600 had been withdrawn from the market, at least for the time being, the long-suffering sales force threatened to quit.

"No, you're not going to quit," said Casebolt. "We're going to start a time-sharing business over here, just as GE is doing around the United States."

Casebolt went on to describe GE's Dartmouth program and the subsequent successful introduction of time-sharing computer services by Don Knight and his group. "It's the wave of the future," proclaimed Casebolt. "We're going to order us a GE 265 and start a time-sharing service right here. Nobody quits!"

The DLRB group was fired up by Casebolt's enthusiasm, and in 1967 inaugurated Europe's first time-sharing service bureau in London. Using the pricing formulas developed by Knight for the United States, DLRB priced the service 10 percent higher than in the United States. To the delight of all, they were sold out in a few months at a monthly gross of about a million dollars annualized. Casebolt quickly floated an appropriation request for a second system.

One of the positive aspects of Machines Bull was the company's affiliate companies in Europe and Latin America, most of them hungry for modern computer products to sell. It didn't take long for DLRB's successful time-sharing program to become a subject of excited conversation amongst the 20 affiliates located in 20 countries in Europe and in Latin America, and Casebolt was quick to capitalize on the opportunity. In a short time, there were GE 265 time-sharing centers in 11 countries, with connections to 4 smaller countries. They were all to be profitable by 1968 and would play a major role in Bull's resurgence to profitability in 1969.[138]

Another major international move was made by Stan Smith in 1967, with the wholesale replacement of the GE management team that, despite its inability to get Bull "under control," had initiated installation of GE financial controls and other reforms that were to bear fruit later. Art Peltasolo, International Division vice president, had replaced Van Aken (who had resigned) and represented the GE shareholding. Unlike Cross, Smith had delegated considerable responsibility and authority to the position. Henri Desbrueres remained as a figurehead president directeur to preside over both "sides." Bill Smart became directeur general, the operating general manager. Reporting to him were four directeur general adjoints: Jean Pierre Brule who was hired from IBM-France, French operations; Pierre Davous was promoted from within Bull, in charge of engineering and manufacturing; Alva Way, former chief financial officer of GE Brazil, was controller; and Vic Casebolt was brought in from DLRB to handle the affiliate companies, including the time-sharing service bureaus. It turned out to be a strong and effective management team.

Ottorino Beltrami, president of Olivetti-GE was also a very effective manager. He led a dynamic marketing-oriented organization that developed the entry-level system for GE outside the United States, the GE 115.

Smith had been effective in shoring up the European management team, but the transition in the United States from division to group status presented a more difficult problem. He moved cautiously—far too slowly in the estimation of many—before proclaiming the elevation of the computer business to a level where the group executive (himself, in this case) reported to the president and had the authority consonant with this position. When he did so, he reappointed most of the individuals who had been in charge before, but with elevated titles and salaries.[139] Lou Wengert, accountant and professional manager, was appointed general manager, Information Systems Equipment Division; Vern Cooper, wire and cable salesman and professional manager, was appointed deputy division general manager for information sales and service; Jerome Coe, chemical engineer and professional manager, was appointed general manager of the newly established Information Services Division; John Haanstra from IBM, a veteran of several years in the computer industry, and recently vice president of IBM's Federal Systems Division, was appointed general manager of the Advanced Development and Resources Planning Division, reporting to Stan Smith.

The appointment of John Haanstra was greeted with mixed enthusiasm and skepticism by the troops in Phoenix. He was the first computer-literate person to be appointed at a high level in the executive chain of General Electric; however, everyone knew that the "Planning Division" really didn't exist, so that Haanstra had little authority. Hopefully, he was being groomed for a management role.

During 1967 the GE 645 program for MIT and Bell Labs was transferred from Phoenix to the Special Information Products Department (SIPD) in Syracuse.[140] The reason given was that the complexities of the MULTICS project were detracting from the technical efforts required to correct the problems of the GE 600, the commercial version that had been withdrawn from the market. In Syracuse, the project engineer was Walker Dix who had worked alongside John Couleur in the development of the original M2360, from which the 600 line had descended. Twenty-five engineers were transferred from Phoenix to Syracuse to augment Dix's group, among them a manufacturing engineer named Bob Sullivan. Sullivan had worked closely with the Research Laboratory in the development of what would be known as thick film technology to provide a substrate for aggregations of integrated circuits, later to be known to the world as microchip modules, or micropads. It was a technology that would spread around the world, and it was first applied by Walker Dix and his group in the design of the GE 645.

This development spawned a continuous series of reviews, confrontations, presentations, and proposals regarding the viability of the competing Phoenix and Syracuse system logic designs and circuit sets as the basis for the GE 600 line. Dick Shuey of the GE Research Laboratory as well as circuit experts from the GE Electronics Laboratory were called in as consultants. It was at this point that the lack of technical expertise of the Phoenix management caused a problem. The Johnsons, Paivinens, Spielbergs, Allers, Bridges, Couleurs, and so on had disappeared from the scene, and Wengert, a reasonable manager in GE terms, was buffeted with several who had personal agendas related to the original 32-bit product line and wished to eliminate the 36-bit GE 600 from the company's product offerings.

As 1967 went along, a number of organizational changes were made at lower levels within the Information Systems Division. One had to do with the establishment of a Document Handling Subsection at a new facility in Oklahoma City, acquired because GE had reacted to political pressures to salvage this strictly military venture. The Oklahoma City facility was to furnish advanced card readers, card punches, printers, optical readers, and high-speed check sorters to Phoenix for incorporation into computer systems. Cy Statt, manager of manufacturing, welcomed this addition in manufacturing capability because the test and assembly area of the Black Canyon factory was not well suited to the production of electromechanical devices. Tom Vanderslice, general manager of the new Information Devices Department, had come from GE's Vacuum Products Operation to head up this new venture. He worked hard to make the venture a success, but the long lead time to develop equipment of this type prevented the department from contributing substantially to the computer business during its life.

As 1967 passed into history, there were few of the spontaneous parties and barbecues that had previously enlightened the Christmas season. Everyone was too busy dealing with the many problems facing the organization—technical, financial, and customer generated. There was a realization that the entrepreneur phase of the business was ending, and that a major effort would be required to fold the Information Systems Equipment Division into the worldwide structure Stan Smith was attempting to create.

It was a trying time.

CHAPTER 34
A FEW RAYS OF HOPE

Despite the technical problems plaguing the GE 600 line of computers, many machines remained in active service after painful and expensive repairs. One of these, a GE 635, had been installed at Cape Canaveral by Bob Kettlety.[141] The project started out as just another "600 disaster" (according to IBM salesmen and 570 skeptics). The building in which the 635 was to be installed on the beach had not been completed at the time of delivery so the ground crew had stored the computer and its peripheral units in a non-air-conditioned building. When Kettlety opened the crates some weeks later, he could not believe his eyes.

"Every damn circuit board and every mechanical device is completely corroded," screamed Kettlety on the telephone to Phoenix.

"Surely you jest," replied Cy Statt, the unflappable manager of manufacturing. He had personally supervised the packing of each item in moisture-proof plastic.

"These nosey feather merchants opened every package in the process of inventorying the shipment, and they closed them with big clips. Believe me, Statt. The thing's a mess."

"Okay, Bob. Give me a list of the assemblies you need and we'll air ship them along with a couple of technicians to help you put the thing together."

"I'll be back to you in an hour," said Kettlety. "Remember, NASA is counting on the GE 635 to check each of 3,000 critical valves and gauges some 12 times a second, and then it has to interpret millions of bits of data and telemeter refined data to 30 terminals in a control room five miles away. The Apollo launch is scheduled for two weeks from today, and the system has to work perfectly during the final countdown. Don't let me down."

"Easy does it," replied Statt. "We've got lots of good sub-assemblies in inventory because the 600's been taken off the market. Flying Tiger will have the stuff to you in two days."

True to his word, Statt delivered in time to complete and test out the system which was used for the Apollo launch. It was a complete success, and the dual 635 system continued to be a workhorse at the Kennedy Space Flight Center for many years.

Ed Parker, assistant and close personal friend of Lou Rader, had been general manager of the Instrument Division in West Lynn until he joined Rader in 1965. He had served a number of years in Schenectady, first as a design and product service engineer and then as the administrative manager for the GE Research Laboratory. In this assignment he had frequent dealings with academic institutions, one of which was Dartmouth College. Parker became a good friend of Dr. John Kemeny.

One day Parker and Kemeny were discussing the future of computer time sharing. "You know," said Kemeny, "GE seems to have gotten its money's worth out of the investment you people made in the original time-sharing program in our Kiewit Computer Center. It's a wonderful example of the mutually beneficial results that can be achieved through cooperation between a major industry and an educational institution. Do you suppose the relationship might be expanded a bit further?"

"What did you have in mind?"

"Well, the fact is that the GE 265 computer that started it all is now a bit old fashioned in terms of capacity and computing speed. We need to quadruple the number of users we can handle simultaneously. Our faculty is aware of the contract GE signed with MIT in connection with their MULTICS time-sharing project, and they're a bit jealous. We don't have a National Science Foundation grant as we had when our project started, but we're just as anxious as before to work with you in upgrading the service."

"Gee, that's a tall order," said Parker. "You realize, I'm sure, that the GE 625 with the Datanet 355 is a million-dollar-plus machine. Also, it's new on the market and has been having some technical problems."

"I've worked with your field service people long enough to have faith in their ability to keep the machine running. The leasing cost is the big problem. MIT has an ARPA grant from the government, so this covers all their costs. The only bait I can offer is that this generation of our BASIC software is humming like a top, whereas MIT's MULTICS is far too sophisticated and complex to be commercially useful. Enough said?"

"You've made a good point," said Parker. "I'll look into it and see what we can do."

This conversation took place in 1965 during the early stages of the 600 program. Parker's investigation was productive, and he came up with a proposal to install a GE 625 with Datanet 355 at Dartmouth at no initial charge provided that, in addition to serving Dartmouth students and faculty, 50 percent of its capacity would be available to GE to serve its time-sharing customers. Because the system could accommodate 400 users simultaneously, this turned out to be an acceptable arrangement to both parties.[142]

The February 9, 1968 edition of the *General Electric News* was headlined, "GE-625 Reaches Time-Sharing Milestone at Dartmouth." The story went on to say that the computer was serving 47 faculty members and students, 20 additional students from secondary schools in the New England region, and 46 customers of the General Electric Information Services Department located in Boston, New York, and Washington, D.C. According to Dr. Kemeny, the system was expected to grow to 200 or more simultaneous users in the near future.

Despite these bright spots, the GE 600 line, withdrawn from the market for two years pending correction of technical defects, continued to be viewed unfavorably by the users of large computers within GE. Under General Manager John Burlingame, the Special Information Products Department in Syracuse continued to pursue the advanced and highly controversial set of current mode logic (CML) chips developed by Bob Sullivan and successfully prototyped by the GE Integrated Circuits Laboratory. Early in 1968, the fateful decision was made at division/group level to go with the Syracuse design approach. The Special Information Products Department was summarily dissolved, and the entire project group under Walker Dix was moved to Phoenix where they became part of the newly formed Large Systems Department. Dix, appointed manager of engineering of the department, moved quickly to integrate his contingent of 100 technical people from Syracuse with the existing GE 600 project group.[143]

This bringing together of computer engineering talent from the commercial and military sides of GE's electronic businesses was long overdue. Walker Dix, an electrical engineering graduate of the University of Oklahoma just before World War II, had served as a radar technician in the Pacific Fleet and had earned his stripes aboard a destroyer picket ship, battling kamikazis. He joined GE at war's end and spent the next 20 years in a variety of increasingly more complex radar end data-processing programs. He was one of a handful of "engineers' engineers" in Syracuse to earn the informal sobriquet of "hard-shelled baptist." With little concern of organizational perquisites, and much concern for technical excellence, Dix was an excellent choice to bring together the two engineering organizations.

In April 1968, Stanford Smith, VP and group executive of the Information Systems Group, played his ace! A special edition of the Phoenix supplement of the *General Electric News* proclaimed, "Haanstra Is New General Manager–Information Systems Equipment Division." Almost as an afterthought, a sub-headline announced, "Wengert Will Head New Industrial Group Division." (The newly established Constant Speed Drives Division was a part of the Industrial Group under Hershner Cross, vice president and group executive.) Close followers of GE's corporate practices recognized what had taken place. The wizards of 570 had first created a group out of the Information Systems Division so that Stan Smith would retain his seniority next to the presidential level and had then patched together a number of Motor Departments to create a division to which Lou Wengert could be appointed without losing seniority. In parallel, John Haanstra, former IBM engineering manager, had been "sanitized" at Crotonville so that he could be considered a GE professional manager before assigning him to head up the computer operation in Phoenix.

Haanstra turned out to be a breath of fresh air for the Phoenix organization. He had not taken Crotonville very seriously, and it became immediately apparent that he was more interested in computers than in management philosophy. He was affable, easy to talk to, self-confident, and extremely knowledgeable about the computer business. More importantly, he immediately launched himself into the details of the product line on both a technical and a marketing level.[144]

During the period when Haanstra was assigned to advanced planning activities he had made useful contacts with the GE Research Laboratory where a great deal of advanced programming was underway to adapt the GE 600 operating system to provide time sharing, batch processing, and on-line data collection in a single computer. Taking advantage of the MULTICS work at MIT and the time-sharing work at Dartmouth, Dick Shuey and Robin Kerr implemented the system on a GE 600 computer modified with four base registers to provide memory protection, automatic relocation, and optional write inhibit. This Research Laboratory Operating System was a virtual operating system in that it could run GECOS, Mark II, DESKSIDE, and so on, all at once with appropriate bridges between the systems.[145] Haanstra was enthusiastic about the operating system. To be known as GECOS IV, it would provide the 600 series with an important competitive advantage.

Haanstra believed the most important thing he could do to make the Phoenix operation profitable was to build upon the base of the GE 400 and GE 600 systems by the introduction of improved hardware and software features aimed at extending the life of the products. One major problem was that the 400 and 600 series were not compatible with one another, and Haanstra's plan was to develop a computer with about four times the speed of the fastest of the 400s to serve as a bridge between the two series. He negotiated an agreement with Toshiba, GE's affiliate in Japan, whereby the computer would be designed in Phoenix and manufactured in Japan. The machine was referred to as Pi, and the reason for offshore manufacture was Haanstra's concern that the GE Deer Valley factory had about all it could handle with the 400 and 600.

Haanstra was somewhat of a character. One day he showed up in one of the engineering laboratories where an improvement of the GE 600 was undergoing life tests. He approached the computer, coffee cup in hand, and suddenly seemed to stumble, spilling coffee all over the gleaming computer. His audience of engineers and technicians, embarrassed at the apparent gaffe of their boss, rushed to sop up the mess before the hot coffee could seep into the innards of the computer.

Haanstra laughed. "And that's what will happen at least once a week everywhere you install one of these machines—that or something worse! Now, do you have a coffee machine handy? I could use a refill before I go down to the factory."[146]

Haanstra never used the same trick twice. His actions produced the desired result of breaking down communication barriers previously erected by the escalating management levels established by the group/division/department/section/subsection organizational structure. For this he was universally admired by the Phoenix group.

During his years of working on IBM's FAA air traffic control system, Haanstra had acquired a twin-engine Cessna airplane that he kept in the private pilot section of the Phoenix airport.[147] He used it frequently for travel to the various regional and district offices, and he made it a practice to show up unexpectedly at customer sites to chat with GE's field service people. While this was sometimes disconcerting to the regional and district managers, his increasing familiarity with customers and field service personnel made a favorable impact on the whole organization.

The feeling was growing in Phoenix that bigger and better days were ahead. Stan Smith was a fine professional manager, well suited to being a group executive in the General Electric environment. He recognized his own lack of knowledge in the computer field, and he welcomed Haanstra's stewardship in Phoenix. What he may not have realized was that Haanstra had been sheltered at IBM as far as account-ability for short-term profits was concerned—he was basically product oriented, with others taking responsibility for profit performance. This delighted the troops in Phoenix but did little to improve the finances of the Information Systems Division. As 1968 went along, the executive office became increasingly restive, and Fred Borch decided Stan Smith's appointment might have been a mistake.

Meanwhile, a possible successor to Smith had come up through the ranks at GE's Aerospace Group in Valley Forge, Pennsylvania. Hilliard (Hilly) Paige, who had received a BSME from Worcester Polytechnic Institute in 1941, went through the GE Test Program and Advanced Engineering Program and then left GE after a brief peri-od. Paige returned to GE in 1951 as manager of operations analysis in the Jet Engine Division. In 1956 he moved to the Missile and Space Division as manager of the Nose Cone Section, and by 1962 he had risen to the position of general manager. When his boss, Jack Parker, was made vice chairman and a member of the newly formed GE executive office, Paige ascended to the position of group executive, Aerospace Group.

During his tour at Valley Forge, Paige was a customer and user of the Computer Department's computers and time-sharing system and became an enthusiastic sup-porter of time-sharing services as a business. At one point, he had proposed to take over the government sector of the time-sharing market. To his disappointment, 570 instead decided to consolidate all time-sharing services in Bethesda.

In 1968, the volume of the Aerospace Group's business, though still quite prof-itable, began to flatten out at about $1 trillion. Paige reflected on the fact that loss-es in the computer businesses were almost twice the profits of his own business. In late 1968, when Jack Parker and Fred Borch, dissatisfied with Smith's progress with the Information Systems Group, asked Paige to leave the Aerospace Group and take on the Information Systems Group, he was agreeable. Smith, more relieved than dis-mayed, was made group executive of the newly formed International Group and Paige took his place at the end of 1968. The announcement of the change said the following in part: "At the same time, Mr. Borch named Hilliard W. Paige, vice pres-ident and group executive of the Aerospace Group, to succeed Mr. Smith as head of the Information Systems Group. He brings to his new position outstanding sys-tems management and technological skills."

The change in group executives did not cause much of a stir among the troops in Phoenix. They had become hardened to the corporate management convulsions and resigned to the probability of trickle-down changes in directions and policy. However, they were pleased at the performance of their division manager, John Haanstra. Perhaps, they hoped, the era of micromanagement from 570 had come to an end.

PART VI

Denouement
January 1969
to
October 1970

DRAMATIS PERSONAE

DICK BLOCH. Former Honeywell product planner, assigned by Paige to develop the specifications and make a financial forecast for the Advanced Product Line.

REGGIE JONES. GE vice president for finance.

PAUL SAGE. Manager of Computer Services under Paige.

JOHN McKITTERICK. GE vice president for long range planning.

ROGER ROSBERG. Minneapolis sales representative for Computer Department.

JIM BINGER. General manager of Honeywell Computer Division.

STEPHEN KEATING. President of Honeywell.

CHAPTER 35
SHANGRI-LA AND A TRAGIC ACCIDENT

As 1969 opened, one of the more exciting systems projects of the Information Systems Division seemed to be coming to fruition. This was Project ISIS, originated by corporate Marketing Services and transferred to Phoenix in 1965 during Lou Rader's administration. It was to be a retail information system involving a magnetic merchandise ticket containing coded price and product information that could be read automatically by a point-of-sale device called TRADAR. A multiplicity of TRADAR terminals, spread throughout a department store, were to be connected to a GE 425 computer where the product information would be decoded and flashed back to the TRADAR where the customer's charge slip would be printed out. Simultaneously, the store's inventory account would be adjusted and the sale recorded. At the end of the day, without human intervention, management reports would be issued, customer charge accounts adjusted, and vendor orders prepared in accordance with the store's inventory-control procedures.

The software required for the ISIS system bore a family resemblance to the ERMA demand deposit accounting software, and the system concept whereby the merchandise ticket acted as the input to the computer was reminiscent of the MICR technique whereby the check became the input medium.

In April 1969, J.C. Penney Co. announced the signing of a $10 million contract with GE for a new, unique information system designed for the retail department store industry. It was called the TRADAR Retail Information System.

J.C. Penney's plan was to install the system in one of its Los Angeles stores on a trial basis, and, if successful, the company would equip 50 stores in the Los Angeles area with 1,500 new TRADAR point-of-sale devices. J.C. Penney claimed the new system would achieve faster sales, increase salesclerk productivity, improve customer service, inventory, and general store operation, and reduce credit losses and cash-till irregularities.

Clint DeGabrielle, one of the many remaining members of the original Sheeley sales organization, was closely involved in the J.C. Penney test program.[148] The system worked perfectly, but the process of encoding every product ticket at the department store level was cumbersome. Neither GE nor J.C. Penney had enough clout in the retail market to sell the industry on uniform product encoding at the manufacturer level. The system was ahead of its time, but the trial did prove the feasibility of the TRADAR point-of-sale terminal. It was unfortunate that neither J.C. Penney nor GE had an "A1 Zipf type" to carry the torch for a common product-encoding language. Had GE retained its ties with NCR, created during the ERMA period, the substantial expenditures of the TRADAR project might have resulted in a more positive approach to the central problem of product-encoding standards.

The most positive event in early 1969 was the renewal of volume shipments of the GE 600s (615/625/635) using the GECOS III operating system.[149] The 600, after two years of debugging and redesign, had developed into a very solid and reliable product—and quite competitive from a price and performance standpoint. The marketing people were overjoyed, and they clamored for specific bells and whistles to exploit various customer opportunities. Sadly, budget constraints had caused prior management to cancel the development of a peripheral system to permit interfacing the 600 with the MICR-quipped high-speed check sorter. This essentially ruled out GE as a competitor for the follow-up version of GE's own ERMA system.

George Snively, who had followed the Bank of America program closely, reported as follows, "IBM ultimately 'bought' the business, but part of the price IBM paid was to pay GE's $250,000 monthly maintenance fees for any months IBM was late in delivering. For nearly 18 months IBM paid the monthly bill of $250,000 for GE's service of ERMA—a total of $4.5 million to eliminate one competitor from one key customer. This was the kind of game GE was not willing to play."[150]

One of the things that irked the marketing people was the fact that, while Bull and Olivetti were beginning to reach the threshold of profitability through the exploitation of the time-sharing systems developed at Phoenix, and through manufacture and sale of 400 and 600 computers, there was no reciprocal dividend for the Information Systems Division, either in terms of new products for the U.S. market or in terms of a share of the profits generated overseas by the sale of products developed at great expense to the Phoenix profit and loss statement but manufactured and serviced by the affiliates.

Chuck Ettinger, marketing manager for small computers, had persuaded management that this situation could be changed if the key field sales people visited Italy to obtain an on-the-spot introduction to the Olivetti product line of small computers.[151] The salesmen jumped at the opportunity to spend a week in Italy studying the Olivetti product line while taking note of the many other attractions of the region. They returned with an appreciation of the Italian way of life and a few samples of Olivetti's 100 line of small machines that were going well in the European market. The product planners, anxious to experiment on something new, predicted sales of 3,000 to 4,000 on the U.S. market. Thus was born the GE 115, advertised to the industry as a workstation-type terminal for the 600 line of time-sharing systems. Unfortunately, the device lacked a number of features that would have made it into a bestseller even though it was sold within General Electric as a remote terminal (cards) and output (printer) station.

Meanwhile, Hilly Page had decided it was vitally important to develop a new product plan that would provide upward software compatibility and time-sharing capability across the board from small to large systems. The GE 200, 400, and 600 series were inward compatible; for example, the 215, 225, 235, and 265 were compatible among themselves, but the 200s, 400s, and 600s were not compatible with one another. Of most importance, there needed to be a bridge between the 400 and 600 series. Haanstra had his Pi program aimed at solving this problem through a software bridge, but this rather esoteric approach was not welcomed by the product planners who visualized a completely new series of products designed to be upwardly compatible at every step. Dick Bloch, brought in from Honeywell by Stan Smith to head product planning at group level, was selected by Paige to organize and head up a team to develop a plan for such a product line.[152] (The story from Phoenix was that Bloch had attempted such a project at Honeywell; an effort costing time and money and ending up with zero results.) Bloch was given the mission of gathering together product planners, engineers, software people, and "marketeers" from throughout the Information Systems Division, GE Bull, and GE Italia to create the specifications for a worldwide product line that would make GE a clear number two behind IBM.

One of the management techniques popular in GE at the time was the "retreat" whereby individuals with diverse and sometimes conflicting viewpoints would be gathered together and isolated from outside pressures while they debated the issues. In the case of Shangri-la,[153] as this very secret project was called, there were 60 participants, divided into 12 groups, each of which would report its findings to the body as a whole for comments and criticism, after which the process would be repeated. It was hoped this process would gradually produce a consensus in which all parties—the French, the Italians, and the Americans—would cooperate to evolve the company's Advanced Product Line (APL).

The Diplomat Hotel in Hollywood, Florida, was picked as the venue for Shangri-la. The participants were mainly product planners and market researchers. John Haanstra was not to be a part of the study team, nor were the many others who were closely associated with ongoing programs and product lines. There was some logic to this philosophy as a means of eliminating the NIH (not invented here) attitude. The price paid for this independence of thought was the virtual elimination of input from those who had the most knowledge of the computer business, gained from combat in the arena.

While the APL project moved ahead, Paige became increasingly concerned with the conduct of John Haanstra. Not only did the Information Systems Division continue to be unprofitable, but Haanstra continued to be difficult to control. Haanstra, not acclimated to the GE way of doing things, had few friends at the executive level.

His negotiations with Toshiba in connection with his Pi project were strictly outside of company channels, and he did little to explain and justify his approach to the product line. Gradually convinced that Haanstra was not the right man for the job, Paige decided to replace him.

GE had a rule that company executives could fly only in private aircraft with two engines and with a co-pilot. Haanstra had a twin-engine plane, and GE, surprisingly, had made an exception about the co-pilot in his case. During vacation, he had brought his family to New York, and Paige decided this was as good a time as any to break the news. It was a painful interview, but both men seemed relieved when it was over.

Not long after this meeting, Haanstra was flying between Oklahoma City and Albuquerque when one engine died. No problem it seemed, but he feathered the wrong engine and the plane came down like a rock, killing him, his wife, and his 14-year-old son.[154] The sad news burst like a bombshell over Phoenix. The natural anguish at this human tragedy was accentuated by the sobering realization that the troops had lost a strong leader who, they felt, understood the computer business.

Equally saddened was Hilly Paige, troubled by the thought that his removal of Haanstra had somehow led to the tragic event. The news came to Paige while he was on vacation at Boca Raton. He had already come to a decision about Haanstra's replacement, and his considered choice was John Burlingame, former general manager of the Special Information Products Department where the forerunner of the GE 600 had been developed under John Couleur. He had also taken over the responsibility for the MULTICS program with MIT, assigning the project to Walker Dix, whose guys did such an outstanding job that Stan Smith had convinced Borch to transfer the entire department to the Information Systems Division.

Burlingame had been invited to take over the merged group, but he was not a fan of either Smith or Haanstra. He elected to leave GE and join RCA as general manager of the division that developed the TV and antenna system for the LEM module on the Apollo program. He was not unhappy at RCA, but he found he missed GE where he had spent 18 years of his business life. He found, on the average, that his former GE associates were a cut above the RCA people he was working with. Also, Burlingame thrived on challenge, and he found that RCA didn't provide the type of challenge GE did. He had occasion to discuss this with GE's Jack Parker when the two met during a missile launch at Cape Canaveral. Parker had been quite supportive of Burlingame in earlier years, and he was receptive to the thought that the man might return to GE at the appropriate time. Shortly after the meeting with Parker, Burlingame received a call from Paige.[155]

"John, how would you like to return to General Electric and become Haanstra's replacement as vice president and general manager of the Information Systems Division?" Burlingame recognized the magnitude of the challenge and was quick to accept Paige's offer. The two men reached agreement on details, and, by the end of September, 1969, Burlingame was back in GE and ensconced in his Phoenix headquarters.

Vic Casebolt returned from Europe in 1969 to become manager of information sales and service, reporting to Tom Vanderslice.[156] Casebolt was full of ideas to make the GE 600 more versatile and customer friendly, and he persuaded both Vanderslice and Burlingame that a proposal should be made to 570. In October 1969, Casebolt, Vanderslice, and Paige met in New York. Casebolt had prepared for the meeting with care, and he arrived with detailed back-up, including schedule and cost commitments from both engineering and manufacturing. The cash-flow projections showed a rapid payback, and specific customers were identified. Casebolt was sure he had a winner.

"We'd like your permission to initiate and carry out a very specific set of projects to increase sales and profits for the GE 600," began Casebolt. "The 600 is already a fine machine with most of its initial teething problems taken care of. We have a plan to extend the line by adding additional models and power and by providing controllers for a few key peripherals such as high-speed check sorters."

Casebolt went on to describe the proposed improvements, concluding with the statement, "This series of upgrades will establish the 600 as one of the hottest products on the market, and they can be accomplished at very low development cost because the architecture and operating system are already developed, and the higher speed circuitry is available off the shelf."

Paige was pressed for time, and he may not have listened to Casebolt as carefully as he should have. His mind was centered on the APL program in Florida. "I have only a few minutes left before I have to shove off for La Guardia. Leave your proposals with me and I'll discuss them with Dick Bloch. We can't afford to make a major investment in a program that doesn't fit in with the Advanced Product Line, but I'm sure Bloch will give you a fair hearing."

Later in the year, Casebolt was invited to visit the super-secret Shangri-la group in Florida to review and critique the results of the three-month think-in.[157] One of the first questions on arrival was, "What did the group think of our proposal for the GE 600 enhancements?"

It turned out that Paige and Bloch had discussed it briefly and concluded that any actions of this sort should wait until APL had been proposed to the executive office and approved. One of the study participants, a friend of Casebolt, told him frankly, "There's no place here for GE 600 enhancements that might compete with the APL. Bloch's objectives are to conceive of a new line of products that would have a 30-percent price-performance advantage over IBM across the 370 spectrum, so we've all been inventing bigger and better IBM clones. We're now in the process of trying to compute the cost of developing the various computer types in parallel and deciding what bits and pieces will be developed by Phoenix, GE Bull, and GE Italia. The general concept of an integrated, software-compatible product line is certainly a good one, but most of us are willing to sign off on most anything so we can get out of here and go home."

Casebolt listened to several days of presentations covering the APL. He felt almost all the presentations were heavy with then-current buzz words and little concrete technical detail behind them. It was Casebolt's opinion that the proposal was devoid of substance.[158]

On his return to Phoenix, Casebolt described his experience to Burlingame and Vanderslice. He was despondent concerning the future of the business in which he had grown up. "John," he said, "we're systematically stunting the growth of our present products at just the time we can visualize a profitable business, and the Florida project, which was supposed to be our future, is a sham. Is there no way we can get to 570 to get the facts across to Fred Borch?"

"You may be right, Vic, but our group executive, Hilly Paige, is the one responsible for the Shangri-la project, so his own reputation is dependent on his ability to sell the APL to the board. He's certainly not going to let us give a negative story to Borch. If I should oppose his pet project, I'd be out of this job in a minute."

"Do you mind if I make an unofficial approach through the financial organization?" said Casebolt. "Al Way, who was chief financial officer of GE Bull when I was there, is a good friend of mine. He's now in the executive office working for Reggie Jones, and he must have an avenue to the top."

"Go to it."

Casebolt, desperate to get his story across, traveled to New York and made his way to Al Way's office at 570 Lexington. He was greeted warmly by Way and, over coffee, the two men reminisced about people and experiences at Machines Bull.

"It was a wonderful experience," concluded Casebolt. "I really felt I was making an important contribution to GE's success in Europe. Now that I'm back home, I'm finding that things are taking a step backward, and I'm here in the hope that you can help me get the facts to the executive office."

"Fire away, Vic."

Casebolt laid out his concerns to Way, concluding with the statement that he was going to start looking for another job, "because we are on the verge of being a strategically bankrupt, failing business."

"Don't do it, Vic. Please stay with it a little longer; there's a remedy in the works that will solve the problem. I can't reveal the exact nature of the remedy, but I think you will be happy with it."

"Okay, Al, I'll give it a shot, but not for too long."

Later, on the plane back to Phoenix, Casebolt struggled with the conundrum presented by Al Way. Try as he might, he couldn't conceive of any way out of the hole he believed Bloch was digging.[159]

While Casebolt was agonizing, Paige and his key staff people were preparing to meet with Wall Street's financial analysts. It was not often that GE's financial management permitted any single GE business entity to interact with the wizards of Wall Street, but this was an unusual situation. Ever since the *Forbes* article calling the computer business "GE's Edsel," the financial press had been rife with speculations concerning the company's dedication to the information-processing industry.

With Paige in his office were five people selected in part because of their positions in the organization and in part for their ability to make convincing presentations. One was Tom Vanderslice, representing the Phoenix marketing organization. Then there were three representing the group's international businesses: Arthur Peltasolo, general manager, International Information Systems Division; Henri Desbrueres, directeur general, GE Bull; Ottorino Beltrami, managing director, GE Information Systems Italia; and, finally, Paul Sage, general manager, Information Services Division (Time Sharing), Bethesda, Maryland.

"I've been instructed to give the analysts a presentation concerning how well we're doing in the computer business," said Paige. "The board hasn't yet approved the plan for the Advanced Product Line so we'll have to stick with the existing product line and try to jazz up the presentations with some of the more spectacular applications. Any suggestions?"

"How about the GE 635 at Cape Canaveral that monitors thousands of valves and gauges of the Saturn V booster 12 times every second? The press is still excited about the moon landing a couple of months ago, and I can probably get a statement from Rudy Burns, chief of the Cape Kennedy Data Systems Division, saying how important the GE 635 was in making the mission a success."

"Good. That will help counter the claims in the technical press that the 600 was a disaster."

"It seemed like it a couple of years ago, but it's turned out to be a tremendous machine. Now that we've renewed the marketing push for the 600 series, the customer acceptance has been immensely gratifying."

"Anything else newsworthy from Phoenix?"

"Well," said Vanderslice, "one of the interesting things is that the GE 200 line, particularly the 265 time-sharing version, which had been thought obsolete three years ago, is still doing well. We're beginning to see the kind of advantage enjoyed by IBM, in which equipment out on lease has been fully depreciated but continues to generate lease income. The 200 line is quite profitable and will continue to be cumulatively profitable."

"How about you, Art?" said Paige, turning to Peltasolo.

"We're doing very well with the GE 400, which is now being manufactured in our Angers plant in the Loire Valley, and we're now importing the GE 600 into Europe in increasing numbers. The Europeans are excited about the '3-D' capability—the ability to do remote time sharing using the new Datanet 355 communications processor as well as to do local data processing, remote data, batch, and conversational time sharing all at the same time.

"Then," Peltasolo went on, "we have two lines of small computers developed in Europe: the GE 50 series designed and produced in France, and the GE 100 series designed and made in Italy. More than 1,000 GE 50s have been produced and sold in France, and 1,500 GE l00s have been sold in Italy. At the moment, these lines aren't compatible with one another, nor is either compatible with the 600. We're working on this problem.

"Finally," said Peltasolo, "I should mention the importance of remote time sharing in improving our financial performance in the overseas markets. By the end of 1969 we'll have more than 75 systems serving 100,000 users in 21 countries and five continents."

"Good stuff for the analysts." Paige turned to Paul Sage with the question, "What do you have to say about the domestic computer services business?"

"We're number one in the country, and our volume is building up fast as we add new users to our existing network. As you know, the time-shared computer service business is very capital intensive. We have to make an initial investment in buildings, computers, communications facilities, and programming before we receive any income, and then we have a frantic period where we sell the service to all sorts of customers: scientists, engineers, universities, banks, and other businesses. Once we hit the break-even point, the rest is gravy. It's sort of like the cable television business, though far more complicated. Anyway, our computer service business is already profitable and growing better every day."

"Okay, then," said Paige. "I'll start the meeting off with a description of our organization worldwide, numbers of employees, and so on, stressing GE's strong commitment to the computer business and with a few general remarks on each of our divisions. I'll then give each of you 10 to 15 minutes to tell your division's story and answer questions. Then I'll give a 5-minute summary.

"Remember, fellows, there's to be no mention of the Advanced Product Line or Bloch's study program in Florida. I'll answer any questions about this if the analysts bring it up, and my answer will be that this is simply a continuation of our long-range planning activity."

The session with the analysts went well, resulting in a favorable article in the Wall Street Journal. The text of the presentations, complete with photographs, was subsequently made into a very attractive publication, "Progress Report on General Electric's Performance in the Information Systems Business." Issued in December 1969, it was the most positive statement ever made by GE in connection with its computer business.[160]

Back in Phoenix, the troops were confused. Most were aware the Shangri-la report had been issued to the executive office calling for a phase-out rather than a build-up of the existing product line, in parallel with the creation of an Advanced Product Line at an estimated cost rumored to be between $500 million and $1 billion. Those who had participated in the APL study realized the plan was highly speculative and based almost completely on achieving a product line that matched IBM's but with improved performance and lower selling prices. There was some faint hope that the bullish progress report released by 570 to the financial press represented a vote of confidence in enhancing the existing product line rather than going the "me, too" route of APL.

John Burlingame, general manager in Phoenix, had been isolated from the APL study and was never given a chance to critique the APL report. Given the assignment of holding the line while the fundamental discussions were going on elsewhere, Burlingame put emphasis on slimming down the organization. Over a period of six months he separated 2,500 persons, of whom he was able to place 95 percent—a remarkable achievement. Suddenly the financials were beginning to look up. Unfortunately, this garnered little attention at an executive office struggling with the APL results.[161]

CHAPTER 36
VERDICT OF THE THREE WISE MEN

When Paige received the final version of the APL report, he paid special attention to the financial projections to meet the program's objectives. The product planners had included $200 million for hardware and software development and an equal figure for factory tooling, special testing equipment, and other facilities necessary to produce prototypes and tool-up for quantity production. Paige felt they had omitted an important element of cost, which was that of training and recruiting the greatly enlarged service organization and sales force necessary to handle the new product line. He increased the total to $600 million.[162]

As the plan was finally submitted to the executive office in late 1969, the projected cost was set forth clearly, but there was some lack of substance as to the means of accomplishing the objective.[163]

The year 1969 was not a very good time to contemplate a cash drain of great magnitude. GE had been facing and still faced a series of costly strikes. The company had three major businesses still hungry for dollars: computers, nuclear energy, and commercial jet engines. In the latter two cases, GE had long before established an industry position as either number one or number two in the country—these had been nourished by the U.S. government during World War II and were considered core businesses. In computers, GE had entered the business late and was still playing catch-up. It was the philosophy of the time that only a plan predicting an eventual number-two industry position would be accepted, and with this in mind the Shangri-la study group had started at the desired end point and worked backward.

The APL program projected the desired outcome to occur within five to ten years, based on a product line that would be highly competitive with IBM technically and would lease for 20 percent less across the board. There were many assumptions in this prediction including the supposition that IBM would stand meekly by and not take punitive action in response to GE's challenge.[164] But, there was another more serious flaw in the APL proposal. It clearly failed to address the needs of the General Electric Company as a whole, nor did it build on the strengths of the company. It was a proposal of a follower rather than a leader, and, above all, GE executives considered themselves leaders.

It was clear to many that any product line established in the computer field should serve the company as a whole including industrial, utility, military, appliances, communications, commercial, and so on. Each Operating Department of the company needed computers in one form or another in its product development, manufacturing, marketing, and service functions. Fulfillment of these needs alone would justify the existence of a major business entity (just as Western Electric was justified as a subsidiary of AT&T in the telecommunications field). Bloch had no understanding of the General Electric Company, and even Hilly Paige's aerospace operation had been apart from most company businesses. Forgetting that the rest of the company would have to foot the bill for the $600 million (plus) APL program, Bloch had failed to provide any incentives for the internal customers.[165]

Faced with the impending cash drain and a general lack of enthusiasm on the part of several division managers, CEO Borch appointed Reggie Jones, GE's vice president for finance, to study the company's three "problem" businesses.[166] Actually, nuclear energy and commercial jet engines were in little jeopardy, so the study boiled down to an investigation of the feasibility of the Advanced Product Line by three corporate vice presidents. One was Reggie Jones himself. The other two were Bob Estes, vice president and general counsel, and John McKitterick, vice president for corporate planning. The trio were quickly dubbed the "Three Wise Men."

Reggie Jones, although a financial man, was known to speak up readily on marketing or technical matters. John McKitterick, an advocate of strategic planning as the basis for the company's actions, was firm in his opinion that GE should not be in any business where the company could not be either number one or number two. Bob Estes, who at one time had been counsel to Doc Baker's Electronics Division in Syracuse and had signed off on the original ERMA contract, was considered a sound and conservative business man.

The first decision made by the task force was to keep the nuclear energy and commercial jet engine businesses. In both cases, the decisions were based on the fact that these two were core businesses where GE was either number one or two and where no great technical obstacles were foreseen. In retrospect, one might question this assumption in the case of nuclear energy, but no amount of strategic planning could have anticipated the impact of Three Mile Island or Chernobyl on the business.

As the task force increased the intensity of its study of the APL, the major omissions in Bloch's Shangri-la study program became evident.[167] No representatives of the Industrial Group or the Aerospace Group had been invited to participate in the study; as a result, these two powerful groups had no commitment to the APL or to the large dollar amount projected to achieve the project's objectives. When called upon by the Three Wise Men for opinions, the management of these two groups rightly commented that the APL was strictly of benefit to the Information Systems Group rather than being a project of the company as a whole.

By February of 1970 the task force came to the conclusion that the APL program was too risky to warrant the gamble of what they felt would be at least a billion dollars. They also accepted the premise that only as number two to IBM should GE remain in the computer business. They investigated the possibility of an acquisition of another company as a means of obtaining the additional volume necessary to achieve the desired market share, but the U.S. Department of Justice informed Estes that purchasing another computer firm would probably violate antitrust regulations.

Based on these considerations, the task force recommended to Fred Borch that GE sell its information systems business. This recommendation was made in an atmosphere of great secrecy, and it was withheld from the organizational units involved—any general leakage of management's plans would cause an immediate exodus of key people and greatly reduce the value of business. Reggie Jones was given the job of selling the business.

Back in Phoenix, the troops were unaware of the decision to dispose of the business.[168] They were aware of the study being made by the task force, but it was generally assumed by most that the decision in question related to a go/no go for Bloch's APL rather than for the computer business as a whole.

John Burlingame knew better. He had spent some time trying to convince "the powers that be" that an evolutionary development of an integrated product line, starting with the successful 600 system and creating a midsize and smaller clone, was a reasonable way to go, but prior disappointments had produced such a negative attitude that no one would buy the approach. He was contacted once by the Three Wise Men, but they were seeking his opinion concerning a possible buyer or partner rather than how to improve the existing business. He suggested Honeywell as a possible acquisition that would make GE number two in the industry, but Estes told him the U.S. Department of Justice wouldn't approve—however, they would approve Honeywell buying GE's computer business. Burlingame got the idea.

On April 13, 1970, GE issued a press release to the Phoenix newspapers that concluded as follows:

> As GE facilities and production of information systems have grown in Phoenix, so has the scope and influence of what was originally known as the Computer Department. What began with 50 Phoenix employees in 1956 is now the worldwide GE Information Systems Group headquartered in New York City, employing 25,000 people, and spread to every free corner of the globe.

CHAPTER 37
THE SELL-OFF

Roger Rosberg was district manager of the Computer Department's Minneapolis district office during the spring of 1970 when GE held its annual shareholders meeting in that city, and he was the first one of the troops to know GE was selling the Information Systems Division. It happened in the following way.[169]

As the local manager, Rosberg had been asked by President Borch's office to be responsible for all the local arrangements for the annual meeting, including transportation, breakfast, luncheon, cocktail parties, banquets, and so on. It was an interesting experience during which he met the major corporate figures such as Borch, Reggie Jones, Bob Estes, and Jack Parker (vice chairman). They came a day early to avoid incidents with a group of environmentalists who were expected to picket the meeting to protest GE's nuclear business (by coincidence, it was the original "Earth Day").

Rosberg was asked to find some space where big papers could be spread around, so he arranged for the room where they would have the cocktail party that evening. He gave them the key and left them alone after ordering an assortment of liquor, ice, and mix. It was mid-afternoon when he returned to check out the liquor supply. Jones answered his knock and was reluctant to let him in until the papers were covered. Rosberg knew something was up.

The next morning—the day of the annual meeting—Rosberg was notified that Borch would be going to his room after lunch and would be joined by Jones, Estes, Parker, and a few others whose names were not given. Rosberg made the usual arrangements for refreshments, including keeping a couple of limousines for their later use.

After the luncheon, he saw four men going into Borch's suite by the back door, and all he could tell was that they knew each other. Late that afternoon, he was sitting in one of the big limousines waiting for the affair to end. Finally, the four men came out of the hotel acting very pleased with themselves. One of them looked like Jim Binger of Honeywell—he'd seen his picture. They were all quite distinguished.

Then the GE group came out. Rosberg helped them with their luggage, asking a few polite but leading questions to Reggie Jones. The answers were noncommittal, but the look in Jones' eyes made it clear it was none of Rosberg's business.

The next day, Rosberg got hold of a Honeywell annual report. All four men who had been at Borch's meeting were pictured in the report, including the distinguished

Stephen Keating, Honeywell's president. At this point, he was sure what had happened. He knew GE wouldn't be allowed to buy Honeywell, so the computer business was obviously being sold.

Several years later, Rosberg happened to be on a sales call with Jim Binger. When their business was completed, they had a couple of scotches together and started talking about the 1970 meeting.

"You know," said Binger, "I had a call from Fred Borch saying that it might be useful for GE and Honeywell to get together to explore possible joint opportunities in the computer business. He invited me to visit him the next time I came to New York on business.

"Well," continued Binger, "I called my guys together and told them we were going to New York to discuss possible deals with GE. After we got there and they had a lunch, and Borch talked a lot of philosophical stuff about the computer business, he finally paused. I looked at him and said, 'Fred, are you buying or selling?' and he said, 'I'm selling.' And that's the way it was about the first of February, 1970."

While Fred Borch was the front man during the sale to Honeywell, Reggie Jones was the architect of the project.[170] He knew Honeywell didn't have enough cash to buy the business from GE, so he crafted an agreement that appeared on the surface to be a joint venture of the two companies to establish a new company to be called Honeywell Information Systems (HIS). The new company would be owned $81\frac{1}{2}$ percent by Honeywell and $18\frac{1}{2}$ percent by General Electric, though the fine print would show that GE had a requirement to divest itself of the HIS stock within ten years. In addition, GE would receive $110 million in notes and Honeywell stock valued at about $125 million. It was a win-win agreement for both companies, given GE's reluctance to stay the course. Honeywell was extremely anxious to acquire the GE 600 computer line, which would fit in very nicely with its medium-speed offerings, and they also placed great value on obtaining the Bull and Olivetti sales and distribution networks. GE would substantially recover the company's 14-year investment in computers along with posting a net profit of $1.5 million in 1970.

The corporate sale went so smoothly that a number of business schools, including Harvard, conducted case studies of what they considered a classic corporate divestiture. Reggie Jones quickly became a celebrity within GE and, in fact, would become GE president in 1972.

But Jones came close to making an important mistake when he was tabulating the business entities and assets that would be transferred to Honeywell as a part of the transaction. He had carefully excluded the process control and communications businesses, but he had included the prosperous computer services time-sharing business located in Bethesda, Maryland. McKitterick, bullish on time-sharing, insisted this not be a part of the sale, and it was quietly withdrawn. Jones's financial wizardry was in contrast with RCA's withdrawal from the computer business a year later at a net loss of $210 million, or Xerox's write-down of $85 million in 1975.

Transmutations of the GE Computer Department plant on Black Canyon Highway, Phoenix. Machines Bull Computers, originally controlled by GE, then by Honeywell, later combined with Nippon Electric to buy controlling interest in Honeywell Information Systems. The Bull sign is complemented by a "For Sale" sign in the yard.

The Phoenix edition of the *General Electric News*, dated May 28, 1970, contained a message from Chairman Borch, quoted in part as follows:

> The formation of the new company with Honeywell establishes a strong, new contender in the computer industry. . . . The new company will have human, financial, and physical resources sufficient to take advantage of emerging technologies and will have abundant opportunities to further improve efficiencies. . . . *Finally, and very important to our share owners, General Electric continues to have a major interest in the computer industry itself with its investments in both Honeywell and the new company.*

The last sentence of Mr. Borch's message was of course untrue in view of the requirement that GE divest itself within ten years of all HIS or Honeywell stock acquired as a result of the transaction. The deliberately misleading phrasing was an obvious attempt to soften the blow to the 25, 000 employees world-wide who otherwise might have jumped the traces. In the main, it was successful.

Five months would elapse between the initial announcement and the final legal agreement. On September 30, 1970, the day before the so-called merger, John Burlingame, as his last act as general manager, invited his staff to the Camelback Inn for a luncheon at which he presented each man with a beautiful ice bucket, engraved with a tombstone inscribed, "I.S.E.D.,* 1.1.68–9.30.70, R.I.P."

The next day the "Computer Department," which most of them still called it despite nomenclature changes from above, became a part of Honeywell Information Systems, Inc.

*Information Systems Equipment Division.

PART VII

Aftershocks
October 1970
to
May 1994

Dramatis Personae

J.A.N. LEE. Editor in chief of the Institute of Electrical and Electronics Engineers (IEEE) *Annals of the History of Computing*.

KEN FISHER. Salesman for both the Computer Department and Honeywell information systems—the Honeywell subsidiary created after the sale by GE.

ED SPENCER. CEO of Honeywell.

DICK ROSENBERG. Chairman and CEO of the Bank of America, circa 1992.

MARIO GIANNINI. Son of A.P. Giannini.

ELTON WHITE. President of NCR.

ROBERT WEBER. Western manager of Pitney Bowes Corporation.

KATIE VOGELMAN. Manager of GE's Western U.S., Canada, and Latin America Information Services Division.

CHAPTER 38
"BLACK CANYON COMPUTERS"

G E's annual report for 1970 indicated that most of the professional managers were well rewarded for their tours of duty in the computer business.[171] John Burlingame was vice president, Corporate Employee Relations Operation; Jerry Coe was vice president and general manager, Industry Components and Metallurgical Division; Hershner Cross was senior vice president; Len Maier was vice president, Corporate Consulting Services; Hilliard Paige was senior vice president, Art Peltasolo was vice president and general manager, Information Services Division; Stan Smith was vice president and group executive, International Group; Tom Vanderslice was vice president and general manager, Electronic Components Division; and Lou Wengert was vice president and general manager, Control and Drives Automation Division.

It is not surprising to find that none of the individuals who created the Computer Department and fought in the trenches ended up as General Electric vice presidents. However, a great many became presidents or vice presidents of substantial businesses and made major contributions across the board from computer time sharing to scientific golfing. Many became millionaires many times over, and the achievements seem balanced between those who left on their own initiative and those who were fired. Apparently, a couple of years of survival in the GE Computer Department was a guarantee of lifelong success elsewhere.

When the business was sold to Honeywell, a number of engineers and manufacturing people—particularly those associated with the 600 line—stayed right where they were and continued with their projects. According to Walker Dix, engineering manager of the 600 line, the transition was well handled. The GE people were treated fairly and equitably, with pension benefits retained and other benefits being essentially equal.[172]

Dix stayed with HIS until 1978, when he moved to Intel as engineering director of Intel's Memory Division. During his period with HIS he experienced seven organizational changes. Shades of General Electric!

John Couleur, who had been a consultant to GE during the transition period, also joined HIS and lasted until 1980. He left at the point where Machines Bull, invigorated by 600 production, time sharing, and support from the French government, bought HIS from Honeywell. A strange turn of events.

One remarkable result of the 14-year adventure of the Computer Department was the creation of the GE Computer Department Alumni Association, which has gathered in Phoenix every four to six years. John Couleur had an interesting slant on history as he mused on the events that had taken place over the years at the Black Canyon Highway plant. He presented it at the regular meeting of the "Liar's Club."[173]

"You know, one of the things that has bothered me for a long time is that you fellows founded a business that turned out to be fantastically successful, but very few people know about it. They keep moaning about why GE went out of the computer business. As you well know, I spent a lot of time in Silicon Valley where everybody talks about start-ups—entrepreneurs, venture capitalists—and you tend to look at things like a business enterprise. And so, one way to explain this thing—and in the talk this morning with J.A.N. Lee (editor, Institute of Electrical and Electronic Engineers' *Annals of the History of Computing*) we kept bouncing back and forth saying things like, 'that happened during Honeywell' or 'that was during General Electric'—and I realized that we were talking about 'Black Canyon Computers,' and we had two venture capitalists.

"We had one venture capitalist when Barney went out and sold the ERMA system—went to his favorite venture capitalist who put up the cash to found the enterprise. And a lot of you guys contributed to that business—you laid a solid foundation for the business.

"Along the way the first venture capitalist decided that we didn't know how to run the business, so he sent in the carpetbaggers—the first team. They were nice fellows who knew how to build locomotives and make diamonds. One thought COBOL was some sort of blue, precious metal, and none of them could even understand Bob Sullivan's circuit specs. And the first venture capitalist sold out the business and left with his tail between his legs, so the second venture capitalist came in.

"Meanwhile, the troops stayed here along with the same product line. Good ole Black Canyon Computers kept rolling merrily along with its new venture capitalist. And all of sudden, a salesman named Ken Fisher came along and said, 'If you guys don't cut the price of the 2000—that's what the new venture capitalist called our 600—in half, we aren't going to sell diddly squat.' So they cut the price in half and, sure enough, a Honeywell sales mogul named Chris Lynch said, 'Well, if you can cut the price in half I can sell 300 a year.' Our manufacturing guy, Norm Feldman, said, 'If you can sell 300 computers a year and you'll guarantee it, I'll cut the cost by a factor of four. He was one of the few people that understood the finance of this business and realized that 80 percent of his shop cost was overhead, so if he could sell 300 computers a year, the shop cost would go down drastically. In fact, he made a fortune in incentive compensation because every time a computer was sold, the book cost would go down.

"Anyway, to make a long story short, we were soon selling the HIS 2000 (GE 600) at a rate of 350 to 400 a year and grossing a billion dollars a year. Sure, we added additional COBOL instructions, extended the base address, added a cache memory—all things our original venture capitalist wouldn't finance, and we kept extending the capability through the years.

"In 1980, the Black Canyon Computer Company, which you guys helped found, was doing pretty well. Ed Spencer, the head of Honeywell, came to visit us and said, 'Well, our Boston Computer Company is losing a little money, like $50 million a year, and our Paris Computer Company is doing about the same, but your Phoenix Computer Company is contributing half of Honeywell's total profits this year.' And if you guys are worried about whether it was Honeywell that funded it, or whether it was General Electric that funded it, I think you just ought to think of it as Black Canyon Computers, and say, 'Hey, I helped make it a success.'"

It was at this same reunion that George Snively, a numbers man to the last, put a different spin on the 14-year history of the General Electric Computer Department.[174]

"You know," said Snively, "I hear a lot of bitching about why General Electric couldn't hack it in the computer business. Some say it was because 570 insisted on trying to prove that a competent professional manager could manage any kind of business, including something as revolutionary as computers. Some say the company created constant instability by changing executives and managers every time a new crisis arose. Many of you think that a few bad apples, like Hershner Cross and Vern Cooper, were allowed to decimate the organization and make sweeping policy decisions in areas where they were ignorant. There's probably a lot of truth in all these theories, though my own opinion is that the best-kept secret of the computer industry is that General Electric made a substantial financial success in computers. For example, GE made a 'cashless' entry into the computer business, with progress payments from the Bank of America for ERMA, and from National Cash Register for the 304 computer, creating positive cash flows for the first two years. GE took advantage of conservative bookkeeping for the rental of computers to create tax shelters for several years. GE made several important contributions along the way, including—together with Dartmouth and MIT—the creation of time-sharing and networking technology that paved the way to the information superhighway. GE negotiated a profitable sale of the hardware portion of the business, structured so there was no recapture of the tax deferments.

"And, finally, GE continues to develop large profits from the substantial time-sharing and networking business that it retained. I rest my case," said Snively.

EPILOGUE
ERMA Revisited

Founder's Day, May 6, 1992. A brilliant northern California sun greeted the group of Bank of America executives, retirees, employees, and guests as they gathered at the bank's Concord Technology Center, in part to celebrate Founder's Day, the birthday of the bank's founder, A.P. Giannini. On this day, the bank chose to honor a team of people and a lady who had made an historic and lasting contribution to the welfare of banking and millions of customers. The lady's name was ERMA—a creation of transistors, magnetic ink, whirling reels of magnetic tape, and a device that read, shuffled, and sorted bank checks at a rate faster than the human eye could follow. ERMA, her hypnotic voice stilled after years of faithful service to the bank, had been retired with honors some 22 years previously.

Actually, there had been 32 ERMAs installed throughout California to automate the checking-account bookkeeping system of the bank's vast network of branches. Only one ERMA remained on Founders' Day, resurrected from storage, lovingly restored to mint condition, and installed in a place of honor and prominence in the Bank of America's Concord Technology Center as a memento of the time the Bank of America, Stanford Research Institute, and the General Electric Company joined forces to launch the banking industry into the age of computers.

As the ceremony proceeded, Dick Rosenberg, chairman and CEO of the bank, reviewed the past accomplishments of A.P. Giannini and his son Mario in bringing new banking services to California citizens, ranging from financing the allegedly "impossible" Golden Gate Bridge to the backing of *Snow White*. It had been in this spirit that the bank, stymied by the apathy of the office-equipment industry, had contracted with nearby SRI to develop a research prototype of an automation system to meet their needs.

Tom Morrin, director of electronics research for SRI, had been responsible for the multimillion dollar program resulting in the prototype first demonstrated to the press in 1955. Still spry almost 40 years later, Tom stepped to the podium to accept an award from the president of the bank. Other awards followed, with the greatest applause being given to Al Zipf, former executive vice president, the boss of the ERMA program.

The bank also honored those in industry who had taken the laboratory prototype and refined it to the point where it could be produced in quantity. This was to be one of the world's first commercial transistorized computers, and it would include a revolutionary technique for reading checks and converting the data to computer input. Bob Johnson had been the General Electric project engineer from beginning to end, meeting and surmounting severe technical challenges that arose every step of the way. Retired from industry, Bob was professor of computer science at the University of Utah. He smiled his appreciation as he received the award.

The honors continued. National Cash Register had been a principal contractor for General Electric, responsible for check sorters, proof machines, and printers, all representing advances in the art. The president of NCR, R.E. (Elton) White, had flown in from Dayton to accept his company's award. Also there was Robert Weber, western manager of NCR's major subcontractor, Pitney Bowes.

The final award was for the General Electric Company, which had launched its computer business with ERMA, had gambled on its ability to meet the technical challenge, and had delivered the entire quantity of ERMA systems on schedule and within rigid technical specifications of accuracy and reliability. Barney Oldfield, the original entrepreneur who obtained the ERMA contract and was the first general manager of GE's Computer Department, had long since left GE and could not be located. GE was represented by Katie Vogelheim, manager of GE's Western U.S., Canada, and Latin America Information Services Division, who accepted the award graciously.

Bob Johnson, who had hoped the award would be accepted by Jack Welch, GE's dynamic president, considered Welch's absence a rebuff. It was ironic, he thought, that ERMA was being celebrated for its revolutionary role in transforming American business data processing when, at the time of its creation, top management of GE had never met with the senior executives of the bank nor had they any interest in competing with their good customer and supplier IBM. As Bob joined the rest of the audience outside to witness the unveiling of the new Al Zipf Building, he reflected on the fact that, when the ERMA computer had finished its natural life at the end of the 1960s, the General Electric Company had not even bid on its successor. What a colossal waste![175]

Not exactly a waste, Bob!

Most of the thousands of General Electric employees who had "graduated" from the Computer Department—from choice, by being fired during periods of management turmoil, or by being laid off when the business was sold to Honeywell—went on to productive careers in the industry they had helped to create. A surprising number rose to top management positions, and many founded prosperous businesses based on lessons learned while chasing IBM's golden apple.

In addition, General Electric had ended up with one of the world's largest computer time-sharing networks, a part of the business that had generated substantial profits at a time when IBM was to embarrass its stockholders with its worst loss in history.[176]

The GE Computer Department did not evolve exactly as expected by its ambitious founders, but the end result could have been a lot worse. The 14-year adventure in computerland had been painful at times, but as one GE veteran expressed it, "It was one hell of a ride!"[177]

ENDNOTES

PART I

1. Homer Oldfield and George Trotter, GE Industrial Computer Section Proposal ICB-1100101, "ERMA, Electronic Recording Machine Accounting," 3 Feb. 1956.
2. Deposition of Fred Borch (former GE president), *United States v. IBM*, US District Court, Southern District of New York, pp. 8–20, Molly Danish, reporter (1974).
3. Author's personal recollection.
4. "Magnetic Ink Character Recognition, The Common Machine Language for Check Handling," Bank Management Publication 138, 21 July 1956, Technical Subcommittee on Mechanization of Check Handling, American Bankers Association.
5. Howard Lief (Bank of America vice president and controller), brief resume of the ERMA project, 7 May 1971.
6. James McKenney and Amy Fisher, "The Development of the ERMA Banking System," IEEE *Annals of the History of Computing*, Vol. 15, No. 1, 1993, pp. 50–52.
7. James McKenney and Amy Fisher, "Manufacturing the ERMA Banking System," IEEE *Annals of the History of Computing*, Vol. 15, No. 4, 1993, p. 10.
8. Howard Lief, letter to author, 28 June 1993.
9. Homer Oldfield and George Trotter, GE Industrial Computer Section Proposal ICB-1100101, "ERMA, Electronic Recording Machine Accounting," 3 Feb. 1956.
10. Homer Oldfield and George Trotter, GE Industrial Computer Section Proposal ICB-1100101, "ERMA, Electronic Recording Machine Accounting," 3 Feb. 1956.
11. Homer Oldfield and George Trotter, GE Industrial Computer Section Proposal ICB-1100101, "ERMA, Electronic Recording Machine Accounting," 3 Feb. 1956.
12. "Dr. Robert Johnson Interview," IEEE *Annals of the History of Computing*, Vol. 12, No. 2, 1990, p. 131.

13. Homer Oldfield, George Trotter, George jacobi, and Robert Johnson, GE Industrial Computer Section Proposal ICB-1100101A, "Initial Study of Simplified ERMA Design for Reduced Capacity Operation," 5 Mar. 1956.

14. George Snively, "General Electric Enters the Computer Business," IEEE *Annals of the History of Computing*, Vol. 10, No. 1, 1988, pp. 72–78.

15. Homer Oldfield and George Trotter, GE Industrial Computer Section Proposal ICB-1100101, "ERMA, Electronic Recording Machine Accounting," 3 Feb. 1956.

16. W.R.G. Baker (GE vice president and CEO, Electronics Division), letter to Howard Lief, 6 Apr. 1956.

17. George Jacobi, letter to author, 8 May 1993.

18. Joe Weizenbaum, letter to author, 31 July 1993.

19. "Report of Site Selection Survey," Industrial Computer Section, GE, 29 Aug. 1956, Homer Oldfield, Raymond Barclay, Kenneth Geiser, Clair Lasher, Kenneth McCombs, and Arthur Newman..

PART II

20. Bob Johnson, letter to author, 8 Apr. 1993.

21. Bob Johnson, letter to author, 8 Apr. 1993.

22. Bob Johnson, letter to author, 8 Apr. 1993.

23. George Jacobi, letter to author, 31 Jan. 1993.

24. George Metcalf, *Making Waves in the Information and Space Age*, Binford and Mort Publishing, Portland, OR, pp. 77–78.

25. George Metcalf, *Making Waves in the Information and Space Age*, Binford and Mort Publishing, Portland, OR, pp. 77–78.

26. Gerry Allard, letter to ERMA fellows, March 1993.

27. Plant appropriation request for GE Industrial Computer Section, GE, 24 Sept. 1956.

28. George Jacobi, letter to author, 17 Dec. 1994.

29. Herb Grosch, *Computer Bit Slices from Life*, Underwood-Miller.

30. George Snively, "General Electric Enters the Computer Business," IEEE *Annals of the History of Computing*, Vol. 10, No. 1, 1988, p. 75.

31. Joe Weizenbaum, letter to author, 31 July 1993.

32. "Dr. Robert Johnson Interview," IEEE *Annals of the History of Computing*, Vol. 12, No. 2, 1990, p 131.

33. Arnold Spielberg, letter to author, 4 Jan. 1994.

34. James McKenney and Amy Fisher, "Manufacturing the ERMA Banking System," IEEE *Annals of the History of Computing*, Vol. 15, No. 4, 1993, p. 21.

35. Herb Grosch, *Computer Bit Slices from Life*, Underwood-Miller.

36. IBID

37. Bob Johnson, letter to author, 16 Dec. 1993.

38. James McKenney and Amy Fisher, "Manufacturing the ERMA Banking System," IEEE *Annals of the History of Computing*, Vol. 15, No. 4, 1993, p. 31.

39. James McKenney and Amy Fisher, "Manufacturing the ERMA Banking System," IEEE *Annals of the History of Computing*, Vol. 15, No. 4, 1993, p. 31.
40. James McKenney and Amy Fisher, "Manufacturing the ERMA Banking System," IEEE *Annals of the History of Computing*, Vol. 15, No. 4, 1993, p. 31.
41. Janet Carter (Bank of America research consultant), letter to author, 10 March 1993.

PART III

42. Short stories of Alexander Botts, super-salesman of the Earthworm Tractor Company, *The Saturday Evening Post*.
43. Clair Lasher, letter to author, early 1993.
44. Ken Geiser, memorandum to Clair Lasher, 4 June 1959.
45. Bob Johnson, letter to author, 30 Mar. 1993.
46. George Snively, letter to author, 30 June 1994.
47. Mrs. Pat Barclay, letter to author, 30 Mar. 1993.
48. Mrs. Pat Barclay, letter to author, 30 Mar. 1993.
49. George Snively, letter to author, 8 May 1993.
50. Arnold Spielberg, letter to author, 14 Nov. 1993.
51. Arnold Spielberg, letter to author, 14 Nov. 1993.
52. Vic Casebolt, letter to author, 7 Apr. 1994.
53. Business plan, Computer Department, GE, 22 June 1960.
54. George Snively, letter to author, 17 May 1993.
55. Business plan, Computer Department, GE, 22 June 1960.
56. Robert Flaherty, "GE's Edsel," *Forbes*, 1 Apr. 1967, pp. 21-26.
57. "Frontiers of Progress," GE Computer Department national sales meeting, Apache Junction, Arizona, 15-18 May 1961.
58. Clint DeGabrielle, letter to author, 6 July 1994.
59. Clint DeGabrielle, letter to author, 6 July 1994.
60. Clint DeGabrielle, letter to author, 6 July 1994.
61. Robert Flaherty, "GE's Edsel," *Forbes*, 1 Apr. 1967, pp. 21-26.
62. John Couleur, letter to author, 6 July 1994.
63. Business review, Computer Department, GE, 5 Dec. 1962.
64. Business review, Computer Department, GE, 5 Dec. 1962.
65. Business review, Computer Department, GE, 5 Dec. 1962.

PART IV

66. Harrison Van Aken, telephone interview by author, 23 June 1995.
67. *The Computer Headliner* (GE Computer Department newspaper), 13 Feb. 1963.
68. George Snively, letter to author, 17 May 1993.
69. John Couleur, letter to author, 6 July 1994.

70. Bob Johnson, letter to author, 3 July 1994.
71. *The Computer Headliner*, 8 Apr. 1963.
72. *The Computer Headliner*, 26 Mar. 1963.
73. Bill Bridge, letter to author, 20 June 1993.
74. "The Computer Revolution," *Dartmouth Alumni Magazine*, 1964.
75. John Couleur, letter to author, 6 July 1994.
76. Mrs. Pat Barclay, letter to author, 25 Aug. 1994.
77. Bill Bridge, letter to author, 20 June 1993.
78. Mrs. Pat Barclay, letter to author, 10 Aug. 1994.
79. *The Computer Headliner*, 31 Dec. 1964.
80. *The Computer Headliner*, 31 Dec. 1964.
81. Bob Johnson, letter to author, 19 May 1993.
82. Robert Flaherty, "GE's Edsel," *Forbes*, 1 Apr. 1967, pp. 21-26.
83. Ed Parker, interview by author, 19 July 1993.
84. Ray Barclay, letter to author, 6 May 1993.
85. Lou Rader, letter to author, 9 July 1994.
86. Lou Rader, letter to author, 9 July 1994.
87. *The Computer Headliner*, 31 Dec. 1964.
88. Harrison Van Aken, letter to author, 4 May 1994.
89. John Couleur, letter to author, 27 May 1993.
90. John Couleur, letter to author, 27 May 1993.
91. Don Klee, interview by author, Port Charlotte, Florida, 24 Mar. 1995.
92. Don Klee, interview by author, Port Charlotte, Florida, 24 Mar. 1995.
93. Don Klee, interview by author, Port Charlotte, Florida, 24 Mar. 1995.
94. Bud Feeley (Martin-Marrieta), telephone interview by author, May 1995.
95. Paul Shapiro, letter to author, 26 Mar. 1995.
96. Paul Shapiro, letter to author, 26 Mar. 1995.
97. Paul Shapiro, letter to author, 26 Mar. 1995.
98. Paul Shapiro, letter to author, 26 Mar. 1995.
99. Paul Shapiro, letter to author, 26 Mar. 1995.
100. George Snively, letter to author, 6 Apr. 1995.
101. Paul Shapiro, telephone interview by author, 15 Mar. 1995.
102. Paul Shapiro, telephone interview by author, 15 Mar. 1995.
103. Paul Shapiro, telephone interview by author, 15 Mar. 1995.
104. Curt Hare, letter to author, 28 Mar. 1995.
105. Curt Hare, letter to author, 28 Mar. 1995.
106. James Richter, letter to author, 28 July 1995.
107. Lou Rader, letter to author, 5 Dec. 1994.
108. John Couleur, letter to author, 27 May 1994.
109. John Couleur, letter to author, 27 May 1994.
110. George Snively, letter to author, 16 Jan. 1995.
111. George Snively, letter to author, 16 Jan. 1995.
112. George Snively, letter to author, 16 Jan. 1995.
113. Vic Casebolt, letter to author, 20 May 1994.
114. Vic Casebolt, letter to author, 20 May 1994.

115. Tom O'Rourke, letter to author, 3 Aug. 1993.
116. George Snively, letter to author, 19 July 1993.
117. Tom O'Rourke, letter to author, 3 Aug. 1993.
118. Don Knight, interview by J.A.N. Lee, Phoenix, Arizona, 29 May 1994.
119. Karsten Solheim, interview by author, Phoenix, Arizona, 27 May 1994.
120. Business review, Computer Department, GE, 15 July 1965.
121. *The Computer Headliner*, 21 Dec. 1965.
122. *The Computer Headliner*, 21 Dec. 1965.

PART V

123. Business review, Computer Department, GE, 15 July 1965.
124. R.B. Curry and W.L. Lurie, letter to Hershner Cross, 15 Aug. 1965.
125. *The Computer Headliner*, 15 Mar. 1966.
126. Lou Rader, letter to author, 9 July 1994.
127. George Snively, letter to author, 8 May 1993.
128. Warren Prince, letter to author, 14 July 1993.
129. Warren Prince, letter to author, 14 July 1993.
130. John Couleur, letter to author, 8 May 1993.
131. John Couleur, letter to author, 8 May 1993.
132. John Couleur, letter to author, 8 May 1993.
133. John Couleur, letter to author, 8 May 1993.
134. Lou Rader, letter to author, 9 July 1994.
135. Information Systems Division presentation to GE Executive Office, 31 March 1967.
136. Bob Johnson, letter to author, 19 May 1993.
137. Vic Casebolt, letter to author, 20 May 1994.
138. Vic Casebolt, letter to author, 20 May 1994.
139. *General Electric News*, 28 Nov. 1967.
140. Walker Dix, letter to author, 3 Aug. 1993.
141. Bob Kettlety, telephone interview by author, 11 June 1993.
142. Ed Parker, interview by author, Sarasota, Florida, 19 July 1993.
143. Walker Dix, letter to author, 3 Aug. 1993.
144. George Snively, letter to author, 8 May 1993.
145. Dick Shuey, letter to author, 16 Dec. 1994.
146. George Snively, letter to author, 3 Aug. 1993.
147. Annual report, GE, 1969.

PART VI

148. Clint DeGabrielle, letter to author, 26 May 1993.
149. Walker Dix, letter to author, 3 Aug. 1993.
150. George Snively, letter to author, 3 Aug. 1993.
151. Vern Schatz, letter to author, 5 July 1994.

152. "The King is Dead, Long Live the King," *Data Management*, July 1970.
153. "The King is Dead, Long Live the King," *Data Management*, July 1970.
154. Lou Rader, letter to author, 5 Dec. 1994.
155. Hilliard Paige, telephone interview by author, 25 Aug. 1995.
156. Vic Casebolt, letter to author, 7 Apr. 1994.
157. Vic Casebolt, letter to author, 7 Apr. 1994.
158. Vic Casebolt, letter to author, 7 Apr. 1994.
159. Vic Casebolt, letter to author, 7 Apr. 1994.
160. "Progress Report on General Electric's Performance in the Information Systems Business," Dec. 1969.
161. John Burlingame, letter to author, 23 Aug. 1995.
162. Hilliard Paige, telephone interview by author, 25 Aug. 1995.
163. "Why and How GE Left the Computer Field," *Wall Street Journal*, 12 Jan. 1976.
164. "Why and How GE Left the Computer Field," *Wall Street Journal*, 12 Jan. 1976.
165. Dick Shuey, letter to author, 8 June 1995.
166. "Why and How GE Left the Computer Field," *Wall Street Journal*, 12 Jan. 1976.
167. Dick Shuey, letter to author, 19 May 1993.
168. Vic Casebolt, letter to author, 7 Apr. 1994.
169. Roger Rosberg, interview by author, Phoenix, Arizona, 28 May 1994.
170. Robert Slater, "The New GE," *Business One*, Irwin, Homewood, Illinois, 1993, p. 21.

PART VII

171. Annual report, GE, 1970.
172. Walker Dix, letter to author, 3 Aug. 1994.
173. John Couleur, "Liars' Club" address, 1994 reunion of the GE Computer Department Alumni Association, 29 May 1994.
174. George Snively, telephone interview by author, 20 June 1994.
175. Bob Johnson, letter to author, 8 Apr. 1993.
176. George Snively, letter to author, 21 Dec. 1993.
177. Cy Statt, letter to author, 16 June 1993.

Glossary

(In approximate order of appearance)

ENIAC	Electronic Numerical Integrator and Computer. The world's first working electronic digital computer.
FORTRAN	A computer language used primarily for scientific applications.
UNIVAC	Universal Automatic Computer. An early vacuum tube computer.
OARAC	Office of Air Research Automatic Computer. GE Electronics Division's first digital computer, circa 1954.
R & D	Research and Development.
GE	The General Electric Company.
SRI	Stanford Research Institute, now called SRI International.
MIT	Massachusetts Institute of Technology.
OMIBAC	Office of Management and Information Automatic Computer. GE's first digital computer, circa 1950.
ABA	American Bankers Association.
NCR	National Cash Register Corporation.
MICR	Magnetic Ink Character Recognition.
TI	Texas Instruments Incorporated.
RCA	Radio Corporation of America.
BSEE	Bachelor of Science in Electrical Engineering.
ROUTE 128	The highway ringing Boston on which many successful "High Tech" businesses are located.
PRODUCTRON	Analog computer developed by GE for factory planning and scheduling.
FIFTY K	Fifty thousand.
IBM	International Business Machines Corporation.

CAL TECH	California Institute of Technology.
AMPEX	Prominent producer of magnetic tape systems.
EDP	Electronic data processing.
BIZMAC	RCA's first digital computer.
MISTRAM	GE's Heavy Military Equipment Department system for control and guidance of the ATLAS missile.
ASU	Arizona State University.
J & L	Jones and Laughlin Steel Company.
MOSAIC	The GE Computer Department's planned 32-bit line of software compatible computers.
IUE and IBEW	Trade unions (electrical).
STRETCH	IBM's largest supercomputer.
CDC	Control Data Corporation.
SEAC	The National Bureau of Standards computer; the world's fastest operational computer as of 1950.
GECOM	A GE Computer Department operating system.
SHARE	An organization of IBM computer users, devoted primarily to the sharing of software information and applications.
MBA	Master of Business Administration.
SNECMA	A large French jet engine manufacturing company.
BASIC	Dartmouth's simplified programming language.
PROJECT MAC	MIT's ambitious time-shared computer project.
MULTICS	Software system for Project MAC.
DECCA	Large British electronics company.
SBIC	Small Business Investment Corporation.
McAUTO	McDonnell-Douglas data processing subsidiary.
BANKPAC	GE Computer Department software for banking applications.
COBOL	A programming language developed mainly for large computers.
BSME	Bachelor of Science in Mechanical Engineering.
ISIS	GE's trade name for a computer-based retail system.
TRADAR	GE's trade name for an ISIS workstation.
APL	Advanced Product Line.
HIS	Hospital Information System.